A THOUSAND KISSES DEEP

Love and Relationship on the Buddhist Path

Shantigarbha

Windhorse Publications
38 Newmarket Road, Cambridge CB5 8DT
info@windhorsepublications.com windhorsepublications.com

For General Product Safety Regulation (EU) queries, the authorized representative for Windhorse Publications Ltd is:
Buddhistisches Tor Berlin
Buddhistische Gemeinschaft Triratna (Berlin) E.V.
Grimmstrasse 11B-C
10967 Berlin-Kreuzberg
info@buddhistisches-tor-berlin.de

Cover design: Katarzyna Manecka Typesetting: Tarajyoti

British Library Cataloguing in Publication Data:
A catalogue record for this book is available from the British Library.

ISBN 978-1-915342-67-6

Appreciation for *A Thousand Kisses Deep: Love and Relationship on the Buddhist Path*

It is not enough to understand our interconnectedness: we need to embody that realization in the ways we love and show compassion when needed. *A Thousand Kisses Deep* provides a truly comprehensive and much-needed overview of the role of love in our spiritual lives. – **David Loy**, author of *Loving the World as Our Body: The Nondual Path in a Dangerous Time*

A Thousand Kisses Deep brings a conscious practice of compassion and love into the intimate, messy terrain of human relationships. Shantigarbha invites us to understand love not simply as a feeling, but as a practice of honesty, empathy, freedom, responsibility, and care. Warmly written with courageous vulnerability, this book offers a rich companion for anyone seeking to love with greater awareness. – **Manasi Saxena**, CNVC Certified Trainer and Founder, enCOMPASSion

A Thousand Kisses Deep weaves Buddhist insight with poetry, story, and science, revealing love as a major pulse of awakening. This is a nourishing, reflective work for anyone – monastic or lay, single or partnered – who wishes to understand how love, in all its faces, can become a path of wisdom and awakening. A worthy read for Buddhists and anyone with an abiding interest in love and the threats to it. – **Christopher Titmuss**, author of *The Buddha of Love*

From the outset, Shantigarbha invites readers into a conscious relationship with the text, encouraging them to notice their response rather than simply accepting what they read without question. Drawing on lived experience, he weaves Buddhist wisdom, personal vulnerability, poetry, and contemporary psychology into a transformative vision of love, offering teachings that readers can test in their own experience. His reappraisal of 'compassion fatigue' merits wide attention. – **Amitaśūrī Yule**, NHS Healthcare Chaplain

Contents

	About the Author	vi
	Preface	vii
	Author's Acknowledgements	xi
	Publisher's Acknowledgements	xii
	Audio Recordings	xiii
	Introduction	1
Part One	Love in Buddhist Practice	13
1	The Art of Loving	15
2	The Science of Love	31
3	Opening the Heart	45
4	The Great Love of the Bodhisattva	71
5	Love, Beauty, and Friendship	89
6	The Garden of Love	119
Part Two	Love in Buddhist Partnership	135
7	Self-Love	137
8	How to Say 'I Love You'	153
9	The Shadow Side of Love	169
10	Love and Sex	183
11	Different Strokes	197
12	Lost Loves	215
13	Growing Together	227
14	Growing Apart	241
15	Final Thoughts: Towards a Culture of Love	257
	Notes	267
	Index	281

About the Author

Shantigarbha (meaning 'He whose inner nature is peace') is a Buddhist teacher, activist, Nonviolent Communication (NVC) trainer, and dedicated mapper of the human heart. Since his ordination into the Triratna Buddhist Order in 1996, he has spent three decades exploring how the stillness of the meditation cushion can coexist with the beautiful, messy collisions of human relationship.

A former student of classics and philosophy at Oxford, Shantigarbha has traded ancient Greek texts for the modern practice of reconciliation. He has led peace-building workshops and restorative circles from the West Bank to the caste-divided communities of India – yet he remains convinced that some of the most profound 'peace work' happens at the kitchen table over a morning cup of tea.

When he isn't writing or teaching, he can be found in Bristol, likely contemplating the intersection of spirituality and environmental activism with the Triratna Earth Sangha, or simply practising the radical art of listening. *A Thousand Kisses Deep* is his latest invitation to treat love not as a fleeting feeling, but as a path of deep, courageous, and slightly stubborn devotion.

For more information about his work, visit: https://seedofpeace.org/.

Preface

Shantigarbha's *A Thousand Kisses Deep* takes its title from a much-loved Leonard Cohen song – a fitting choice. Many Buddhist practitioners have adopted Leonard Cohen, along with poets Rumi, Mary Oliver, Rilke, and Thich Nhat Hanh, as a patron saint quoted on retreats. Cohen's five years as a Zen monk in California lend his work a deep spiritual resonance.

Shantigarbha's book invites us to explore love – sexual, romantic, platonic, social, and spiritual – and to recognize its unique importance in human life. He reminds us that love can fill our consciousness without reason or justification, defying the intellect.

The book explores love as something far deeper than physical attraction. Sex sought for gratification exploits and damages love, and brings much suffering. We need to know the difference between 'making love' and 'having sex'.

Love and the Buddhist path

'The Science of Love', 'Love, Beauty, and Friendship', 'The Shadow Side of Love', 'Love and Sex', 'Growing Together', and 'Growing Apart' – these and other chapter themes show the range of his enquiry. Although the subtitle focuses on

'Love and Relationship on the Buddhist Path', the book reaches beyond the Buddhist network. Shantigarbha draws from science, psychology, literature, spirituality, and religion to illuminate the transforming power of love.

Love, he shows, functions as a liberating force overcoming violence, hatred, and blame. The author quotes the Buddha's teaching on *metta* – love/loving-kindness/deep friendship. The power of *metta* enables one to respond with understanding rather than reactivity.

Buddhist tradition reminds us, 'We do not blame the lettuce for failing to grow.' Likewise, people's harmful behaviours reflect both internal and external conditioning. We remain vulnerable to absorbing the harmful behaviour of others in childhood and adulthood and repeating the harmful history.

The four Immeasurables

A section of the book explores the Buddha's four Immeasurables: love, compassion, appreciative joy, and equanimity.

- Love untethered from wisdom can turn into obsession or aversion in the frustration of desires.
- *Karuna* (compassion), derived from the Indo-European word *krs*, means 'movement' – the same root as found in the word 'karma'. *Karuna* means 'to go forward to address suffering'.
- Appreciative joy arises as a heartfelt openness to others' happiness, freeing us from envy and competition.

- Equanimity means to stay steady and grounded in our response to what arises. Equanimity bears no relationship to neutrality or to a passive view.

Personal and practical wisdom

Drawing on his own life – from teenage love to his current partnership, Shantigarbha bridges Buddhist practices with first-hand experience and occasional humour. Guided meditations and reflective exercises at the end of chapters translate insight into application, allowing readers to apply these principles within their own relationships.

His approach echoes the spirit of the bodhisattva, beings who act from compassion within the ordinary world. Love, loss, acceptance, and letting go can form a sequence of experiences to develop clarity and understanding. The book shows how cultivating awareness within such experience leads to freedom.

The power of non-anger

A pivotal verse from the *Dhammapada* supports an insightful perspective:

> Anger does not cease through anger;
> anger ceases through non-anger.

Buddhist tradition often translates 'non-anger' as 'love'. Following Sangharakshita, Shantigarbha reframes non-anger in positive terms – as cherishing, protecting, and helping others to grow. The Buddha recognized that moving from hatred to expressions of love can ask too much of those who have suffered at the hands of others or know of the suffering inflicted on others in various environments.

A book about love in all its forms

Shantigarbha treats love as an energy to dissolve both individual and collective suffering. Society must still guard against exploitation and cruelty, take necessary steps, and develop ways to end the infliction of pain on others, regardless of rationale.

A Thousand Kisses Deep weaves Buddhist insight with poetry, story, and science, revealing love as a major pulse of Awakening.

This is a nourishing, reflective work for anyone – monastic or lay, single or partnered – who wishes to understand how love, in all its faces, can become a path of wisdom and Awakening.

A worthy read for Buddhists and anyone with an abiding interest in love and the threats to it.

Christopher Titmuss
Author of *The Buddha of Love*

Author's Acknowledgements

This book exists because of a vast web of connection, and I am deeply grateful to those who helped me spin it.

To Urgyen Sangharakshita, my preceptors and the Triratna Buddhist Order: deep gratitude for giving me a name to live up to and an order within which to flourish.

To Marshall Rosenberg and the NVC community: for providing the inspiration and tools to turn 'invincible defeat' into opportunities for connection.

To Windhorse Publications: thank you for your patience, your encouragement, and your confidence that there is something here that needs to see the light of day.

To Gesine – my partner, co-director at Seed of Peace, and constant companion on this path of love and relationship. Thank you for sharing the 'thousand kisses' of our daily life.

To the reader: thank you for picking this up. May these pages help you find the light through the cracks, and may your own journey be at least a thousand kisses deep.

Publisher's Acknowledgements

We would like to thank the individuals who supported this book through our 'Sponsor-a-book' campaign (www.windhorsepublications.com/sponsor) and the Friends of Windhorse Publications initiative (www.windhorsepublications.com/friends).

Windhorse Publications wish to gratefully acknowledge a grant from Future Dharma and the Triratna European Chairs' Assembly Fund towards the production of this book.

FUTURE DHARMA

Triratna
European Chairs Assembly

Audio Recordings

A Thousand Kisses Deep has been produced with accompanying guided meditations by the author.

They are indicated by this image:

These can be streamed directly from the web.

Please go to: https://tinyurl.com/TKD-audio

Introduction

> Not by hatred are hatreds ever pacified here (in the world). They are pacified by love. This is the eternal law.
>
> The Buddha[1]

When you pick up a book on love in a Buddhist context, you want to know something about the person who is writing it – what qualifications or experience do they have? I've been following the Buddha's teachings since 1985, when I was nineteen. That means I've been meditating, studying, and teaching the Dharma for forty years. In 1996 I was ordained into the Triratna Buddhist Order and given the name Shantigarbha, which means 'He whose inner nature is peace'.

I've also been sharing Nonviolent Communication (NVC) since 2004, and using the skills I've learned to support couples who are struggling to communicate with each other. You start to see patterns after a while, especially if you also reflect on your own experience of partnership. I've been with my current partner, Gesine, since 2014, and she'll be helping to write some of the more intimate sections relating to our heterosexual partnership.

This book came from something that happened about ten years ago. I was at the Bristol Buddhist Centre for Parinirvana Day, the annual festival to celebrate the Buddha's final passing away. The person who was leading the day invited us to reflect on our own deaths. What did we want to be remembered for? I didn't have an immediate answer, but stored the question away in my mind and heart as a koan – a spiritual question or paradox.

As I reflected, I rephrased the question: what qualities did I want to develop by the end of my life? Not in a self-conscious way. Just, what qualities did I want people to remember me for? After several months of wrestling with this question, I came to the conclusion that I wanted to be remembered as a loving person. I wanted to love and be loved. It was as simple as that. It meant fulfilling the possibilities of life, or at the very least learning to love it!

I knew that I didn't want to repeat the romantic mistakes of the past. And I knew that I didn't want to die in emotional poverty. So it seemed to me that developing love would bring me a sense of completion on both psychological and spiritual levels.

I decided that I wouldn't worry too much about the distinction between love and the Buddhist quality of *metta* (loving-kindness), which is more impartial and inclusive. I would deal with that later. This decision gave me clarity, a sense of purpose, and permission to look in all sorts of places. It allowed me to reorganize myself around the principle of love. I felt energy, excitement, and enthusiasm for my quest.

So how was I going to develop this quality of love? The immediate issue I faced was emotional warmth. Of course I wasn't completely without it – sometimes I felt very warmly towards people and things. However, I found it all too easy to lose this warmth. I knew that I needed to make a daily practice of it in order to change that. I imagined that, if I could raise the overall sea level of emotional warmth, it would gradually envelop and transform any emotional wrecks still lurking at the bottom!

I had known about and practised loving-kindness meditation for many years, but my practice of it had gone stale. I would need to breathe fresh life into it. I had kept a gratitude diary for several years, so would recommit to this. I would pay particular attention to empathy, for myself and others, as I know that empathy is received as love. And finally, I would seek out or create new practices, both on and off the meditation cushion. I resolved to do one of these things every day for at least a year.

This book is the result. More accurately, it's an account of the journey I've been on. It's a reflection on what's worked and what hasn't. It's also a celebration. My preliminary finding is that writing about love is itself a heart-opening activity! I hope reading it will be too. It's possible to enter into the mysteries of love, and the practice can transform us into great lovers.

The languages of love

Poetry, song, and music are the native languages of love. A character in Plato's *Symposium* playfully asserts that everyone becomes a poet when Love comes knocking![2] So it seems inevitable that I would use a poetic metaphor for the book's title. 'A thousand kisses deep' is a song by Leonard Cohen, 1960s poet and ladies' man turned Zen monk.

The song comes from his monastic cell, an older man wondering whether to revive his love life. He still has the occasional triumph, but the end ('invincible defeat') is in sight. There's an air of tragedy about his passion, as in so many of Cohen's songs. Take for example his most famous song 'Hallelujah', where he describes love as a hollow victory.[3]

What I love about Cohen is the way he expresses love on different levels – physical, sexual, emotional, and spiritual. In 'A thousand kisses deep' he says,

And sometimes when the night is slow,
The wretched and the meek,
We gather up our hearts and go
A thousand kisses deep.[4]

What could 'a thousand kisses deep' mean? The phrase has ancient echoes. The Roman poet Catullus tells his lover, 'Give me a thousand kisses, then a hundred, then another thousand, then a second hundred, then yet another thousand, then a hundred.'[5] There's a sense of urgency. He wants to consummate his love as soon as possible, while there's still life in them.

In Cohen's version, the mood isn't urgent but sombre and reflective. It's the wretched and the meek who must gather up their hearts, when the night is slow. 'A thousand kisses deep' is an almost mystical phrase. Perhaps it's a state of total absorption, a loss of a sense of self and a merging with the other. At the same time, Cohen seems to be speaking about a state of meditative absorption, a thousand kisses deep.

He looks back at his career as a lover, and realizes that he has come to the end of the road. He's become a scavenger, searching for scraps of comfort and satisfaction where there weren't any. The question is: when will he cut his losses? This is a question for all of us. When do we cut our losses with a relatively limited romantic love and let go into the 'masterpiece' of a more encompassing form of love – perhaps being in love with life? How will we bring about this transformation? Cohen describes how he gets to the forward deck of the ship. From this vantage point, he sees that there is only a remnant of the fleet he set sail with. Compassion arises as he contemplates the impact of loving and ageing, and he blesses the fleet. Then consciously, with awareness, he allows himself to be wrecked, a thousand kisses deep.

This time the phrase clearly suggests the profound depths of love. This is a more encompassing love, entered into with awareness, choice, and a profound sense of compassion for the limits of our human state. This is a mystical song, suggesting how we can transform relatively limited passion into unlimited compassion, a thousand kisses deep.

Passion and compassion

Passion and compassion often seem at odds in the Buddhist tradition. When people think of Buddhism they imagine 'desireless' monks, or Enlightenment as being the eradication of the 'poisons' of greed, hatred, and delusion. Framed like this, Buddhism can come across as heavy, even nihilistic. Where's the fun? Where's the joy? Where's the passion?

And yet, what are we to make of the Buddha's statement that 'Not by hatred are hatreds ever pacified here (in the world). They are pacified by love. This is the eternal law'?[6]

And this statement from Padmasambhava, the semi-mythical bringer of Buddhism to Tibet?

> I am Padmasambhava the sorcerer.
>
> Mine are the counselings of the Dharma that transmutes the five poisons.
>
> I do not bid farewell to pleasures, I take them with me on the path.[7]

The poisons that Padmasambhava transmutes can also be translated as 'passions'. Is it even possible to integrate passion and compassion? How can we make connections between our experiences of falling in love and the Buddhist ideal?

In the ancient Indian languages of the Buddhist texts, *metta* or *maitri* means 'boundless loving-kindness', 'universal friendliness', 'benevolence', 'goodwill', or 'love'. *Metta* is an aspect of the creative mind. 'The creative mind loves where there is no reason to love', as my Buddhist teacher Urgyen Sangharakshita wrote in an early pamphlet.[8]

Let's take a step back in order to understand this. According to the Buddha, the cycle of rebirth, the whole of conditioned existence, is kept spinning by three things: greed, hatred, and ignorance. This may come as a bit of a shock to us. We're not used to thinking in these terms. Can it really be true that these are what keeps the wheel of samsara turning? I guess that we're used to seeing ourselves as more high-minded, more dignified, more human. But once we've seen the power of these three forces in our lives, we can start to look for alternatives. And of course the alternative to greed is generosity, the opposite of hatred is love, and the antidote to ignorance is awareness.

Generosity, love, and awareness give us a clear direction. Psychologically, it's easier to focus on qualities that we *want* to cultivate than remember what to avoid. So generosity, love, and awareness might prove more useful than their opposites. They also give us a direct flavour of the enlightened heart/mind. Awareness is permeated by unconditional love. Being awake is not different from love. Awareness is inherently loving, because it is curious, responsive, and empathic.

Our hearts are dying to be known. And yet it's really difficult for us to express what is in them. It's a hugely vulnerable experience to allow love to flow towards us, to know that love is in the world, and to know that we are capable of giving and receiving it. Because it is so vulnerable, we create veils around our hearts, and these are greed, hatred, and ignorance.

A lot has been said in recent years about the importance of awareness or mindfulness, so here I want to concentrate on love. In fact, we could talk about following the Buddha's teaching purely in terms of embodying the 'love mode'. If we could switch from the 'power mode' to the 'love mode', everything else would follow.

Of course this isn't new. Jimi Hendrix, a famous figure from the 1960s counterculture, said, 'When the power of love overcomes the love of power, then there will be peace.' Actually, it wasn't Jimi Hendrix! This is one of those fake quotes that you find on the internet. But you'll be even more surprised to know who *actually* said it. It was William Gladstone, a nineteenth-century British prime minister: 'We look forward to the time when the Power of Love will replace the Love of Power. Then will our world know the blessings of peace.'[9] But I'm sure that Jimi Hendrix would have sung it if he'd thought of it!

So what is the love mode? It's a spirit of helpfulness and tenderness towards the whole world. It's the happiness that comes from our capacity to open ourselves to others. The love mode is nonviolence, the most direct and important manifestation of the spiritual act of going for refuge to the three jewels of the Buddha, Dharma, and Sangha. It can lead to a relaxation of the belief in a separate, unitary self.

But are we prepared to give up the advantages of the power mode, of greed and aversion? In this context, power is the capacity to use force. Violence is using this capacity to negate the being of another, whether physically, mentally, or emotionally. We may feel personally estranged from such power. However, all living beings have the capacity to use force, and therefore possess power. Humans possess more power, both materially and psychologically, than many other living beings, so we have a particular responsibility in this area.

The power mode is all around us, it's in our environment. We are both 'victims' of the power mode and 'perpetrators', maintaining its existence. Moving from the power mode to the love mode means a complete change in our centre of gravity, a turning about in our basic orientation. My teacher Sangharakshita suggests two principles here: if you ever 'have' to operate in the power mode, subordinate it to the love mode. An example would be a parent forcibly restraining a child from harm. Secondly, the spiritual community is ideally based on the love mode. If you act from the power mode, you temporarily put yourself outside the spiritual community.

As love is a spiritual principle, there is no limit to the number of ways in which it can be applied. We can all act more or less skilfully, depending on whether we are in the love mode or the power mode. As nonviolence or love is the most direct manifestation of the act of going for refuge to the three jewels, its potentialities are infinite.

There are no advantages to the love mode. It's a pristine spiritual quality. What helps us to move from one mode to the other is that Buddhism proposes an ethics of *intention* or *volition*. What is in my heart, when I act with body, speech, and mind? I can ask this question again and again. What is the nature of my relationship with the other person? How do I see myself and them? Am I open to them? Do I want a connection? Perhaps I don't feel a sense of wellbeing in their company. Nevertheless, am I open to them? Or do I want to compete with them, to get the better of them, even by blanking them out?

Sometimes I notice that I rationalize that I'm doing something 'for the other person's good', when actually I'm trying to meet my own needs. It can be very subtle. If at any moment I feel that my sense of identity is being challenged, I try to exploit the other person so that I seem bigger and they seem smaller.

How often do we try to convince ourselves that 'I'm right, they're wrong'? All the time we are trying to find ways to come out best, to meet our own needs at the expense of those around us. These are all aspects of the power mode: keeping ourselves big, trying to reduce the size of the other, trying to fix ourselves as 'this is who I am' to bolster a sense of identity. Does this sound familiar?

The distinction between power mode and love mode is similar to a more recent distinction between *power with* and *power over*. 'Power with' implies using resources in ways that ensure safety and respect for others. 'Power over' implies using resources in ways that do the opposite. So the love mode has a very strong overlap with, and is almost identical to, 'power with'.

Skilful emotions are very important in Buddhism. If you only cultivate mindfulness (awareness), you can get very dry and disconnected from the people around you. So *metta* or loving-kindness is an important counterbalance. You develop *metta* by becoming aware of your feelings. You give special attention to your friendly responses and develop them more widely and more continuously. In this way, you develop a broad range of positive and creative emotions. We'll return to this in Chapter 3, 'Opening the Heart'.

We all have the experience of feeling kind and loving in certain situations. For some of us it's when we see a loved one or close friend. For others, it's a beautiful summer's day or a rock concert. Buddhism offers a reliable way of feeling like this, a way to feel kind and loving all the time.

Part One of this book, 'Love in Buddhist Practice', explores the aspects of the Buddha's teaching that we'll be drawing on. Part Two, 'Love in Buddhist Partnership', applies these teachings to the way many of us are actually living – in partnership.

At the end of every chapter, there are guided reflections to help us engage with our own experience. I suggest that you find a quiet and comfortable place to do these exercises, and look for help online if you need advice about sitting posture. It can be useful to have a pen and paper to hand for your thoughts and reflections.

In the *Karaniya Metta Sutta*, the Buddha says that love can help us to become more ethical, support our meditation, and take us all the way to Enlightenment. So what are we waiting for? Let's gather up our hearts and go a thousand kisses deep!

Part One

Love in Buddhist Practice

1

The Art of Loving

> The more knowledge is inherent in a thing, the greater the love. [...] Anyone who imagines that all fruits ripen at the same time as the strawberries knows nothing about grapes.
>
> Paracelsus[10]

When I was eighteen, I got depressed after an unhappy love affair. Then I read *The Art of Loving* by Erich Fromm, the German psychoanalyst. On the first page, I read that my attempts at love were bound to fail unless I tried to develop my total personality. I wasn't going to find satisfaction in individual love without the capacity to love my neighbour, without humility, and with courage, faith, and self-discipline. I felt hopeful for the first time in months. Maybe there was something to be done with my life, after all.

I had believed that love was a matter of feeling something special for a special someone. I had romanticized this experience as a form of idealism. Fromm pointed out that it's very common for people to believe that nothing is easier than to love, and there is nothing to be learned about love. The truth, he claimed, is that love is an art, which requires knowledge and effort. It's not a pleasant sensation that we experience by chance.

Most people see the problem of love as one of *being loved* rather than *the capacity to love*. They put effort into being lovable – by being popular, or having sex appeal. According to Fromm, this misses the point: love is not about an object – it's a faculty. It's not primarily a relationship to a specific person. It is an attitude, an orientation of character, which determines the relationship of a person to the world as a whole.

He gave the comparison of a person who wants to paint pictures, but refuses to learn the art of painting, claiming that, if they just wait for the right object to come along, they will paint beautifully!

Falling in love, he argued, is a temporary state that is very exciting and satisfying at the time. When it comes to an end, it is taken as failure. Could we examine the reasons for this and study the meaning of love? Love is an art, and mastery of this art involves theory and practice. Like any art worthy of the name, achieving mastery is a matter of ultimate concern.

Up until that point, I'd believed the capacity to love was something that we were simply born with. Experience seemed to be suggesting otherwise, so it was reassuring to hear that love was an art, a skill that I could learn. The thought softened my sense of failure. If it was learnable, then I could learn it. And learning it could give my life meaning. I might even be of use to the people around me. So I took back control of my life, with the motivation that I could learn how to be of use to the people around me. The arrangement seemed fair enough to me – I might even enjoy it along the way.

Coming back to Fromm, he didn't undervalue love, even if he thought it wasn't as simple as we might think. He claimed that the deepest need of humanity is to overcome its separateness, to find communion. The full answer to this need lies in the achievement of interpersonal union, of fusion with another person, in love. This is the mature answer to the problem of existence.

I learned that mature love is union with integrity. It's different from the symbiotic fusion of falling in love. It's an active power, an action that can only be practised in freedom. And it's primarily about giving, rather than receiving. So there's nothing passive about love: it's a power that produces love in the other being.

Rereading *The Art of Loving* more than forty years later, I'm still struck by the depth of Fromm's insights. For instance, he suggests that there are four elements common to all forms of love: *care*, *responsibility*, *respect*, and *knowing*.

In *care*, love is an active concern for the life and growth of that which we love. Like farming, gardening, or parenting, the essence of love is labouring to make something grow. *Responsibility* is not duty, it is voluntary. To be responsible is to be ready to respond to the needs of the other being. *Respect* means to be aware of the other being's individuality, and to support them to grow as they are. There is an absence of exploitation. We don't treat the other person as an object for our use.

And finally, it's not possible to respect a person without *knowing* them, recognizing their individuality, seeing them on their own terms, not as you imagine them to be. Knowing here isn't about the facts, it's an understanding of a deeper truth, the secret of life, of our common humanity, a form of existential knowledge. Love is the only way of gaining this kind of knowledge. In the act of loving we find ourselves, each other, and humanity.

Cherishing, protecting, and maturing

My Buddhist teacher Sangharakshita considered the same problem in his ground-breaking contribution to Buddhist ethics, *The Ten Pillars of Buddhism*. If we want to use the word 'love' to translate *ahimsa* or 'nonviolence', the basic ethical principle of Buddhism, he suggested that we need to clarify what we mean. 'Love' as a translation of *ahimsa* is not erotic love, parental love, or even friendly love. It's a *cherishing, protecting*, and *maturing* kind of love. He described this kind of love as having the same effect on the spiritual being of others as the light and heat of the sun have on their physical being.[11]

Cherishing means treating with fondness and affection. It comes from the French *cher*, meaning 'dear', which in turn comes from the Latin *carus*, 'dear', 'costly', 'beloved'. It implies intense liking and emotional warmth. It means not withholding love, but loving unreservedly and fully. It means valuing and holding dear. It's what Carl Rogers described as unconditional positive regard. In this context, it means holding all beings in our hearts, with affection. It means wishing beings happiness and the causes of happiness. In the words of the Buddha, 'May all beings be happy and secure, may their hearts be wholesome!'[12]

Cherishing represents the absolute affirmation of another's being. It's the light that – like the sun – illuminates their unique qualities and the warmth that instils in them a love of living. Cherishing is notably absent from Fromm's four elements, which focus on the more cognitive and existential aspects of love.

Protecting corresponds to Fromm's attributes of *care* and *responsibility*: being responsive to another being's needs and protecting them when necessary. The Buddha gives the example of a mother who would protect her only child, even at the risk of her own life. In just this way, the Buddha invites us to cultivate a boundless heart towards all beings.[13] So protecting means protecting all beings, not just the ones we like. It can lead us to a love of the earth and its myriad inhabitants. It means protecting all beings from harm, and protecting their spiritual being from unwholesomeness and unskilfulness – theirs and those of others.

Maturing means supporting beings to learn and grow. It corresponds to Fromm's *care,* labouring to make something grow. Vietnamese Buddhist teacher Thich Nhat Hanh famously said, 'If the lettuce isn't flourishing, you don't blame the lettuce. You look for reasons why it isn't doing well.' It may need fertilizer, or more water, or less sun. Whatever it is, you never blame the lettuce. By contrast, if we have problems with our family members or friends, we tend to blame them. Blame has no positive effect at all, nor does trying to persuade them using reason and argument. What they need is understanding (what I call empathy), rather than blame or advice. If we know how to take care of our nearest and dearest, they will grow well, like lettuce. Nhat Hanh concluded, 'If you understand, and show that you understand, you can love, and the situation will change.'[14]

The parable of the rain cloud from the *White Lotus Sutra* also speaks of maturing. In the mountains, along the streams, in the valleys, and on the land there are plants, trees, thickets, forests, and medicinal herbs of all kinds. The rainy season comes and a dense cloud spreads over the whole land, pouring rain down everywhere equally. The moisture fertilizes the plants, trees, thickets, forests, and medicinal herbs, as well as the roots, stalks, twigs, and leaves of different sizes. Every growing thing receives its share. From the rain of one cloud, each grows according to its nature, opening its blossoms and bearing fruit. Though they grow in the same soil and are moistened by the same rain, they remain different.[15]

The rain cloud represents the Buddha, who proclaims his teaching in many worlds to many different kinds of beings. He declares that he is enlightened, and can show the way to Enlightenment for others. He notices that beings have different capacities and natures, so he teaches them in various ways. Like the water from the rain cloud, his teaching has one form and flavour, and yet beings grow individually. Maturing means providing a vision of human potential and support for beings to grow in their own way. Modern research confirms that love, or unconditional positive regard, is essential for healthy development. We'll return to this in Chapter 2, 'The Science of Love'.

The maturing aspect of love brings us back to the Paracelsus quotation at the head of this chapter. You need to really know a person in order to help them grow. Anyone who imagines that all fruits ripen at the same time as the strawberries knows nothing about grapes! This is the existential knowledge and sense of union that Fromm describes as *knowing*.

But, if love plays such an important role in Buddhism, why did the Buddha appear to emphasize its 'selfish' aspects? Let's unpack a William Blake poem to find out.

The clod and the pebble

The pithy poem below, titled 'The clod and the pebble', is from Blake's *Songs of Innocence and of Experience*. Each poem in the book contrasts these two contrary states of the human soul. Who is telling the truth, the clod or the pebble?

'Love seeketh not itself to please,
Nor for itself hath any care,
But for another gives its ease,
And builds a Heaven in Hell's despair.'

So sung a little Clod of Clay
Trodden with the cattle's feet,
But a Pebble of the brook
Warbled out these metres meet:

'Love seeketh only self to please,
To bind another to its delight,
Joys in another's loss of ease,
And builds a Hell in Heaven's despite.'[16]

The clod sings the song of innocence and altruism. We learn from the accompanying engraving that the clod is at the bottom of a stream, and cattle tread on it when they come to drink. So it's an image of absolute service. The clod sees the world as a despairing hell of selfishness. Its response is to offer itself to others to build a heaven of unselfishness. This echoes a common Christian sentiment of the time, 'Love feels no burden, thinks nothing of troubles, attempts more than it is able, and does not plead impossibility.'[17]

The pebble exists in the same brook (stream) as the clod.

Being smooth, round, hard, and discrete, it's the image of perfect isolation, in contrast to the soft, pliable clod. The pebble sings the song of experience, and according to Blake its response is 'meet' – timely or appropriate. The pebble paints a very different picture of love: there is nothing altruistic about it. It's only self-seeking. It attempts to bind another for its pleasure, and delights in their discomfort and loss of freedom. In this way it creates a hell where heaven might have been.

So who are we to believe, the clod or the pebble? We might agree with the clod on an ideal level, but agree with the pebble that in practice it's very difficult to be completely unselfish. There's usually more than a trace of self-interest in our love. If we start asking the poem this kind of question, we may find that the tables turn and the poem interrogates us: what do we really believe about love?

But when we turn to the early Buddhist texts, the Buddha comes down firmly on the side of the pebble.[18] In one story, the Buddha has defeated Mara, the pantomime devil of the scriptures. Mara is sitting dejected on the ground nearby. However, his daughters haven't given up. They tell their discouraged father that they will catch the Buddha with the snare of lust and get him under their control.

So Mara's daughters, Tanha, Arati, and Raga, approach the Buddha and tell him that they are at his service. The Buddha, unsurprisingly, pays no attention. The daughters reason that men's tastes are diverse, so each one transforms into a hundred maidens and they approach again, announcing that they are at the Buddha's service. Again, no response. The daughters try variations on this theme, but nothing works.

The daughters complain that, if they had approached any other ascetic who wasn't devoid of lust, his heart would have burst, he would have vomited hot blood, he would have gone mad, or he would have dried up and withered away. They ask the Buddha if he's alone and unmoved because he is depressed or a fugitive from justice. The Buddha responds that he has discovered the bliss of meditating alone, genuine peace of the heart.

In a later version of the story, Mara is identified as Kamadeva, the god of sensory desire, or Cupid.[19] Like Cupid, he fires arrows to strike love into the heart of his 'victims'. Mara gives the Buddha a lengthy warning, then fires his arrow, which turns out to be... his daughters and sons. Characteristically, the Buddha takes no notice and continues meditating.

What does this tell us about the Buddha's attitude? He is set on Enlightenment, and won't be distracted by love and sexual attraction. He has found bliss and unutterable peace. He seems to have no need of friends in the ordinary sense, or intimate connections. Why is this?

As Blake's pebble points out, there's an element of greed in most forms of love. How quickly does love turn to hatred, when we don't get what we want? This is because hatred is the reflex of frustrated greed. So what is greed? It's appropriating the object of attention for your exclusive possession. This object could be a thing, person, or experience. It involves a narrowing down of our focus, a loss of perspective. It has to be *this* person, and no other one will do. We can lose our freedom, and start treating that person or those people as objects, rather than as sovereign beings. With this loss of perspective, we are much more likely to start making demands and using the power mode.

The Buddhist tradition is rich in words to describe this sort of attachment. As we've seen in the story, two of Mara's daughters are called Raga and Tanha. *Raga* means 'cupidity-attachment' and is a passionate attachment to one's object. It's a form of craving (*lobha*) and is a purely 'negative' emotion. Neither *raga* nor *lobha* can be translated as 'desire', because desire is not necessarily negative. For example, the desire for all beings to gain Enlightenment is utterly skilful.

Raga and *lobha* are 'negative' because they involve desiring pleasure from the object that one is attached to. This puts us more or less squarely in the power mode, unless we are lucky enough to find an object that ceaselessly obliges us without coercion.

Mara's third daughter, Tanha, or 'thirst', denotes a very powerful, primordial drive. If you were dying of thirst, you would do anything for a drink of water. The same is true when you are passionately attached. At its root, *tanha* is the thirst for continued existence. You just want to go on being you. You cannot bear any threat to this state of affairs. You don't want to change. You want to keep going with the same old habits.

Elsewhere, the Buddha mentions *pema*, which means 'sticky affection'. Think of images of kittens on social media.

So craving, passionate attachment, and sticky affection are always unskilful, but desire in itself is not. The Buddha recognizes that desire can be skilful or unskilful: *dhammachanda* or *kamachanda*. *Kamachanda* is sensory desire, seeking pleasure through the five senses. It's listed as the first of the five hindrances or obstacles to higher meditative states. By contrast, *dhammachanda* means the desire for the spiritual life itself, the desire for Nirvana or Enlightenment.

So, in this formulation of the Buddhist path, we have a stark choice. *Kamachanda* will keep us on the wheel of continued existence, but *dhammachanda* offers us a way to get off the wheel entirely. Both involve desire; the question is, desire for what?

For most of us this choice is too stark to engage with. Perhaps we need a way in. Could we start by distinguishing between our wants and needs? As the Rolling Stones sang in a moment of clarity, when the clouds of marijuana smoke had parted, 'You can't always get what you want. But if you try sometimes, you may find, you get what you need.'[20]

It's a mark of growth and development to find out that we need something that we didn't even realize we wanted. We are creatures of appetite. The heart is an organ of desire. It says 'no' to something only on the way to saying 'yes' to something else. Whether we mine the insights of Buddhism or anthropology, the story is the same: we are group-dwelling mammals, and our behaviour is driven by habit and social copying. Social media and related advertising muddy the water between our wants and our needs. We end up buying what they want us to buy.

There is nothing unskilful about these experiences or objects in themselves. However, there is something unwise about craving in general, and passionate attachment in particular. We are trying to get satisfaction from an object that just can't give it to us, by its very nature.

Reality is in essence inconceivable and ungraspable. Trying to grasp it creates suffering for ourselves and others. The solution? To get realistic about what kind of satisfaction things can give us. What kind of satisfaction is an intimate relationship capable of giving us? Could we distinguish our wants from our needs, and make realistic plans about how to meet those needs?

I seem to be leaning on the language of needs. If we're going to use this language, we'll need to clarify that needs can be physical, psychological, and spiritual. We'll also need to explore a variety of ways to address them. Our culture promotes satisfying needs *externally*, in the form of objects, people, and experiences. This is the basis of consumerism – that we need to consume something in order to experience satisfaction. However, there is another way to meet needs, and it's *internally*.

I grew up believing in romantic idealism. Perhaps you did too? I believed that, one day, I'd find someone to love and settle down with and live out my own 'happily ever after' story. But there are risks to this kind of idealism. To explore these, I would like to turn to another poem, this time by John Keats, one of the greatest of the English Romantic poets.

Bright star! would I were steadfast as thou art –
  Not in lone splendour hung aloft the night
And watching, with eternal lids apart,
  Like nature's patient, sleepless Eremite,
The moving waters at their priestlike task
  Of pure ablution round earth's human shores,
Or gazing on the new soft-fallen mask
  Of snow upon the mountains and the moors –
No – yet still steadfast, still unchangeable,
  Pillowed upon my fair love's ripening breast,
To feel for ever its soft swell and fall,

> Awake for ever in a sweet unrest,
> Still, still to hear her tender-taken breath,
> And so live ever – or else swoon to death.[21]

I love the mesmerizing tenderness of the scene. And yet, though it may seem sacrilegious, I want to use this poem to identify the shadows of Romantic idealism lurking beneath. These pitfalls include: self-obsession, the desire for worldly fame, using art for worldly gains, romanticizing death, naive attempts to gain immortality through art, and sentimentality towards the natural world.

Romantic idealism is clearly a form of idealism. And yet it is of a limited and delusive nature. The love it promotes can easily slide into attachment, possessiveness, and even hatred. So, if you've grown up with Romantic idealism, as I have, how do you transcend it? One useful approach is through imagination. Imagination allows us to step outside our own limited experience and enter someone else's perspective. This shift can help us to foresee more clearly the possible consequences of our actions. When we are swept away by sexual-romantic passion, the past and future disappear. So remembering the past or imagining the future can be helpful in giving us the clarity we lack in the moment.

Shelley, another great English Romantic poet, speaks of morals in terms of imagination. He argues that

> the great secret of morals is love; or a going out of our own nature, and an identification of ourselves with the beautiful which exists in thought, action, or person, not our own.[22]

By exploring this ethical aspect of imagination, we can begin to transcend Romantic idealism.

Kissing the joy as it flies

We can also explore alternatives to appropriating the object of our love. William Blake suggests *appreciating* rather than appropriating:

> He who binds to himself a joy
> Does the winged life destroy
> But he who kisses the joy as it flies
> Lives in Eternity's sunrise[23]

Did Blake just give us a glimpse of Enlightenment, in the Buddhist sense of the word? Blake calls it 'Eternity's sunrise'. Just imagine the sun coming up on eternity. What are the colours in the sky? Are other beings present? Which desire did you just transform, and which bliss are you now experiencing?

Blake's poem reminds me of the glorious and beautiful descriptions you find of Buddhist 'purelands'. These are heavenly realms in which everything is supportive of Enlightenment. Imagine millions of rays and beams springing up, intersecting and weaving themselves into incredibly pure, beautiful patterns. Rainbows appear and disappear. Trees shine and flash with nets of multicoloured gems. Flowers fall like rain. At the centre of this splendour sits the Buddha of the Mahayana, the eternal Buddha. All rays converge into a canopy above his head. Flowers are strewn at his feet. His unnumbered audience sit in ecstasy and devotion on all sides.

I've come to see 'The clod and the pebble' as another koan or spiritual paradox. The references to heaven and hell remind us of Blake's earlier book, *The Marriage of Heaven and Hell,* in which he tries to heal the dualistic split between body and soul, good and evil. The book climaxes with the memorable 'Proverbs of hell', which include such paradoxes as 'The road of excess leads to the palace of wisdom', 'Prudence is a rich, ugly old maid, courted by Incapacity', 'He who desires but acts not, breeds pestilence', and the thunderous 'Sooner murder an infant in its cradle than nurse unacted desires.'[24]

Blake rejected the conventional Church-based morality of his time, preferring to present the voices of both innocence *and* experience. Can we entertain both viewpoints and hold them without collapsing into one or the other? Can we see desire as something life-serving without shutting it down? Blake is convinced this is how insight can arise. In further chapters, we'll explore how to work with this.

The teaching that I follow goes back 2,500 years to the time of Gautama the Buddha. However, I was also born in the West, and I'm intrigued by how modern scientific studies can throw light on ancient problems. What does science say about love? Why do we love? What are the benefits? So the next chapter explores the science of love.

In the meantime, I invite you to join me in dwelling on and cultivating the three aspects of boundless love. Let's give it up for cherishing, protecting, and maturing!

Guided reflection: cherishing, protecting, maturing

- Purpose of this activity: to dwell on and cultivate the three qualities of boundless love: cherishing, protecting, and maturing.
- Time: 15 minutes.

2

The Science of Love

> Of this, I am actually certain. After collecting thousands of stories, I'm willing to call this a fact: **A deep sense of love and belonging is an irreducible need from the moment we're born until the day we die.** We are biologically, cognitively, physically, and spiritually wired to love, to be loved, and to belong. When those needs are not met, we don't function as we were meant to. We break. We fall apart. We numb. We ache. We hurt others. We get sick.
>
> Brené Brown[25]

As I emerged from adolescence, I was clear about two things. I didn't want to have children – one experience of childhood in a lifetime was enough for me. And I didn't want to get married. I told myself, 'Take no prisoners on the journey of life.' In this chapter I want to take a scientific approach to these painful memories. Can science shed light on the universal and yet deeply personal phenomenon of love? Could it help me to understand my history and life choices? It's a personal thing. With understanding, perhaps I could do things differently in the future.

So this chapter takes the form of a scientific whodunnit: what led to such painful memories? It will be characterized by the gradual accumulation of evidence and, hopefully, some kind of revelation. A popular misconception of science is that it consists of moments of sudden revelation. That's not to say that sudden revelations don't happen. It's just that scientists I've spoken to are more likely to point to the thousands of hours of accumulating evidence, relieved by a hopeful result or a gradual shift in understanding as the evidence falls into place.

So let's get to it. As Sherlock Holmes cried out to the sleeping Dr Watson, 'Come, Watson, come! [...] The game is afoot!'[26]

What is love, from a scientific perspective? Evidence from various scientific disciplines confirms that love is central to human experience. Ultimately we rely on it for our health, wellbeing, and survival. However, the same studies also confirm that love is a complicated phenomenon, and not reducible to one explanation, such as the popular conception of neurochemicals swishing around our brains.[27]

Survival is at its centre, with many layers outside. It has elements of addiction and attachment. In the West, romantic love tends to be overestimated, while friendship-love is underestimated – more about this in Chapter 5. There are genetic and neurochemical components. There are social aspects including rules about who and how many people we can love. There is a religious component, such as love of god(s) or other spiritual figures. And finally, with love come motivation and manipulation.

Human beings get to experience love in many different forms. There's romantic love, love for children, family, friends, and spiritual figures, including god(s), if you believe in them. Then there's love for pets, community, celebrities, and in the future potentially even for humanoid robots. Love infiltrates every fibre of our being. As we shall see, it's not an emotion but a *need*, as fundamental as the food we eat and the air we breathe.

Why do we have love? In the previous chapter we looked at the benefits of *metta* or love from a Buddhist perspective: peace of mind, emotional awareness, kindness, affection, and protection. The scientific answer is simply that *we need each other*. Humans are the most cooperative species on the planet.

In our evolutionary past, we needed to cooperate to hunt animals and butcher them. We needed to cooperate to find water and build shelters. Then there's learning: humans are the only species who actively teach each other. We are masters at social learning. Then there's raising children. Humans have brains that are six times larger than those of other mammals of our size. We also walk on two legs, so we need relatively narrow hips to do this. The evolutionary workaround is that human babies are born much sooner than other mammals, to get that big brain through the narrow birth canal. The downside is that human babies are born especially helpless – another reason for cooperation.

To make sure that we invest in our survival-critical relationships, evolution has come up with love as a form of biological glue. With love, we feel warm, content, and even euphoric as we start and maintain relationships with our partner, children, friends, and so on. In this way we build a network of relationships. So love is the force that motivates us to overcome the difficulties of group living, to cooperate at a level unmatched by any other species.

In the Buddhist tradition, this survival-critical network is represented by the sangha or spiritual community. At its highest, the Sangha is one of the three jewels, or ideals of Buddhism, and consists in the community of enlightened beings. On a more mundane level, it represents your spiritual teachers and friends. As one of the jewels, it is regarded as of essential importance, as an end in itself.

You might argue that we only needed to cooperate in order to survive when we were hunter-gatherers – that no longer applies today. We can order pretty much all that we need from the comfort of our sofa. However, love is still very much about survival. There's subsistence: even when we are ordering stuff from our sofa, we are cooperating with thousands of people up the supply chain. There's learning: our world is becoming ever more complex and technological. And, finally, raising children involves cooperating with dozens, if not hundreds, of people. As the saying goes, it takes a village to raise a child.

There are two specific areas of research that confirm that love is still about survival. Firstly, love plays an enormous role in the likelihood that you will survive illness. Secondly, recall that human babies are born much sooner than other mammals, to get their big brains through the relatively narrow birth canal. This comes with an evolutionary cost: the brain takes another two years to develop fully. During this time, the infant is unable to look after itself, and relies on the care and protection of others. Love plays a central role in securing the attachment between the infant and their caregiver(s).

How could love play a role in whether you survive illness or not? Large-scale studies have looked at the correlation between social networks and how likely you are to survive chronic illness, and even how long you will live. It turns out that the impact is massive. Being in a supportive social network reduces the risk of mortality by *50 per cent*. That's the equivalent of quitting smoking.

Other studies have confirmed that the biggest factor is the nature of your relationships, your *love*. This goes for surviving illness, your mental and physical health, life satisfaction, and length of life. Love keeps you healthy and helps you live longer! It does this by bringing practical and emotional resources, so it's still about survival in a basic sense.

People whose early life is untroubled tend to be straightforward, open, and receptive. People who have struggled in early life tend to be suspicious, reserved, and wary. Now we have a scientific explanation for this. How much love you receive, particularly in the first two years of your life, is your very foundation. Children who don't experience love from a parent or caregiver are more likely to suffer from mental-health problems, addiction, and social problems.

Researchers have observed how an infant interacts with their parent or caregiver. Imagine a room with the caregiver and infant seated and toys on the floor. Infants who are *securely attached* explore the room while their caregiver is near, occasionally returning to them for reassurance. They are capable of soothing themselves when disturbed. They treat their caregiver as a secure base from which to explore the world.

By contrast, infants who are *anxiously attached* stay close to their caregiver. They appear to be worried that their caregiver will leave them. They don't explore the room and seem nervous about taking risks. Infants who are *avoidant* in their attachment appear to be independent emotionally and physically from their caregiver. They don't explore the room.

They appear unconcerned if their caregiver leaves the room, and ignore or avoid them if they return.

Secure attachment is a specific set of feelings and behaviours that offers a relatively objective measure of love. The feelings and behaviours are key markers of deep love, signalling the intense and enduring form of companion-love that will see us through to the end of our lives. Attachment theory acknowledges that the attachment between infant and caregiver is the foundation upon which all others are built. This is in contrast to the passionate sensations that come up in the earliest stages of a relationship.

So yes, love is definitely about survival, in various ways.

When it comes to neurochemicals, the story is one of addiction. It's the funky groove of 'Love is the drug' by Roxy Music, or the heavy-metal tension and glorious vocal harmonies of 'Victim of love' by The Eagles:

> Some people never come clean.
> I think you know what I mean, oh.
> You're walkin' the wire, pain and desire,
> Looking for love in between.[28]

We are addicted to love in the same way that people are addicted to heroin. The biological glue is a set of neurochemicals that motivate us to start and maintain our survival-necessary relationships. Roxy Music sang about love as if it was only one drug. In fact, it's four. So let me introduce you to oxytocin, dopamine, serotonin, and beta-endorphin.

Oxytocin is probably the most familiar. Oxytocin lowers your inhibitions by quieting the amygdala, the ancient part of your brain that assesses threats. This makes you more confident, giving you an unusual sense of calm as you take the first step in forming a relationship.

Dopamine is also fairly well-known, as it's the brain's general reward. It is released along with oxytocin. If you just received oxytocin, you might feel so relaxed that you wouldn't actually get up out of your chair and walk across the room to talk to that interesting person. Dopamine motivates you to make a move.

Serotonin is mainly known for its role in depression, and even this is questioned nowadays. It seems to provide the obsessive component of falling in love. You can't stop thinking about this new person and sending photos of them to your friends. Unusually, serotonin levels go *down* when people fall in love.

And finally, beta-endorphin is the hormone of long-term love. It underpins long-term platonic relationships. As a drug, it's so powerful that we never develop a tolerance to it. It is a natural opiate, like heroin. Beta-endorphin is released in many different ways, including through touch, laughter, singing, and chanting. Its benefits are multiplied if these activities are done in a group setting. So next time you are absorbed singing in a choir or chanting a mantra with others, remember that your feelings of euphoria are courtesy of beta-endorphin!

We always wonder if these things are determined by our genes. So are there genes for love? Yes, there are genes that underpin receptors for oxytocin, serotonin, and beta-endorphin. However, the impact of these genes is fairly minimal in comparison to other factors such as environment and nurture. So it would be very difficult to make any sort of argument from genes alone.

Looking at neurochemicals and genes gives us a general answer to the question: how do we love? But without testing me for neurochemicals at key points in my life, or testing me for particular genes, it doesn't give Sherlock Holmes a motive, opportunity, or means. Back to the psych. lab to pursue a different line of enquiry.

A 2019 paper by Spanish psychologist Enrique Burunat argues that love is not an emotion. According to Burunat, love is a need or motivator, like hunger, thirst, or fatigue. It's a motivation or drive to ensure that we seek out the resources we need to survive. There are two main arguments for seeing it in this way.[29]

We experience feelings or emotions for relatively short periods of time. As we have seen, love resembles addiction in its power to orient us towards a particular person, object, or experience. So it is clearly a driver. It encompasses a wide range of emotions, but is much more than this. It persists through time, sometimes decades, and this strongly argues against it being a short-lived emotion.

Secondly, oxytocin and dopamine figure prominently in the onset of love. Dopamine is the hormone of *motivation* – it gives you the kick to make a move. Brain-scan studies confirm the close overlap between the neural fingerprint of love and the dopamine/motivational circuits of the brain. The fingerprint of love *is* the fingerprint of motivation. It's a motivation that ensures that our survival-based needs are met over the course of our lives. The feelings associated with love give us feedback about how we're doing.

Love is a driver of change. It motivates people to fulfil their potential. It primes us for action in relation to another person.

There's experimental evidence that being a parent makes you want to fulfil your potential, in order to provide a role model for your child.[30] Love can motivate us to achieve great feats. The medieval code of chivalry is all about love as *action*: going on quests, submitting to ordeals, killing dragons, rescuing princesses, and so on. It's not enough to love. You have to prove your devotion. It's love that enables us to achieve these apparently impossible goals. For a relatively modern reference, think of Marvin Gaye's song 'Ain't no mountain high enough', and you're there.

Sherlock has discovered more about the importance of love. However, he still hasn't managed to tie this back to my painful childhood memories. Perhaps it's time to go back to attachment theory. The theory states that human infants, along with other animals, rely on attachment figures for protection, support, and help with managing their emotions. In the first two years, when our brains are rapidly growing, these attachment relationships to our caregiver(s) are hugely influential on our development.

We form further attachment relationships as we grow into childhood, adolescence, and adulthood. These attachments follow similar patterns. They can be secure, meaning that they increase our confidence to navigate social situations and support our mental and physical health. Or they can be insecure in two ways: anxious or avoidant.

The game is in the balance. Sherlock summons all the main actors to the parlour. He declares that there is a piece missing. The information about attachment was fascinating, but how does it apply to me, Shantigarbha? He asks me to fill out various attachment questionnaires on the spot. The results?

As a child, I had a secure attachment to my father and an insecure attachment to my mother.

Early memories flood back of looking up to my dad and my mother being unable to comfort me. Things changed in adolescence. I got closer to my mum, explored my nurturing aspect, and learned how to cook with her. At the same time, I felt more distant from my dad, rejecting his free-market ideology. Then, as an adult, hearing other people's impressions of me: 'You're a distancer.' 'You keep on disappearing, literally and metaphorically.'

Why did I reject marriage and choose not to have kids? On one level, I could see that these things weren't going to give me the meaning and satisfaction I sought. And yet... Sherlock suggests that I talk to my mother about the time of my birth. She told me that we were living in a flat in Dorking, Surrey, with damp walls. She had two children under the age of two. She was exhausted from looking after my brother Simon, who was very active. She may have suffered from depression.

I was a quiet baby and slept a lot. She felt relieved, as her hands were already full. She thought that it was okay to let me sleep. She thought that it would be easy to wake me up and stimulate me, the way she had my brother. She was surprised when it wasn't. I just kept on sleeping.

There we have it – a quiet avoidance, or at least ambivalence. The capacity to put a wall up, to shut the world out, to cut off from painful relationships. So Sherlock has a solution: I was avoidantly or ambivalently attached to my mum.

Nowadays I'm securely attached, but to what? I found refuge in the Buddha, Dharma, and Sangha. I remember the moment as if it were yesterday. It was April 1985 and I was nineteen. I was living in a community and working with other Buddhists. One Saturday we drove up to Conway Hall in London to celebrate the founding of the Friends of the Western Buddhist Order (FWBO), now the Triratna Buddhist Community.

For the first time I took part in a puja – a devotional ritual. I remember sitting on the floor and reciting the opening words of the *Heart Sutra*:

> Form is no other than emptiness,
> Emptiness no other than form.
> Form is only emptiness,
> Emptiness only form.[31]

I felt convinced that I'd heard these words before. Or perhaps I'd known them before and just forgotten them. They reminded me of the connection between form – everything that can be seen, heard, touched, tasted, or thought about – and emptiness, that nothing is fixed and final. Everything is empty of a fixed self, full of the rest of the universe. Nothing is permanent; there is only flow, process, interaction, and interpenetration. But I wasn't thinking about it rationally, I was feeling, absorbing, remembering, and *realizing* it.

Sitting astride those cushions in a crowd of people reciting the sutra, I was filled with a deep sense of coming home. And that feeling has never left me. There has been no going back.

So now, instead of feeling angry about my relationship with my mother, I can see that she was overwhelmed, and possibly struggling with her emotional health. I can see her as a separate person, with her own difficulties, rather than as an extension of me. I've re-established a relationship with both my parents on an adult basis, and it's deepened over the years. I can see that my tendency to avoid things is also my capacity to focus strongly on tasks and inner processes. It's given me an instinct for self-preservation that has sometimes saved my skin.

However, even now I react to feeling hurt by putting up a wall. I can hear my internal voice saying, 'How dare you! Nobody speaks to me like that!' It can last two or three days if I get really strongly triggered. So maybe these things just lessen in intensity, rather than disappear completely.

As Sherlock's latest case closes and the credits roll, I realize that I want something different from what I thought. I want to tell my parents that I love them, that I'm grateful to them for bringing me into the world and for their love and support. I want to say that I'm grateful for the gift of life. What did you think of Sherlock's latest case?

* * *

A moment of revelation isn't something that you can engineer. However, practising meditation opened my heart and mind to the words of the *Heart Sutra*. We know that we feel better when we are kind and loving. But, as I've noted, these feelings come and go. Is there a more reliable way to open your heart? In the next chapter I'll suggest how to open your heart more consistently.

But, before we go, let's take a moment to experience the love that secure attachment can bring.

Guided reflection: secure attachment and love

- Purpose of this activity: to experience the power of love in secure attachment to yourself, a close friend, a loving figure from childhood, and a 'spiritual' figure.
- Time: 15 minutes.

3

Opening the Heart

> Just as a mother would protect her only child at the risk of her own life, even so, let [them] cultivate a boundless heart towards all beings.
>
> The Buddha[32]

In the previous chapter we acknowledged the evolutionary origin of love as the biological glue that cements our survival-necessary relationships. Now let's turn to some of the Buddha's teachings, to help us work with the *tanha* or craving that arises.

In the *Karaniya Metta Sutta*, the Buddha's primary teaching on *metta*, he encourages us to develop a boundless heart towards all beings with the intensity of a mother protecting her only child. To evoke this intensity, I asked my partner Gesine about her feelings towards her firstborn son, Jesko. Would she have risked her life for him?

She told me that there was an immediate sense of belonging. He lay on her stomach, and she felt that they belonged together. At the same time, everything was new. The nurse took Jesko to the next room overnight, so that Gesine could get some rest. There were other babies around, and some were crying, but when Jesko cried she recognized his sound immediately. She knew that he was her baby.

Gesine's intense feelings for her son led me to reflect on my own experience. Most people learn to take responsibility in their lives by having children. I chose not to have children of my own. Early on, I realized that I needed another way to mature. I did this by taking on spiritual responsibilities within the Buddhist community. Could I match Gesine's intensity with my love for all beings, even at the risk of my own life? I doubt it. I've suffered from a lack of emotional warmth and a tendency to hold grudges.

It's hard to get to grips with the intensity of love that the Buddha is pointing to here. In another place, he says that *metta* 'burns and shines and blazes forth'.[33] This brings out the incandescent, passionate aspect of *metta*, rather than what we usually think of as a 'spiritual' emotion. *Metta* is passionate! It shines from the faces of those who cultivate it.

Terms such as 'friendliness', 'loving-kindness', and 'goodwill' don't come close to expressing this intense and expansive energy. We tend to have a weaker vocabulary for 'spiritual' emotions than for unrefined emotions such as hatred, anger, jealousy, fear, anguish, and despair. This creates the unfortunate impression that these emotions are more 'real' than more 'spiritual' emotions, and certainly more interesting.

It's difficult to imagine developing healthier emotions to anything like the intensity of the passions. If we do experience intense emotion, there tends to be an element of possessiveness or aversion in there somewhere. It's not easy to transform our emotions into vigorously wholesome ones like *metta*. To do so, we need to bring the passion of the unrefined emotions into the refined and balanced emotion of universal goodwill.

As Leonard Cohen makes clear in his song 'A thousand kisses deep', in our desire to be near the object of our passion, we experience the energy and intensity that eventually characterize our experience of *metta*/love. And, if we achieve union with the object of our passion, we may briefly experience the blissful calm, balance, and harmony that characterize *metta*.

Metta is both dynamic and calm, harmonious and fiery. It can even be ecstatic, in the sense that it can carry us outside of our normal sense of self. In its fullness, *metta* is blissful, a naturally expansive desire to brighten the whole world, even the whole universe!

We tend to assume that *metta* practice began with the Buddha; however, this is not the case. It was already established, and the Buddha simply endorsed it as conducive towards Enlightenment. The benefits of cultivating *metta* are listed in the *Anguttara Nikaya*, and discussed by the fifth-century Sri Lankan Theravadin commentator Buddhaghosa in his *Path of Purification*.[34]

According to Buddhaghosa, if you cultivate *metta* you will sleep in comfort, wake in comfort, and have no nightmares. People and animals will treat you with warmth and affection. The gods will protect you! Fire, poison, and weapons cannot touch you. Your mind will become concentrated quickly. Your habitual expression will become serene. You will die without getting confused. And finally, if you don't enter into the stream leading to Enlightenment in this lifetime, you will be reborn in a heavenly realm.

We could also add some more psychological and emotional benefits: you become more deeply emotionally aware, more open-hearted, kinder, more loving, more patient and able to deal with frustrations, more emotionally buoyant, more at ease with yourself, more spontaneous and engaged with life. You become better able to relate to different kinds of people and more able to respond to suffering.[35]

In the *Karaniya Metta Sutta*, the Buddha sets out a progressive path of *metta*, leading to Insight and even Enlightenment. In the first verse, he clarifies his aim. He wants to support people who understand what genuinely contributes to life to achieve their ultimate goal, the state of peace or Nirvana. The Buddha doesn't present the achievement of this goal as a commandment. He understands that spiritual development is a matter of skill and training, rather than blind faith or following rules. He simply invites those who wish to attain the state of peace to practise in certain ways, clarifying the implications of certain courses of action.

In this way, the Buddha appeals to our spiritual intelligence, respecting our individual responsibility to assess the situation and choose to act accordingly. There is no sense of coercion here, or anywhere else, in the Buddha's teaching. The Buddha simply shows the way. It's up to us to decide for ourselves whether we want to follow it or not.

With this in mind, the Buddha suggests that the first qualities you need to develop if you want to follow a spiritual life are to be able, vigorous, and capable. Once you are resourceful and resilient, you can turn your attention in any direction. The Buddha suggests that you direct your attention to becoming straightforward in your behaviour and dealings with other people. This implies communicating honestly. Once you've developed this, the Buddha suggests that you also practise speaking in a kindly, helpful, and harmonious manner. He offers some qualities or characteristics that might support this: being flexible or amenable to others, having a mild and gentle manner, lacking conceit.

So we could say that the Buddhist path begins with the conscious development of the ordinary qualities of a happy, healthy human being.[36] Once you have developed these happy-human qualities, the Buddha suggests that the next step is developing contentment. This presupposes a degree of integration and individuality. Contentment is not so much about cutting yourself off from the external world – it's more a state of openness and freedom. You don't need to hold onto anything in order to be happy.

Contentment tends to manifest in a simple, uncomplicated lifestyle. Such a lifestyle will give you space to practise meditation and reflect. If there are people who support you with resources, the Buddha advises you to be modest in relation to them. He suggests that you refrain from being greedy for gifts, or taking advantage of your supporters, or seeking their approval. Live with a calmed mind, appreciating rather than appropriating what comes through your senses. Develop the practical wisdom to keep out of trouble from a spiritual point of view. This includes choosing circumstances that support contentment and the practice of meditation. Acknowledge the importance of supportive conditions, even 'guarding the gates of the senses' at times.

If you think, feel, and act according to your values, you will become more ethical. And, as you become more ethical, you will quite naturally wish for others to enjoy health, happiness, security, and peace of mind. So the second section of the sutta is concerned with the technique of meditating on loving-kindness. It begins with a phrase that sums up the generosity, the sincere and heartfelt regard for others, which characterizes *metta*. Simply wish that beings may be *happy*, *secure*, and *happy-hearted*. The word translated as 'happy-hearted' implies that it is not dependent on external circumstances. Happiness is not something you *have*, it's something you embody.

The Buddha suggests that we direct our loving-kindness towards different categories of living beings: the weak, the strong, beings of various shapes and sizes, right down to those not visible to the naked eye, those far away, those near, those born, and those unborn. May all beings be happy!

We need a systematic way of developing *metta* towards as many beings as possible. It needs to be methodical, otherwise we are likely to get overwhelmed with all the beings. At the same time, we need to develop *metta* in relation to specific people, otherwise our emotions won't get involved. A systematic approach will also counteract any dislike we may have for certain categories of people, such as the rich, the poor, or people with differently coloured skin.

There are many variations on the cultivation of *metta* as a practice, including a version by Buddhaghosa in five stages, which we will explore later on in this chapter. The main thing is to get your *metta* flowing, and bringing to mind different people, or categories of people, seems to be the most effective way of doing this. Once you have got your *metta* flowing, it doesn't really matter which method you follow, as long as you include all beings, everywhere.

Metta isn't just about wishing others well. It manifests in how you *respond* to them. Can you keep the *metta* flowing even when they are doing things that you're not in alignment with?

Responding with *metta* also means not deceiving others, or despising anyone at any time or place. It means not wishing any harm or suffering upon another, in a flash of anger or in settled hatred. Hatred, rather than anger, is the real enemy of *metta*. It is the fundamental wish to do harm to others. By comparison, momentary anger is a relatively healthy reaction. Sometimes letting off steam in a safe context is healthier than bottling it up.

It is at this point that the Buddha shifts from meditating on *metta* to how it can lead to Insight. We can begin this with a reflection on the nature of hatred. Hatred is the antithesis of human growth and development. So how does it arise?

If we have a painful feeling, we tend to look for an external cause. If we think we've found the cause, we tend to respond with hatred towards that cause. So hatred is a combination of an idea and a feeling. We hate whatever we see as responsible for the unhappiness we feel. We don't just want to remove this thing, we also have an urge to retaliate by inflicting the same or greater suffering. In other words, we're longing for some kind of balance for our pain, some understanding for its particular intensity. The best way we know of getting this balance or understanding is by inflicting the same or greater pain.

Spelled out in this way, it seems crazy. What are the chances that the other person will really understand us? They are much more likely to react to *their* experience of suffering. They will blame *us* for it and retaliate, thus perpetuating the cycle of suffering. Every time we allow a memory of supposed wrong to run through our minds, hatred accumulates, and an 'enemy image', a fixed attitude, develops.

However, this cycle isn't inevitable. If you have a painful experience, you don't need to manufacture hatred from it. From a Buddhist perspective, feelings themselves, whether painful or pleasant, are karmically neutral. They are the results of your previous actions. How you deal with them is of decisive karmic importance. If you react with hatred, you are likely to continue to experience painful feelings in the future, as you are creating fresh unskilful karma. Hatred isn't something that happens to you: it's something that you *do*.

To complicate matters, our dislikes and resentments are often not based on anything that a person has actually *done*. We tend to project certain qualities onto certain people, based on our early childhood conditioning. As we saw in the previous chapter, people whose early life was relatively untroubled tend to be straightforward, open, and receptive. People who have struggled in early life tend to be suspicious, wary, and reserved. When one object of resentment departs, another black sheep appears to take its place.

In trying to cultivate *metta*, we are to some extent swimming against the tide of evolution. Hatred is a basic human trait. We are always trying to protect ourselves against the threat of attack – not just our bodies, but also the fragile sense of who we think we are. We have a sense of ourselves as human beings. We identify with a 'self' in a limited sense, and this makes us susceptible to hatred.

So if you succeed in sustaining *metta*, this would suggest that you no longer experience a sense of threat, and that you no longer identify with a contingent personality. In other words, Insight has arisen in you! Before this, we can make use of our irrational reactions to develop awareness and put down the psychological burdens we have been carrying.

For instance, when we feel hatred towards someone for an apparently trivial reason, we can start to notice that the situation doesn't seem to justify it. Just notice the incongruence, the lack of proportion, and reflect on it. Is there something else going on here? Does the situation trigger painful memories? If so, do they suggest a deep-seated need that went unmet at the time? Does the current situation remind you that this need is still 'hungry'? Are there relatively healthy and skilful ways you could get this need met in the present moment? In this way, we can free ourselves of our early conditioning.

At this point the Buddha introduces the analogy of a mother's love, as quoted at the top of the chapter. The analogy suggests the emotional depth that we are trying to develop. The Buddha emphasizes that it is her *only* child. He chooses maternal love to make this point because it is a nurturing love. Romantic love can have this intensity, but it doesn't so obviously have this element of nurturing.

Metta is like a mother's love in that it is intense, selfless, nurturing, and even intuitive. However, in another way *metta* is quite unlike a mother's love. A mother's love tends to be limited to her own offspring, whereas *metta* is universal and unlimited. A mother views her child as an extension of herself, and loves it as part of herself. It's only by extending this love to others that a real transcendence of self can occur.

As the next verse makes clear, *metta* is unbounded: 'Let [their] thoughts of boundless love pervade the whole world; above, below and across, without any obstruction, without any hatred, without any enemy.' In other words, nobody is beyond the reach of this love and goodwill. *Metta* continuously expands to take in more and more beings. It opens out, becoming free of any specific reference or object. It continues shining whether or not there is someone there to receive it.

In this respect, *metta* is a movement within consciousness, or even a medium within which consciousness moves. This manifests in a tendency to be more and more inclusive of others, and less focused on your own interests at the expense of others. Perhaps we could call it enlightened self-interest.

If you develop *metta* at all times, as long as you are awake, whether you are sitting, walking, or lying down, it can seem as if you are living in a divine state. But Buddhism doesn't stop here, in reaching a heavenly state. Its goal is Enlightenment, and this means escaping the cycle of birth and death completely.

So, in the final verse of the sutta, the Buddha clarifies the connection between *metta* and Enlightenment. He says that, if you don't fall into mistaken views, if you're ethical and dwelling in Insight, if you discard attachment to sense desires, then you'll never again be reborn. In other words, you will have escaped the cycle of birth and death and gained Enlightenment.

Metta is related to Insight, because it deepens our emotional involvement with the truth of *anatta*, or no-self. The unenlightened take their own self as the fundamental and absolute reality of things. *Metta* is inherently expansive, and yet thinking of ourselves as separate from others will have a limiting effect on our experience of it. Only when *metta* is permeated by Insight do our emotions finally go beyond the range of self.

Directly experiencing Insight into the truth of no-self is the first real breakthrough on the way to Enlightenment. It is traditionally known as 'entering the stream', and marks the first point where progress towards Enlightenment is assured. The stream entrant has broken the fetter of self-view, and understands directly and intuitively that the separate self is only an idea, albeit an idea that is the source of unhappiness and lack of fulfilment. They experience this insight in the form of a fully developed emotional positivity.

In the Pali Canon, the earliest record of the Buddha's teachings, there is a monk called Subhuti. He's the younger brother of Anathapindika, a wealthy merchant who donated a large park to the Buddha and his disciples. Subhuti became famous for living at peace in the forest. He gained Insight, or became an arhat (holy one), through meditating on *metta*. Because he had cultivated *metta*, he was declared to be especially worthy of gifts from laypeople. The story of Subhuti directly links the cultivation of *metta* with gaining Enlightenment.[37]

There are times when we feel love for many people, perhaps at a rock concert, at a religious gathering, or when witnessing a natural disaster. Is there any limit to this feeling? The Buddhist tradition has been exploring these questions for over 2,500 years. It has developed many practices to help us to respond creatively. These practices can help us to become more loving towards ourselves and others. Learning and practising them can raise our general level of contentment and enjoyment of life.

I learned one of these practices at the Croydon Buddhist Centre in 1985. It was the *metta bhavana* or development of loving-kindness. The particular form comes from Buddhaghosa, the Theravadin commentator mentioned earlier. He describes the practice in chapter 9 of the *Visuddhimaga* (*Path of Purification*).

People often think of meditation as emptying the mind. However, with the *metta bhavana* we deliberately use everyday situations that arouse love, empathy, and their opposites. We let the practice stir up pleasant and unpleasant feelings so that we get to know ourselves more deeply. We acknowledge the 'messiness' of our experience. We may feel disappointed to notice how few beings we can relate to, how little empathy we feel, and how limited our wishes for the wellbeing of others are.

As we use skill, play, and beauty to practise the *metta bhavana*, other people will appear more pleasing to us, and we will start to notice their skilfulness. We will tend to find them inspiring. This allows for genuine communication, trust, and intimacy. And we will want this for others as well.

When we notice that we've got stuck, we can keep returning to this place with kind awareness until something shifts and we can move on. And, if we keep going, this practice can really open our hearts and set up the conditions for the arising of deep wisdom and compassion.

Buddhaghosa has some practical tips to help us get the most from the practice. For instance, he tells us that *metta* arises from being able to see the loveableness in beings. Could we commit to this – seeing the loveableness in beings?

As we've seen above, the Buddha describes how to prepare for this practice. He suggests that we start with a principled and upright life, develop strong positive energy, and take this out into the world. We cultivate a healthy, happy human life. On this basis, we turn to meditating on *metta*. It can seem difficult to get started, so we need to manage our expectations.

The US poet William Stafford was famous for writing a poem every morning, for years. Over the course of his life he wrote more than 20,000. Stafford was once asked if there were mornings when he couldn't write. He replied that there weren't: 'I think that anybody could write if [they] would have standards as low as mine.'[38] In other words, if you're struggling to develop *metta*, lower your standards! *Metta* is a slow, warm dawning rather than a sudden lightning flash.

It's also an honest practice. We start where we are. It's not about some time in the future when you've got yourself together. You may see yourself as violent – that's a place to start. There's plenty of rich material to work with. You might be depressed and addicted – okay, start there. You might be feeling jealous and giving yourself a hard time – start there. You might think that you're not good enough or that nobody hates themselves as much as you do. These are places to start. There is no other moment that is more spiritually beneficial than this one. Start from where you are.

As we've seen, *metta* is a motivation or drive rather than a feeling. However, we need to be aware of our feelings in order to access this drive. Before we try to improve a situation, it's helpful to get to know and understand it. We can take a kindly interest in what's already there, acknowledging our own feelings and needs as we go through the practice.

What we attend to, we become. This is how karma works. So we make our friendly feelings the centre of our attention and expand them to people we don't like. In this way, these friendly feelings can grow, develop, go beyond their bounds, and ultimately become boundless.

The five stages of the practice consist in developing *metta* towards (i) yourself, (ii) a very dearly loved friend, (iii) someone you're neutral towards, and (iv) someone you find difficult (the 'enemy'), before (v) equalizing *metta* towards all four people and radiating it out, ultimately towards all beings. For further instruction, you can listen to the first three guided reflections at the end of this chapter.

It's important to remember that *metta* is not primarily a feeling. It is a wish for wellbeing and welfare. A first step is self-empathy, acknowledging what you're feeling at the moment. Whether this feeling is pleasant or unpleasant, sensing it is a valid way of doing this stage.

When we can reliably see the loveableness in all beings, we may be ready for the next stage. This is when we encounter beings who are experiencing the extremes of suffering and joy. Can we continue to see their loveableness, even then? How do we make our peace with them? Is there such a thing as compassion fatigue?

The Theravadin tradition emphasizes *metta* or love rather than compassion. This might be because *metta* is easier to practise. When you encounter suffering, it is easy to fall into overwhelm and horrified anxiety. As we've seen, *metta* is what you can practise, what you do. The *Karaniya Metta Sutta* presents this as a complete path. *Metta* is the basic Buddhist emotional response of friendliness, loving-kindness, and love.

Metta promotes welfare and wellbeing. It arises from seeing the loveableness in all beings, and manifests in reducing ill-will and hatred. By contrast, *karuna* or compassion promotes the reduction of suffering. It responds to the suffering of others. It manifests as noncruelty, care, concern, and support. It sees the helplessness of those overwhelmed by suffering. And, when it is successful, it makes cruelty subside.

Metta and *karuna* are the first of four Buddhist qualities known as the *brahmavihara*s – Brahma was the king of the brahma gods in ancient Indian mythology and *vihara* means 'dwelling place', so they are the 'divine abodes'. I like to call them the four flavours of love. The other two are *mudita* or empathic joy, and *upekkha* or equanimity.

The *brahmavihara*s were around before the time of the Buddha. They were practised by the sramanas, the non-Vedic freelance wanderers that Siddhartha joined before he became the Buddha. Sramanas were expected to dwell in the *brahmavihara*s. So Siddhartha would have learned these meditations as part of his training. After Enlightenment, the Buddha encouraged his own students to practise them, and act from *metta* in all matters, privately and publicly, with body, speech, and mind.[39]

These four flavours of love help us to understand how a Buddha relates to unenlightened beings and suffering in the world. They also clarify that a Buddha has equal love and compassion for all beings. A Buddha wishes all beings the highest joy of complete Awakening. So these four flavours are Buddha qualities. Only a Buddha knows the joy of these flavours in their fullness. The rest of us are in training!

The *brahmavihara*s are sometimes referred to as the Immeasurables. They are immeasurable in the sense that their scope is limitless. There is no limit to the number of beings they can be applied to. They apply to all or any beings that you can conceive of. Each of the Immeasurables shares with *metta* the same limitless object. If it really is *metta*, you'll never feel that you have had enough. This is most obvious with *upekkha* or equanimity. Equanimity restricted to a few objects or people would be a contradiction in terms. The essential nature of equanimity is not to make distinctions. In the literal meaning of the word, its nature is to have an 'even mind' towards all.

The *brahmavihara*s are very closely connected, with *metta* underlying them all. If we experience *metta* and encounter a being that is suffering, our *metta* transforms into *karuna* or compassion. *Karuna* is the strong and practical desire to do whatever we can to relieve suffering. We'll want to do something to help. We'll appreciate what they need to thrive and we'll look for ways to support this. So this is a key challenge for our *metta*, how we respond to suffering.

Karuna's natural tendency is to reach out and expand its field of activity, ever further and more powerfully. As we've seen, any skilful attitude has this tendency. We look upon anyone we meet with the love a mother feels for her own helpless child. So it will come as no surprise that the neural fingerprint of compassion in the scanner correlates to brain areas associated with love, especially maternal love, feelings of belonging and gratification.[40]

I've heard experienced meditators say that *karuna* is the most beautiful of the *brahmavihara*s. I have some experience with this. A few years ago I was absorbed in *metta* when I spontaneously brought to mind someone's suffering. The experience went from being loving to being incredibly moving and profoundly beautiful. I was in love with the richness and depth of human experience! So this was really a spontaneous experience of the *brahmaviharas*. It's amazing to imagine that, when a Buddha sees beings who are not yet enlightened, their *metta* becomes this kind of *karuna* or compassion.

You develop *karuna* in much the same way as *metta*. Paradoxically, you don't try to develop *karuna* directly. As we've seen, the basic wish is *metta*. Simply try to develop *metta* towards someone, *including* their suffering. Keep a broad awareness of the person/being and what they need to thrive, rather than focusing exclusively on their suffering.

As mentioned above, *karuna* can be a more challenging quality to develop than *metta*. We can find the suffering of others very difficult to handle. We may not like to acknowledge suffering at all, our own or other people's. We may see it as some kind of moral failure. But this attitude can lead us into indifference or even neglect, which are both unskilful responses, as we will see below. For more specific guidance in developing *karuna*, you can listen to the guided *karuna bhavana* at the end of this chapter.

If you're experiencing *metta* and encounter a being who is happy, your *metta* transforms into *mudita* or empathic joy. *Mudita* is the state of being happy for the happiness of others. It means rejoicing in their merits and skilful qualities. It's inherently expansive, and reaches a peak when you can recognize and rejoice in the skilful actions of people you regard as enemies. You are as happy to rejoice in their merits as you are your friends'.

If you could only rejoice in the skilfulness of your friends, that would be a limited form of *mudita*. If you could only appreciate actions that benefited you in some way, that would be gratitude rather than full-blown *mudita*. *Mudita* is the appreciation of the true happiness of others. If you can't feel happiness in their happiness, then *metta* is not really present.

Ultimately *mudita* expands to include all beings and Enlightenment itself. The poet Shantideva expresses this cosmic vision in his *Bodhicaryavatara* or *Path to Awakening*:

> I rejoice with delight
> In the good done by all beings,
> Through which they obtain rest
> With the end of suffering.
> May those who have suffered be happy!
>
> I rejoice in the release of beings
> From the sufferings of the rounds of existence;
> I rejoice in the nature of the Bodhisattva
> And the Buddha,
> Who are protectors.
>
> I rejoice in the arising of the Will to Enlightenment,
> And the Teaching:
> Those Oceans that bring happiness to all beings,
> And are the abode of welfare of all beings.[41]

If this is too high an aspiration, we could start by developing gratitude for gifts received, which is an essential building block of *mudita*. Once we are comfortable with expressing and receiving gratitude, we can expand this to include other people's skilful actions that only benefit us indirectly, and so on. For more specific guidance, listen to the guided *mudita bhavana* at the end of this chapter.

Metta, *karuna*, and *mudita* come together in *upekkha*, the last of the *brahmavihara*s. Whatever work has been done with the first three provides a foundation for this more complete practice. According to Buddhaghosa, the first three will only take you so far in meditation; *upekkha* will take you much further. This is when you are meditating on the other-regarding aspect of equanimity. It has qualities that make it potentially far more powerful. For more specific guidance, you can listen to the guided *upekkha bhavana* at the end of this chapter.

Sometimes, when we're learning something new, it's helpful to be reminded of what it *isn't*. This is the Buddha's approach in his teaching of near and far enemies. As we've already seen, the far enemies of the four *brahmavihara*s are as follows: the far enemy of *metta* is ill-will or hatred; the far enemy of *karuna* is cruelty; the far enemy of *mudita* is resentment or envy; and the far enemy of *upekkha* is cold, hardened, fixed indifference. The far enemies of the *brahmavihara*s are relatively easy to spot, as they are almost exactly their opposites.

Now let's look at their near enemies, the things that are relatively easily mistaken for them. The near enemy of *metta* is *pema*, sticky affection or sentimental attachment. Remember how many cats you've seen on social media? As you start to develop *metta*, you may experience *pema*. It's easy to mistake it for genuine *metta*. *Pema* is emotional attachment to another being, a craving for some kind of experience from them. It can be subtle or obvious. It can range from a slight tendency to sentimentalize or idealize them, to full-blown sexual desire.

It's not just sexual desire that is likely to be affected by *pema*. Parents may mix a genuine desire for their child's wellbeing with ideas about how they should grow up. This confusion can extend to any relationship between a more experienced and a less experienced person. This is why, in the second stage of the *metta bhavana* practice, Buddhaghosa recommends that we choose someone who is roughly the same age as us. The main point is to cultivate *metta*, or love, and this will get refined in the process.

The near enemies of *karuna* are sentimental pity and horrified anxiety. If we don't know the difference, we can easily fall into these responses when we encounter suffering. We may even mistake them for *karuna*. Both of the near enemies arise from the fear of the feelings stimulated by witnessing another being's suffering. Perceiving another to be suffering is often painful and confusing. We can be unable to respond warmly and open-heartedly to the situation because we are preoccupied with our own discomfort.

Sentimental pity can arise when we shy away from our sense of discomfort and try to cover it up by feeling sorry for the other being. We tell ourselves that it's not possible to relate to them. If we're not careful, this can become a basis for explaining away their suffering. Sentimentality is unearned emotion. It may seem harmless enough, but it stems from a cynical attitude. As the Irish idealist Oscar Wilde shrewdly observed, 'the sentimentalist is always a cynic at heart. Indeed sentimentality is merely the Bank-holiday of cynicism.'[42]

Feeling afraid or confused about another being's suffering is not the same as *karuna*. We're likely just to want to escape the situation. With *karuna* comes a clear seeing of what the being actually needs to thrive. We take the trouble to get involved and find out.

Horrified anxiety is another form of counterfeit *karuna*. It can arise when we allow ourselves to experience the distress that another's suffering stimulates in us. We are so affected by this distress that we're unable to see the other being clearly or what they need. We stiffen and panic, so we're unable to be of any actual use. Since we're feeling *something* in relation to the other being, we may tell ourselves that this is a kind of *karuna*.

These two responses, sentimental pity and horrified anxiety, correspond to the avoidant and anxious attachment styles. Whenever you recognize them in your experience, you can adjust your approach. In the case of sentimental pity, you can acknowledge and engage with your actual feelings about another's suffering. In the case of horrified anxiety, you can acknowledge your anxiety and reflect on how it makes it difficult to see things clearly. As a climate activist, I've noticed how often these two come up for myself and other activists. I explore them in more detail in my book *The Burning House: A Buddhist Response to the Climate and Ecological Emergency*.[43]

The far enemies of *mudita* are resentment and envy. However, they are not as far away as some of the other 'opposites'. The Germans even have a word for it, *Schadenfreude*, which means 'gloating' or taking joy in another's misfortune. As I am temperamentally competitive, I tend to hold grudges. Sometimes I can rationally recognize another being's happiness or good fortune, but inside I feel resentful about it. There's an unpaid account that's still open. Perhaps it will always remain open. This usually arises when I compare myself to others and find that I'm not 'good enough'.

I used to think that I would be happy if I could just get enough acceptance from others. As I hadn't had this kind of acceptance, it was natural for me to think that this was what was missing. In my work as a Nonviolent Communication (NVC) trainer, I had the opportunity to test this out. For years, I received a great deal of appreciation from the groups I supported. I enjoyed this experience; however, I was shocked to realize that it hardly translated into self-value at all. Despite acceptance from the group, I still couldn't accept myself.

Then I realized that self-acceptance was the real deal. So I asked, what would need to be in place in order to accept myself? The answer came back, two Nobel Prizes and Enlightenment! Okay, so I've got high expectations! Nowadays, I describe myself as a recovering perfectionist. One way to support my recovery is to appreciate my own merits, my own skilfulness and contribution to life. I consciously try to let go of the idea that other people will see me the way I want to be seen. We see the world not as it is, but as we are. What I *can* do is to see myself.

By contrast, the near enemy of *mudita* is vicarious enjoyment. This is a sentimental kind of satisfaction in another being's happiness. They represent our *idea* of happiness. We welcome their happiness, perhaps even idolizing them as celebrities, but avoid any real connection to them or any interest in who they actually are. To counteract this tendency, we can pay closer attention to the beings themselves and appreciate what their experience of happiness and good fortune is really like.

The far enemy of *upekkha* is cold, hardened, fixed indifference. Obviously this is in total opposition to all-embracing, insightful love. *Upekkha*'s near enemy is neutrality, a lukewarm, apathetic lack of interest. Our feelings are so weak that it seems pointless to take any interest at all. It's a near enemy because this can easily be mistaken for a skilful, disinterested attitude.

In the *upekkha bhavana* practice we choose to develop *metta* towards a being we feel neutral towards. This is a challenge for our emotional maturity. Can we still relate to them, even though we have no emotional investment in them? With the near enemy of neutrality, we are refusing to really experience this being. We can't be bothered to engage with them.

This gives us an opportunity to work with our own prejudices and preconceptions. The people we find interesting inevitably reflect how we want to see ourselves. In this way the *brahmavihara*s allow us to extend ourselves beyond our present imagination, to look into the lives of others with curiosity and wonder.

The *upekkha bhavana* can't be practised effectively unless there has been preparatory work in the other *brahmavihara*s. *Metta* is fundamental, but we also need some experience of *karuna* and *mudita*. *Upekkha* draws these threads together, allowing us greater insight into how someone we find uninteresting might feel, and what they may need to thrive.

Upekkha takes *metta*, *karuna*, and *mudita* to their highest, most universal level. It allows us to develop greater empathy towards others. This means not just 'equal positivity', but a love that is equally strongly felt towards all. It is the highest possible degree of emotional skilfulness. *Karuna* and *mudita* help us to loosen our attachment and aversion. *Upekkha* is different in that it does not see others in terms of pleasure or pain. It includes compassion towards suffering and gladness that everyone can experience joy and happiness. But it adds the realization that suffering and joy arise from an accumulation of choices. We are all heirs to our previous karma (actions).

Upekkha is an extremely skilful emotion combined with a powerful element of insight. Understanding the universality of actions and consequences gives birth to equanimity. We realize that, even if beings are not immediately responsible, in the long run each of us is responsible for our happiness. This strengthens and deepens the connection between ourselves and others, giving us a new kind of patience and kindness.

So these are the *brahmavihara*s, the four flavours of love. This is what happens when a Buddha encounters beings who are experiencing the extremes of suffering and joy. A Buddha will continue to see their loveableness, and be at peace with them. The *brahmavihara*s provide a template for how we can relate to suffering and joy in the world. They are the Buddhist answer to the 'problem' of suffering. By practising them, we can bring the emotional and aspirational aspect of Enlightenment into our lives.

So is there such a thing as compassion fatigue? Perhaps we have an answer. Skilful qualities such as the *brahmavihara*s are expansive by nature. If they aren't broadening in scope, they aren't fully developed. Like *metta*, the basic response, their tendency is to become universal. They go on expanding, renewing themselves, growing brighter and stronger. If it really is *metta*, *karuna*, *mudita*, and *upekkha*, you'll feel as if you can never have enough of them. So compassion fatigue probably equates to a combination of sentimental pity, horrified anxiety, lukewarm neutrality, and even a touch of indifference.

In the next chapter, we'll explore the great love of the bodhisattva and the tantric approach. Meanwhile, I invite you to reap the benefits of this chapter with guided reflections to develop *metta*, *karuna*, *mudita*, and *upekkha*. We all have different ways into the *metta bhavana*, so I've recorded three different versions, one with verbal phrases, one with empathy and taking a next step, and one using colour and imagery. Feast your senses!

Guided reflection: the *metta bhavana* in five stages using phrases

- Purpose of this activity: to open our hearts to unbounded love using verbal phrases.
- Time: 20 minutes.

Guided reflection: the *metta bhavana* in five stages using empathy and a next step

- Purpose of this activity: to open our hearts to unbounded love using empathy and imagining a next step to enrich life.
- Time: 20 minutes.

Guided reflection: the *metta bhavana* in five stages using colour and imagery

- Purpose of this activity: to open our hearts to unbounded love using colour and imagery.
- Time: 20 minutes.

Guided reflection: the *karuna bhavana*

- Purpose of this activity: to develop the strong and practical desire to do whatever we can to relieve suffering. Distinguishing *karuna* from its near enemies of sentimental pity and horrified anxiety.
- Time: 25 minutes.

Guided reflection: the *mudita bhavana*

- Purpose of this activity: to develop the state of being happy for the happiness of others, including rejoicing in their merits and skilful qualities. Distinguishing *mudita* from its near enemy of vicarious enjoyment.
- Time: 25 minutes.

Guided reflection: the *upekkha bhavana*

- Purpose of this activity: to develop the other-regarding aspect of equanimity, a love that is equally strongly felt towards all. Distinguishing *upekkha* from its near enemy of neutrality, a lukewarm, apathetic lack of interest.
- Time: 25 minutes.

4

The Great Love of the Bodhisattva

> Manjusri then asked further, 'Good sir, if a bodhisattva should look upon all beings in this way [as insubstantial and illusory], how then can [they] have great love for all beings?'
>
> Vimalakirti replied, 'Whenever, Manjusri, the bodhisattva looks upon them with the thought: "It is up to me to teach the Dharma in such a way that these beings comprehend the Dharma," then [they feel] the love which is true and protective of others.'[44]

In the previous chapter, we looked at some of the Buddha's teachings from the Theravadin tradition that can help us to work with *tanha* or craving. In this chapter, we're mining the Mahayana and Vajrayana traditions.

Let's start with the figure of the bodhisattva, the ideal Buddhist of the Mahayana tradition. As the above extract makes clear, the bodhisattva develops a great love for all beings. They do this by reflecting that beings are insubstantial and illusory, and yet they still need to find a way to teach the Dharma in a way that beings can comprehend. When bodhisattvas reflect in this way, a great love arises in them, which is authentic and protective.

What the Mahayana makes clear is that Reality is in essence

inconceivable and ungraspable. Trying to grasp it, to fix it, creates suffering for ourselves and others. In our daily life, we tend to settle into routines. At the very least, we repeat certain actions such as eating, sleeping, defecating, and walking. Sometimes this can lead to boredom and lethargy. However, in reality, every moment of our life is unique. Everyday life is ungraspable. How much more inconceivable is the experience of Enlightenment or Emancipation? When we are imprisoned, the reality of emancipation or freedom is inconceivable. We can try to imagine the experience, but the experience itself is ungraspable.

The Sanskrit word 'Mahayana' means 'the Great Way' (*maha* means 'great', and *yana* means 'way'). The Mahayana is a form of Buddhism that sets no limit upon the spiritual development of the individual. It encourages all beings to aim for the highest goal of the spiritual life – supreme and perfect Enlightenment.

A being who aims for this goal not just for themselves but for the benefit of all beings is known as a bodhisattva (*bodhi*, 'wisdom' or 'awakening', and *sattva*, 'being'). So a bodhisattva is one who is dedicated to Awakening. According to the Mahayana, the bodhisattva is the ideal Buddhist. You become a bodhisattva by developing those qualities that will give rise to the bodhicitta, or Awakening Heart/Mind.

The path of the bodhisattva begins when you take four great vows. These are: (i) However innumerable beings are, I vow to deliver them; (ii) However inexhaustible the passions are, I vow to extinguish them; (iii) However immeasurable the teachings are, I vow to master them; (iv) However incomparable the Buddha-Truth is, I vow to attain it.

It may seem unrealistic or even demotivating to undertake such all-encompassing vows. However, it's more that our ordinary self opens up to the forces of wisdom and compassion that these vows represent, allowing it to be transformed by them. In a sense, we allow wisdom and compassion to work through us, relying on 'other-power' rather than 'self-power'. These four great vows represent the spirit of the Mahayana tradition out of which the *Vimalakirti Nirdesa* (or *Teaching of Vimalakirti* – the text quoted at the top of this chapter) emerged.

Meditating on *metta* and the other *brahmavihara*s is a way of stepping into the broader vision of the Mahayana. It links us to the bodhicitta, the vision and feeling that we need to train as a bodhisattva, to bring all beings to Awakening. As we saw in the previous chapters, *metta* has a protective quality (remember cherishing, protecting, and maturing?). *Metta* can be seen as a protective kind of love. In the *Metta Sutta*, we wish people to be free from enmity. And the *Metta Sutta* itself is regarded as one of the protective suttas, to be recited for protection in times of danger.

We also saw that the *brahmavihara*s are universal and unlimited. So it's no surprise that, in the Mahayana, *metta* (Pali) or *maitri* (Sanskrit) has become *mahamaitri*, the great love. This is the love that is a refuge for others, offering protection and inspiring fearlessness. The whole of the bodhisattva path arises from this.

By comparison, later Buddhist tradition talks about *sunyata-karunagarbha*, the essence (*garbha*) of emptiness (*sunyata*) and compassion (*karuna*). The famous Indian teacher Atisha, who reintroduced Buddhism to Tibet, told his disciples about the importance of *metta* in their practice. He presented *sunyatakarunagarbha* as one quality and the final goal of the teaching. There is no insight (*sunyata*) without altruistic activity (*karuna*).

True wisdom doesn't rest for long. It moves outwards towards suffering through compassion. The historical Buddha sat for seven weeks after his Enlightenment, absorbing the experience. Then he went to find someone to communicate it to. Not long after, he sent sixty disciples out to teach the Dharma for the welfare of the many (*bahujan hitay*). The Buddha spent the next forty years travelling around, meeting people and talking to them, out of compassion.

The *brahmavihara*s also appear in the Vajrayana tradition. The famous semi-mythical teacher Padmasambhava enters into a *samadhi* (profound meditation) on the *brahmavihara*s in order to transform all demons. The *samadhi* is seen as having great magical power. And the Tibetan teacher Longchenpa talks about the *brahmavihara*s. In *sadhana*s (practices to visualize specific Buddhas or bodhisattvas), the *brahmavihara*s come first, as preparation.

Now let's turn to the great love of the bodhisattva. In chapter 6 of the *Vimalakirti Nirdesa*, Manjusri asks Vimalakirti how a bodhisattva should regard all beings. Vimalakirti replies:

> as a wise man would look upon the moon reflected in the water [...] as someone would look upon their face in the mirror [...] as comparable to the water in a mirage [...] as a magician would look upon a man magically created by a magician, as the sound of an echoing voice, clouds in the sky, a clump of foam just as it takes shape.

With these images, Vimalakirti evokes the ephemeral and illusory nature of all beings.[45]

Beings are inconceivable. In a sense, we don't know anything about them. There is a vivid appearance, but, if we look carefully, we can find no essence. Things are indefinable and indescribable. Suffering arises when we try to fix them into some*thing*.

Then Manjusri asks Vimalakirti, 'Good sir, if a Bodhisattva should look upon all beings in this way, how then can [they] have great love for all living beings?'

Vimalakirti replies:

> Whenever, Manjusri, the bodhisattva looks upon them with the thought: 'It is up to me to teach the Dharma in such a way that these beings comprehend the Dharma,' then [they feel] the love which is true and protective of others because it has no object.

Vimalakirti goes on to explain the Mahayana understanding of the other *brahmavihara*s. There is great compassion (giving away to all beings the roots of merit from everything that the bodhisattva does), great empathic joy (when the bodhisattva gives, they are delighted and have no regrets), and great serene equanimity (dedication to the benefit of both self and other).

A goddess appears and showers the assembly with flowers. The flowers don't stick to the bodhisattvas – only to the great monastic disciples. Monastic rules forbid monks from wearing flowers, so this stimulates discomfort for them. In another challenge to monastic literalism, the goddess points out that they are feeling uncomfortable because of dualistic thinking.

So there are two perspectives here. On the one hand, beings aren't ultimately real: they are selfless and insubstantial. On the other hand, it's up to us to teach the Dharma in such a way that beings can comprehend it. It's this intention that gives rise to a great, protective love. This is in fulfilment of the first of the four great vows: however innumerable beings are, I vow to deliver them. The bodhisattva develops living beings in order to create a Buddhaland or Buddhafield. It's a joint creation – no living beings, no Buddhaland. It's a vision of *kalyana mitrata* or spiritual friendship, of personal and collective spiritual development.

In this vision, *mahamaitri* is the great love, nondual loving-kindness. It is *maha* or great because it is fully expanded. It has dissolved the distinction between self and other. It is an expression of *sunyata*, voidness or emptiness. The whole path emerges from this great love. It is a force, a power, free-floating, and effects a miraculous transformation on whatever it touches.

What would it feel like to pursue the bodhisattva path and develop *mahamaitri*? At this point you are like a great beacon of love, ablaze with the fire of well-wishing for all living beings. You care for them as if each one was your only child. You feel incredibly close to them. You're very near to a direct experience of how things are. Just let go of thinking in terms of a 'self' that loves 'others'. Suddenly this duality of self and others will fall apart. You emerge into an indescribable world where there is no separation. It is as natural to care about another person as it is to care about your own hand. There is no 'me' and 'others', only love.

When you experience insight into the nature of things, you realize that your picture of the world is just a useful description of it, rather than how things really are. Simultaneously, three things happen. You experience a tremendous sense of aliveness, freedom, and energy in your heart. This energy has been overlaid by misguided judging and conceptualizing. Now you get a glimpse of what is possible, the inspiring prospect of total freedom. Secondly, your heart opens to the intense suffering you see around you. You feel intensely the pain of a baby crying for its mother, or refugees crossing the Mediterranean in order to escape war and persecution.

And thirdly, as you open to intense suffering, you also realize that a great deal of it is brought about by inaccurate interpretations of the world. At least once in your life you may have fallen into a state that could be described as paranoid. In this state you may have created your own suffering by interpreting everyday situations as threatening or dangerous. However, even if we're not in a state of paranoia, we create much of our suffering through how we interpret our experience. Based on inaccurate interpretations, we make choices that lead to further suffering for ourselves and others. As we saw when exploring *upekkha*, we are all heir to our previous karma (actions).

Someone whose heart is nearly awakened sees a heartbreaking situation. They know that in the depths of every being's heart lie profound joy, freedom, and love. At the same time they can see how those same beings are running around, trying to find an external source of happiness. It takes a great deal of courage to turn towards this suffering and open your heart to it. If you do manage to open your heart to it, then, instead of breaking, your heart opens to its fullest extent. The deepest and most miraculous powers of a human being are drawn out, and you awaken to the great love of the bodhisattva.

As mentioned earlier, a bodhisattva seeks to gain Enlightenment for the sake of all beings. Now we can understand this more deeply. A bodhisattva is set on Awakening to help others escape from suffering. This suffering is brought about by them misunderstanding the nature of their experience. In this way, the bodhisattva finds true fulfilment, realizing their deepest heart-wish for 'themselves' and 'others'.

This state is said to be the result of practice over many lifetimes. However, it is possible to get a direct, intuitive glimpse, even in this lifetime. You could say that a bodhisattva is in the service of wisdom and compassion, and this is what enables them to shine in the world. How much of the suffering in relationships is brought about by greed and hatred? Wars, human-generated global heating, and the destruction of the biosphere all began with movements in people's hearts. They all started from longings for security, ease, freedom, dignity, or empowerment. The war-torn regions, the disappearing rainforests are all expressions of a lack of connection, a lack of belonging, a lack of empathy for other beings.

As suffering originates in the heart, it can also be brought to an end by working to open the heart. We need to start where we are. We can begin this transformation by cultivating ordinary friendly feelings. In these, there is a sense of selflessness. Rather than contributing to the suffering, we can become part of the solution.

And now for a touch of magic! In the previous chapter, we explored love primarily in a Theravadin context. In this chapter, we have expanded our enquiry to include the

Mahayana context of the *Vimalakirti Nirdesa*. Now let's discover how love can be the agent of magical transformation. This is a particular flavour of the Vajrayana or Tantric tradition. The Vajrayana, or Indo-Tibetan Tantric Buddhism, emphasized direct experience and magical transformation.

It's very easy to become fascinated by samsara, the mundane world, and more difficult to become fascinated by Enlightenment. The Vajrayana recognized this by promoting the seductive figure of Kurukulla, a sublimated form of Kamadeva. Kurukulla represents the fascinating aspect of Enlightenment, Enlightenment as all-beautiful. Her name means 'She who causes knowledge'.

Kurukulla is shown dancing vigorously, indicating her energy and activity. She is sixteen years old, symbolizing the peak of physical beauty. She has a beautiful face and voluptuous body. Her colour is vermilion red, signifying the magical function of fascination and enchantment. She has one face because she embodies nondual wisdom. She is naked, signifying that she is unconstrained by discursive thoughts.

She has four arms, signifying the *brahmavihara*s of loving-kindness, compassion, empathic joy, and equanimity. Two of her arms hold a bow and arrow, which are entwined with flowers. She shoots beings with a desire for the Dharma. Her other two hands hold a hook and a noose. Once she has shot her victim, she pulls them towards her with the hook and binds them with the noose.

She wears human-bone ornaments and a necklace of fifty freshly severed heads, embodying wisdom and vanquishing negative emotions. She dances upon a male human corpse as she fascinates and subdues greed, hatred, and delusion. She stands upon a red sun disc, because her nature is hot and inflamed with passion. Under the sun disc is a red lotus blossom, because she is a pure vision of enlightened awareness. Kurukulla's function is to fascinate and subdue. Through her love magic she leads everyone, even the enemies of the Dharma, to fall at her feet.

Kurukulla most likely began life as an Indian tribal deity, an independent goddess associated with magical domination. Later she was incorporated into the Buddhist pantheon as Tara, where she performs the 'red' rite of fascination. She came to Tibet as a deity of power, bringing with her the ritual embodied in her basic tantra, *The Practices of the Noble Tara Kurukulla*.

Tibetan monastics called on Kurukulla when they were building a monastery or starting any enterprise. They relied on her to fascinate and subdue the human or demonic forces that stood in their way. More prosaically, Tibetan traders seeking profit and Tibetan lovers seeking satisfaction called upon her in the rituals established by Indians in her basic texts.

I notice that I am drawn to her crimson colour. My body feels excited and tingly. I am energized by her posture and sense of movement, and curious to see her bow and arrow. However, I am shocked by her semi-wrathful expression, and horrified by the severed heads. I have a sense that I'm in the presence of great power and beauty. At the same time, I'm in grave danger of losing my head, both literally and metaphorically.

Kurukulla embodies the subversive power of Enlightenment. It's a power that can undermine the conventional order of society.

As you may have realized by now, some of the symbolism of the Indo-Tibetan Tantric tradition has its origins in magic. Magical practices of all kinds were very popular in India in ancient times, and continued at least up until the last century. My own Buddhist teacher recalled magical rituals being performed near where he lived in North-East India. On the nights of the new moon he could hear the 'Tak, tak, tak' of little drums in the distance, sometimes all night long. And sometimes he heard a horrible wailing as the magician (*jakri*) danced, beat his drum, and shrieked his incantations.

Suppose you have the misfortune to fall in love with someone who didn't reciprocate your love. What can you do? Since time immemorial, people have relied on love magic. You could perform, or pay a *jakri* to perform, a magical *rite of fascination*, and the object of your passion would just come to you, drawn by an irresistible force.[46] Just think of the moody fascination of a song like 'I put a spell on you', made famous by Nina Simone. 'I put a spell on you... 'cos you're mine.'[47]

The rite of fascination was just one of four magical rites commonly performed in ancient India. If you wanted to harm someone or get them out of the way, there was the rite of *destruction*. If you wanted a person or an enterprise to succeed, there was the rite of *prospering*. And finally, if you wanted to pacify a person or spirit more powerful than you, there was the rite of *pacification*.

The Vajrayana took over these rites, not in their crude magical form, but for their spiritual symbolism. The rites came to be associated with the different Buddha 'families'. Each rite came to be associated with a particular *activity* of the enlightened mind. So the rite of destruction was associated with destroying ignorance, the rite of pacification with pacifying forces inimical to the Dharma, the rite of prospering with spiritual maturation, and the rite of fascination with charming the hearts of all living beings.

When you view Enlightenment through the rite of fascination, it is not only truth, reality, and the supreme good, but also the supremely attractive object. It's what everybody really wants in their heart of hearts, whether they know it or not. It symbolizes this supremely beautiful, seductive aspect of the enlightened mind. Like the figure of Kurukulla, the colour of this rite is bright red, brilliant, crimson, vermillion red. But why red? Red is the colour of blood, so it's the colour of life. Blood has temperature, it is hot. So the colour red is also the colour of warmth, both physical and emotional. Red is the colour of all the *brahmavihara*s, loving-kindness, compassion, empathic joy, and equanimity.

The tantric symbolism of colours didn't end there. The rite of destruction came to be associated with black, and known as 'the black rite'. The rite of prospering came to be associated with yellow, the colour of golden corn. And the rite of pacification came to be associated with white. These aren't literal correspondences. Rather than attaching a rigid meaning to each colour, we can try to conjure up and experience the emotional and spiritual association that the colours possess.[48]

So, according to the Vajrayana, red is the colour of love. The tantric term is *maharaga*. As we saw in the previous chapter, *raga* is almost a violent word. In ordinary literary and psychological contexts it means 'passion'. And *maha* means 'great', but in a special sense. *Maha* suggests *sunyata*, emptiness or reality, the Truth or even the Transcendental.

So *maharaga* doesn't just mean excessive passion, it means passion that partakes of the nature of *sunyata*. It means a passion that has been merged with Reality, plunged into Reality, or purified by the experience of Reality. We could say that it is nondual passion. Like *mahamaitri*, it is great because it is fully expanded. It has dissolved the distinction between self and other. *Maharaga* is an emotion that hasn't lost anything of its emotionality, yet has been purified and thoroughly transformed. We could even translate it as 'transcendent passion', an uninterrupted stream of powerful positive feelings that flows spontaneously from the very heart of Enlightenment in the direction of all living beings.

So how can we use the figure of Kurukulla and her rite of fascination to move ourselves towards Enlightenment? And how can we use them in our relationships?

When we fall in love, we're always thinking about the object of our love. We listen out for their name, we feel energized, alive, in the presence of beauty. Chapter 2 describes how this happens at a neurochemical level. Serotonin provides the obsessive component of falling in love, so we can't stop thinking about them and sending photos of them to our friends! If we could feel like that about our spiritual ideal, our progress would be swift and sure. We would always have the figure of the Buddha and our potential for Enlightenment in mind. We would be fascinated by the Buddha's teachings (the Dharma). We would want to spend time with the sangha. All our energies would be focused on this.

So in the Vajrayana, we don't use the rite of fascination to make someone else fall in love with us. We use it to make ourselves fall in love with the ideal. And perhaps we cooperate with the rite of fascination that is being 'used' on us by Enlightenment or Reality. We could say that Enlightenment or Reality is trying to attract us towards becoming the enlightened person we could be.

This idea is familiar from other spiritual traditions. As Rumi's mentor Shams points out in a poem, 'What I want also wants me, is looking for me and attracting me.' He comments, 'There is a great secret here for anyone who can grasp it.'[49] Then there is Thomas Merton: 'Your life is shaped by the end you live for. You are made in the image of what you desire. To unify your life[,] unify your desires.'[50]

But what do we really fall in love with? We fall in love with beauty, whether it's external, physical beauty or the internal qualities of another person. And as Freud and Jung and other psychologists have pointed out, we tend to fall in love with those qualities that we don't perceive in ourselves.

The faculty that perceives beauty, whether physical or metaphorical, is intuitive – it's neither head nor heart but integrates both. As such, it's very closely related to the Buddhist quality of *sraddha* (confidence, trust). *Sraddha* has been described as 'The response of our total being. The response of what is ultimate in us to what is ultimate in the universe'.[51] The etymology of the word is 'to place the heart upon'. We could translate it as 'heart-knowing'. It's a way of knowing both beauty and truth.

Sraddha is calling us towards Enlightenment. At one time or another, we've all been fascinated by aspects of the Dharma, the Buddha's teaching. We've all experienced a heart-knowledge concerning the direction of our life. Our capacity to experience beauty is very closely related to our capacity for *sraddha*, so we can increase our love of what is ultimate in the universe by increasing our appreciation of beauty.

When you fall in love you become intensely focused on that person, more than in any other experience. They are absolutely fascinating to you, and you become deeply resourceful in how to get to know them! You pay detailed attention to their physical appearance, their particular features. In this focused quality of desire for sensuous experience (*kamatrsna*) can be found the seed of its transformation.

This kind of approach tends to be associated with the Vajrayana or Tantric tradition, where the longed-for deity (*ishta devata*) has a special place. However, it is also present in the earliest accounts of the life of the Buddha. People were simply fascinated by his beauty, the physical beauty of his appearance and the 'ethical' beauty of his enlightened qualities.

Even before he became the Buddha, Siddhartha held a magnetic attraction for those who met him. They became aware of the minute particulars of his appearance. They were enraptured by his beauty. A local king called Bimbisara saw Siddhartha on his alms round, well restrained, his sense-doors guarded, mindful, and alert. Watching from his palace, Bimbisara was immediately impressed. So much so that he commented to the people around him:

> Look at this one, sirs. How handsome, stately, pure! How consummate his demeanour! Mindful, his eyes downcast, looking only a plough-length before him, as one who's not from a lowly lineage.[52]

He immediately sent the royal messengers to find out where Siddhartha was staying. Later he rode out by coach to offer

Siddhartha a position as a general in his army. Siddhartha turned down this offer, telling the king that he had gone forth from sensual pleasures and sought peace in renunciation and striving. This was his heart's desire.

The same was true after the Buddha's Enlightenment. There was once an ascetic called Bahiya, who wore bark cloth. He was already successful, and had a following. But a *deva* (god) told him that he wasn't enlightened and wasn't even on the path to Enlightenment. Bahiya asked the *deva*: 'So who is enlightened?' In response, the *deva* sent him to the Buddha.

Bahiya becomes obsessed with meeting the Buddha. He walks all the way from the west coast of India to Sravasti in the east. That's about 1,200 miles without stopping. When he finally gets there, the Buddha has gone into town on his daily alms round. Bahiya catches sight of him, and it's a revelation. The Buddha seems to him serene, inspiring confidence, calming, his senses at peace, his mind at peace. He seems to have attained the utmost tranquillity and poise. He is tamed, guarded, his senses are restrained, like a well-trained elephant.

Bahiya can only respond to the Buddha's appearance by throwing himself down, with his head at the Buddha's feet, and asking the Buddha to teach him for his long-term welfare and bliss. It is the Buddha's beauty, as well as the teaching that he finally gives, that prompts Bahiya to gain stream entry.

On another occasion, the Brahmin Sela goes to visit the Buddha and sees in him a fulfilment of the prophecy in the Vedas of the thirty-two marks of a great man. Sela speaks in verse, celebrating the Buddha's appearance:

> Perfect your body, shining well,
> well-born, lovely to look at,
> Blessed One, you have a golden complexion,
> you have white teeth, you're vigorous.
> The characteristics of a well-born man,
> the marks of a Great Man,
> are all present in your body.
> Clear your eyes, good your face,
> imposing, splendid, straight upright:
> In the midst
> Of a community of contemplatives
> You shine like the sun.[53]

And finally, at the end of the Buddha's life, his longtime attendant Ananda breaks down with grief at the thought of him dying. The one quality that he remembers about the Buddha is that the Buddha has been 'so compassionate' towards him. We can take this as a summary of the Buddha's life, as Ananda sees his ethical beauty, the beauty of his character. The Buddha responds by rejoicing in Ananda's many qualities and encouraging him to continue to make an effort. Soon he too will gain Enlightenment.

In this chapter we've delved into the great love of the bodhisattva and its context in the Mahayana tradition, and explored how this love can have a magical effect, a particular flavour of the Vajrayana or Tantra. At times it may be useful for us to reflect on the *asubha* or unbeautiful aspects of samsara. However, as we'll see in the next chapter, we also need to develop an appreciation of the *subha* (beautiful) aspects of Enlightenment. Without this, we may fall into a state of spiritual lifelessness. Rather than denying our desires, we lead them where they really want to go, where they will find their ultimate fulfilment. This is the tantric approach.

In the meantime, I invite you to relive the *Vimalakirti Nirdesa*'s evocation of the great love of the bodhisattva.

Guided reflection: the great love of the bodhisattva

- Purpose of this activity: to give space to reflect on how the great love of the bodhisattva arises and absorb its qualities.
- Time: 15 minutes.

5

Love, Beauty, and Friendship

> Desire for anyone flowers into love for someone
> And at last bears fruit as compassion for everyone.
>
> Sangharakshita[54]

As a classics student I was fortunate to read Plato's dialogues in the original ancient Greek. I struggled to make sense of his theory of forms, but was inspired by how he depicted his teacher. Socrates comes across as unconventional, a playful lover of beauty in all its forms. His character shines through *The Symposium*, a semi-fictitious account of an Athenian dinner party.

The party was thrown by a tragic poet by the name of Agathon to celebrate his play's victory at the annual dramatic festival. The all-male guests have finished their dinner, and the evening is still ahead of them. Many are still hung over from the previous night's celebrations, so, instead of hard drinking, they decide to make speeches praising Eros, the god of love.

For the ancient Greeks, Eros could denote any strong desire, but was particularly associated with falling in love, in the sense of intense desire for a person as a sexual partner. Like Kurukulla and Cupid, he uses a bow and arrow to slay his victims. Athenians generally agreed that *eros* was a response to the sight of a person who was beautiful (Greek: *kalos*, 'beautiful', 'pretty', 'handsome', 'attractive'). So most of the guests took the approach that *love is a response to beauty*.

They also assumed that falling in love would primarily occur with other men. Such relations were probably the strongest emotional experience they had known. This may seem strange to modern ears. Despite increasing acceptance of different sexual orientations, modern Western culture defaults to heterosexuality. Things were different in ancient Athens. Homosexuality arose in the context of the segregation of the sexes and comradeship on military campaigns, and wasn't associated with effeminacy. Nobody really had an explanation for its popularity, except that their fathers and grandfathers had done it. They took it for granted that a good-looking boy would excite the same sexual interest as a pretty girl.

One of the first speakers, Pausanias, claims that there are in fact two gods called Eros. 'Popular' Eros is only interested in bodily contact leading to orgasm. This kind of *eros* has given love a bad name. By contrast, 'Heavenly' Eros governs sex within the context of emotional intimacy and the desire for self-improvement. The next speaker takes a doctor's perspective. He declares that it's a doctor's duty to cultivate healthy *eros* in their patients, and reject unhealthy *eros*, the way a musician tunes their instrument. So much for common-sense views on love.

Next comes a comic turn. It's Aristophanes, author of comedies such as *Lysistrata*, *The Birds*, and *The Clouds*, plays that are still performed today. He gives a humorous, mythological account of Eros. Originally, he says, humans were made up of two faces and bodies fused to each other, rather like Siamese twins. They were very strong and attacked the gods, so Zeus cut them in two. Since then, each half has yearned for the other half, from which it was severed.

He points out that the myth neatly explains various sexual orientations. Those who came from a female whole long for their female counterpart. Those who came from a male whole long for their male counterpart. And those who originally came from a hermaphrodite whole long for their 'other half' of the opposite sex. This is why, when humans are in love, they want nothing more than to be welded to each other for eternity. Eros is simply the name we give to the desire and pursuit of wholeness.

Despite its comic overtones, Aristophanes' delightful fairytale reminds us of what it actually *feels like* to fall in love: the intense longing for union, the vast sense of incompleteness without it. Sigmund Freud may have helped us to understand from a psychological perspective that, when we fall in love, we are projecting unrealized qualities onto our beloved. But how much more convincing is Aristophanes' description of the severed halves, who look to Eros to restore them to their former state and heal their wounds.[55]

Now it's Socrates' turn to speak. He describes his meetings with the priestess Diotima, his instructor in matters of love. According to her, Eros is not a god but a great spirit, half-god and half-human, acting as an intermediary between those worlds. The function of Eros is to procreate and bring forth in beauty. Such creation can be either physical or spiritual. Physically, this manifests as people's desire to reproduce and perpetuate the species, or at least their own genes, which will give them a kind of immortality.

However, those who are fertile in their souls bond with another beautiful, noble, and gracious soul, and, by association with their beauty, bring forth the spiritual children of wisdom and virtue in general. This echoes the description of *kalyana mitrata*, spiritual friendship in the Buddhist tradition. The Greek word for 'beauty' (*to kalon*) may even be etymologically linked to the Sanskrit word *kalyana*. When the Buddha corrected Ananda, saying that *kalyana mitrata* is the *whole* of the spiritual life, he was declaring that associating with others on the basis of shared values and ideals is tantamount to spiritual development. Diotima outlines a number of stages in this ascent of beauty that lead to a perfect revelation of the mysteries of love.

The path starts with admiring physical beauty. The guide leads the initiate to fall in love with a particularly beautiful person. It continues with noticing that other people are also beautiful, not just your beloved. Physical beauty in one person is closely akin to physical beauty in any other, so you come to love all physical beauty. Through this realization, you relax your passion for one particular person as being limited.

As you see beauty more generally, you learn to see 'beauty of soul' (ethical qualities and values) as more valuable than physical beauty. You turn your mind to educating the younger generation in these qualities and values. From contemplating these, you come to appreciate beauty as it exists in activities and institutions, and recognize that the beauty in these spheres is ultimately one.

Second to last, the guide in the mysteries of love leads you to contemplate beauty in nature. This is the beauty of a mathematical proof or the Milky Way. The initiate who learns to see beauty in this wider sense contributes profound insights of their own, until at last they catch sight of a beauty to crown all their previous efforts.

This is beauty itself (*auto to kalon*), which is eternal, neither coming into being nor passing away. It doesn't increase or decrease. It's not beautiful in parts and ugly in parts. It is *monoeides*, indivisible and not associated in any way with anything but itself. All other beautiful things partake of this indivisible beauty. Yet, while these things come and go, it remains unchanged.[56]

So this is how you come to experience beauty itself, by a gradual enlargement and refinement of your faculty for perceiving physical and ethical beauty. Once you have seen beauty itself, you will not value lesser beauties as highly. And you will be able to manifest true goodness, because you will be in contact with the truth.

Some years later, it came as a surprise to learn that my Buddhist teacher Sangharakshita regarded himself as a Platonist: not in the sense of Plato's famous dualism between the world of immutable forms and everyday concrete things, which he regarded as eternalist, but in the spirit of the Socratic dialogues, especially *The Symposium*, which he regarded as a great work of art. Sangharakshita saw the ascent of beauty as a kind of Western tantra, and regarded it as essential to the transmission of the Dharma in the West.[57]

There are many references to beauty (*subha*) in the Pali texts. The Buddha told his followers that an enlightened person sees things differently. An enlightened being sees samsara, or the world, as impermanent, insubstantial, and relatively unsatisfactory. These are known as the three marks (*laksana*s) of conditioned existence.

By contrast, unenlightened beings (that's us!) have things upside down, or topsy-turvy. We tend to see the world as permanent, substantial, pleasant, and beautiful. Even if we profess to see the world as 'a vale of tears', we still act as if it is a pleasant place, that our possessions will never be taken from us, and that we are going to live for a few centuries at least! We can smile at this description and at the same time recognize ourselves in it. This is because these topsy-turvy views (*viparyasa*s) are almost as deeply rooted as sentient existence itself.

They can only be turned the right way up by prolonged, systematic meditation on their opposites: impermanence, insubstantiality, and unsatisfactoriness. As the Buddha says in the *Diamond Sutra*:

> Thus shall you think of all this fleeting world:
> A star at dawn, a bubble on a stream;
> A flash of lightning on a summer cloud,
> A flickering lamp, a phantom and a dream.[58]

For a deeper understanding of this, let's look at the Pali terms the Buddha used. *Asubha* means 'ugly', 'horrid', 'disgusting', 'repulsive', or 'impure'. Its opposite, *subha* is usually translated as 'pure', though it really refers to spiritual beauty in the Platonic sense of something shining in a world of its own, above and beyond concrete things. Those concrete things are only called beautiful inasmuch as they participate in beauty's perfection.

When the Buddha tells us that samsara is actually *asubha*, he doesn't mean that we have to regard a flower as ugly, or seek out its ugliness. He means that, in comparison with the beauties of higher planes of reality, those of a lower plane are *asubha*, relatively ugly.

Beauty and ugliness are relative terms. We can only see the *asubha* aspect of samsara when we have seen the *subha* aspect of Reality or Enlightenment. And even within samsara, we need to ascend in meditation to higher planes of consciousness before we can acknowledge the relative ugliness and impurity of our ordinary experience.

There is a story in the Pali Canon that illustrates this. The Buddha had a younger half-brother named Nanda. On Nanda's wedding day, the Buddha asked him to become a monk. Nanda reluctantly agreed. At some point later, Nanda understandably lost his appetite for meditation. When he was ready to give up, the Buddha didn't chastise him. Instead he used the rite of fascination, transporting Nanda to the Heaven of the Thirty-Three, where 500 pink-footed nymphs were ministering to Sakka, lord of the *deva*s. When Nanda saw the nymphs, he had to admit that they were incomparably more beautiful than the Shakyan woman waiting at home.

According to Buddhist cosmology, the Heaven of the Thirty-Three is only two *kamaloka* sub-planes above the human world. Even from this level, Nanda finds the loveliest human face repulsive. Viewed from a higher plane still, the 500 nymphs would seem ugly. We see things as *subha* (beautiful, pure) in comparison with those of a lower plane, and *asubha* (ugly, impure) in comparison with a higher plane of consciousness.

The Buddha guarantees that, if Nanda keeps on practising, he will obtain 500 pink-footed nymphs. Nanda agrees. Later on, Nanda becomes enlightened and so releases the Buddha from his promise. The Buddha showed Nanda a beauty that was relatively near to him. It turns out that Enlightenment is even more beautiful and alluring, or simply more satisfying, than the nymphs. This story suggests a resolution to the 'problem' of love. There is a connection between love and beauty. We love what we find beautiful. If we discover a more complete form of beauty, our attention naturally goes there.

This doesn't seem to have been understood by early Buddhist commentators. Some of them appear to believe that, according to the Buddha, ugliness is real and beauty is unreal. They believe that we progress in the spiritual life by seeing more ugliness and less beauty everywhere and at all levels of existence. Even in the Buddha's time, apparently, some non-Buddhist teachers accused the Buddha of holding the view that, 'When one reaches up to the Release called The Beautiful [...] they regard the Whole [Universe] as ugly.'

The Buddha explicitly rejected this view as belonging to him, saying that, in fact, 'Whenever one reaches up to the Release, called The Beautiful, then they know indeed what Beauty is.'[59] In another place, we learn that you can achieve the heart's release known as 'the beautiful' through developing... *metta*, or love! So love and beauty are joined at the hip in the Buddhist tradition as well.[60]

It may be useful to reflect on the *asubha* aspects of samsara, especially if we are of an acquisitive temperament. However, it's clear from this passage that, in principle, awareness of beauty, the 'positive' factor, is more important than awareness of ugliness, the 'negative' one.

We need to develop an appreciation of the *subha* aspects of Enlightenment. Without awareness of and delight in *subha*, it's very difficult to relate to the other aspects of samsara:

impermanence, insubstantiality, and unsatisfactoriness. All our efforts to convince ourselves rationally that samsara is *asubha* are unlikely to bear fruit, so we continue to swim around in it. It can also lead to an overconceptualization of Insight. As we shall see, *subha* is very important, because it is nonconceptual.

In the Western tradition, beauty is nonconceptual; it is inexpressible, even incomprehensible, beyond the reach of reason. The playwright Christopher Marlowe expresses this when he says that beauty is like the sun:

> The golden ball of heaven's eternal fire,
> That danced with glory on the silver waves[61]

Beauty is intuited, as the philosopher Immanuel Kant suggested, something to be sensed rather than thought about.[62] Secondly, it is intensely pleasurable and engaging, though not necessarily pleasant. We find beauty uplifting, delightful, inspiring, and fascinating. Thirdly, it has an unavoidable tendency towards transcendence. As we appreciate an object of beauty, inevitably we pass from that object to a deeper contemplation. This is the aspect that Plato drew out in the ascent of beauty.

Finally, beauty is ecstatic, in the original Greek meaning of the word, as standing outside of yourself. Beauty draws you out of yourself into appreciating it and other people as *ends in themselves*.[63] You become entranced and absorbed in it. You fall in love! Sangharakshita suggests that this is where beauty can become a gateway to liberation (*vimokkha-mukkha*).[64]

We can lose ourselves in beauty. This contemplation may be more direct and compelling than the gateways associated with the other three marks (*laksanas*). A single smile from Beauty can bring about greater transformations of character than all the frowns of Righteousness! Like them, it can also lead to Insight with a capital 'I'. We do this by exploring these four aspects of beauty *in our experience*. Working from the inside out, we follow our transcending impulses and slowly elevate our desires.

However beautiful our lives may be, there always has to be more. We haven't seen the highest beauty yet. Through poetry and the arts we can contemplate this truth without being turned to stone. This doesn't mean going out of our way to find something *asubha*. Samsara is marked by *asubha*. The question is, can we acknowledge the relative lack of beauty in our daily experience? If we refuse to acknowledge this, we won't take the necessary steps to see beauty. We first need to experience the *absence* of beauty, or Enlightenment, or the Buddha in our lives, in order to experience their presence. Reflecting on *asubha* means acknowledging that 'there has to be more', and knowing where to find it.

By contrast, contemplating *subha* means recognizing the reflections of real beauty in our experience. Beauty can be found in many places, not just what is pretty or lovely. Beauty can also be terrible and destructive. However we imagine it, this full and final beauty is reflected in our everyday experience. Seeing its reflection, we come closer and closer to it, contemplating a higher beauty, a deeper beauty, something further along the path of beauty. And this gives us an intimation of the highest beauty, a direct, unmediated sense that bypasses concepts.

In one of his discourses, the Buddha reminds us of three things that are difficult in practising the Dharma. It's hard to go forth and commit yourself to the Dharma. It's hard to find delight in the Dharma. And thirdly, it's hard to give up the lesser delights of samsara for the greater delights of Nirvana.[65] We need all the help we can get. This is where the arts can come in. The practice and appreciation of the arts and beauty can have an important place in our lives.

The arts have the capacity to enlarge the circle of our consciousness and develop our sensitivity to the world around us, our inner lives and other people. They can help us to become more integrated by finding emotional equivalents for our intellectual understandings, whether of the Dharma or other things. They can provide a channel for emotional energies, leading them to higher levels of expression. In this way they can refine our emotions and open the way to meditative experience. Engagement with the arts can even open up insight.[66]

It's for this reason that Sangharakshita included the importance of the arts in the spiritual life as one of the six distinctive emphases of the Triratna Buddhist Community.[67] Elsewhere, he cites William Wordsworth's 'Lines composed a few miles above Tintern Abbey', where the poet describes the 'beauteous forms' of the Wye Valley:

> These plots of cottage-ground, these orchard-tufts,
> Which at this season, with their unripe fruits,
> Are clad in one green hue, and lose themselves
> 'Mid groves and copses. Once again I see
> These hedge-rows, hardly hedge-rows, little lines
> Of sportive wood run wild: these pastoral farms,
> Green to the very door; and wreaths of smoke
> Sent up, in silence, from among the trees!

Memories from a previous visit have inspired Wordsworth to act in a kindly and generous manner, and prompted more meditative experiences of stillness in which:

> we are laid asleep
> In body, and become a living soul:
> While with an eye made quiet by the power
> Of harmony, and the deep power of joy,
> We see into the life of things.

In these moments, he felt:

> A presence that disturbs me with the joy
> Of elevated thoughts; a sense sublime
> Of something far more deeply interfused,
> Whose dwelling is the light of setting suns,
> And the round ocean and the living air,
> And the blue sky, and in the mind of man:
> A motion and a spirit, that impels
> All thinking things, all objects of all thought,
> And rolls through all things.[68]

Wordsworth's 'see[ing] into the life of things' and 'something far more deeply interfused' parallel the Buddha's teachings on interconnectedness, and demonstrate that Insight is not a uniquely Buddhist phenomenon. Insight is a universal aspect of human potential.

From the arts we can derive something that adds to and supports our Dharma lives. The arts can lend us images of beauty to nourish our imaginations. When we have an aesthetic experience, our normal perceptual framework starts to break down. The subject (us) moves closer to the object (the work of art or the aspect of nature). Our sense of time begins to expand, slow down, recede into the background, even stand still. We cease to be concerned with how this object is related to other objects. Instead we just concentrate on the object's internal relations. The object is not really 'out there', nor is it 'in here'. It hovers between the two.

An image appears or emerges. It's an image because all perception is ultimately image-ination. Through aesthetic experience, the imagination becomes liberated from its moorings in space, time, and causality. The image can live free of its context. The image itself comes alive.

Art has the power to release us from our empirical experience of ourselves, giving us a purer glimpse of ourselves outside time. We can experience the pure image, more refined and subtle than our ordinary experience. We need to experience our selfhood more fully before we can go beyond it and see through it completely.

The language of images takes us beyond the world of representation into another world of knowing: imagination. Our images come from our imagination. We ourselves are images, and all our experiences are imagination. Imagination is our real life, our real knowing. We become 'image perceiving image'.[69]

Enlightenment becomes an image, in fact an inexhaustible fountain of images. Not the end of a journey, but the beginning. This is what art can do for us: it can lead us into the world of imagination, to 'things as they really are'. Imagination brings us closest to the ineffable, indescribable nature of Reality. We are images imagining images.

In the previous chapter we contemplated the image of the historical Buddha. We saw how people were fascinated by his physical beauty and his enlightened qualities. He developed these qualities by learning to see beauty in all beings, and thereby coming to love them. We know this from an incident that occurred shortly after his Enlightenment.

The freshly minted Buddha considered trying to communicate his experience to others. But he told himself that people generally were preoccupied with their own stories about themselves and their place in the world. He realized that it was going to be extremely hard work to get them interested in another way of looking at things. So he decided to enjoy his newfound peace and freedom instead.

Fortunately for us, a powerful god called Brahma Sahampati heard of the Buddha's reluctance, and came to ask him to change his mind. He pointed out that some beings would be open to hearing the Buddha's teaching because they had 'but little dust' in their eyes.

So the Buddha looked out on the world with his newly opened Buddha-eye. It seemed to him as though beings were like a vast sea of lotuses, stretching further than he could see. There were blue lotuses, red lotuses, and white lotuses. He was profoundly struck by their beauty. Some lived and thrived in the water without rising out of it. Some rested on the surface. And some had risen clear of the water.[70] *No mud, no lotus.* This is an organic, living image. We all start down in the slimy dark of the mud. This is the nutriment from which we grow.

A Buddha sees the lotuses simultaneously in two ways. Some beings are like lotuses that have passed through the mud, risen through the water, and broken through the surface of the water to open their petals to the sun and air. These are the ones that have 'but little dust' in their eyes. In terms of the story, these are the beings who can see more clearly, so are more likely to hear the Buddha's teaching. We can celebrate that there are such developed beings.

However, this doesn't exhaust the meaning of the vision. The Buddha also realizes that *all* beings are like lotuses. All beings have their desires and aspirations. All have the urge to grow, to develop, to reach up from the depths towards the warmth and nourishment of the sun. All beings have this potential for growth and development, even the ultimate potential of Enlightenment. We need both of these ways of seeing in order to experience the true spiritual depth of his vision.

Though this story appears in the earlier Theravadin versions of the Buddha's teaching, this belief is central to the later Mahayana schools. In the eyes of a Buddha, *all beings* are beautiful because they have the potential for growth and development. With this one comes to love them, to feel compassion towards them, to want to communicate with them. This is the symbolic birthplace of compassion in the Buddha's life story, and as such is an incredibly important realization on the Buddhist path of love. You can grow to love anyone if you can see their beauty.

Earlier in the chapter I suggested that we could regard the ascent of beauty as a kind of Western tantra. Now perhaps we can understand this more deeply. Instead of denying our desires, we can simply lead them where they really want to go. We can lead them where they will find their ultimate fulfilment.

We are mythic beings existing within time and space. Enlightenment means discovering that myth or pattern, or reflections of it. It means relying on our intuition, our love or longing that seeks ultimate fulfilment. It means faith in the sense of discovering what each one of us 'must' do for our own liberation. It means collaborating with the beauty of Enlightenment so that

> Desire for anyone flowers into love for someone
> And at last bears fruit as compassion for everyone.[71]

Such compassion manifests in profound friendships. The Buddha had such a friendship with Ananda, his cousin and companion for the last twenty-five years of his life. One day Ananda realized how important his contact with the Buddha was for his progress on the path to Enlightenment. So he came to the Buddha and said, 'I've realized that spiritual friendship, spiritual companionship, and spiritual camaraderie are truly half of the spiritual life.' He must have been surprised, even shocked by what the Buddha said next.

The Buddha replied:

> Don't say that, Ananda. Don't say that. Spiritual friendship, spiritual companionship, and spiritual camaraderie are actually *the whole of* the spiritual life. When a monk has spiritual friends, companions, and comrades, they can be expected to make spiritual progress.[72]

The idea may seem strange. In what sense can spiritual friendship be *the whole of* the spiritual life, not just a part of it? What is the role of friendship in Buddhism?

Let's start by examining the words that the Buddha used. The word he used for 'friendship' is simply *mitrata*. The word derives from the Pali word *mitta* or Sanskrit *mitra*, meaning 'friend'. In turn these words are related to *metta* or Sanskrit *maitri*, which as we know means 'loving-kindness' or simply 'love'. So friendship is a vehicle for *metta* or love.

The word I'm translating as 'spiritual' in 'spiritual friendship' is not quite so straightforward. In Pali it's *kalyana*, an adjective meaning 'beautiful', 'charming', 'auspicious', 'helpful', 'morally good'.[73] Sometimes it's also translated as 'lovely' or 'noble'. The word is commonly used to describe the Buddha's teaching, which is said to be *kalyana* in the beginning, middle, and end. It is 'lovely' because it is both good and beautiful. In the time of the Buddha, moral and aesthetic beauty hadn't yet been separated. What was good was also beautiful, and vice versa.

A *kalyana mitra* is a good companion, a virtuous friend, an honest, pure, lovely friend. More technically, a *kalyana mitra* is a spiritual guide, a spiritual adviser. The implication is that the role of the spiritual guide belongs firmly in the context of friendship.[74]

The word the Buddha used for 'spiritual life' is *brahmacarya*, literally 'faring as a god or a brahma'. The Buddha uses it here to mean something like 'the whole path towards Enlightenment'. He confirms this when he explains to Ananda that, when a monk has a spiritual friend, a spiritual companion, a spiritual comrade, it is likely that they will develop and cultivate the noble eightfold path. He goes on to point out that people have gained Enlightenment through having him as their *kalyana mitra*, so this is another way in which *kalyana mitrata* is the whole of the *brahmacarya*.

Kalyana mitrata is a relationship based on the pursuit of a common spiritual ideal. For Buddhists, this ideal is

Enlightenment. If you're aiming for Enlightenment, you will be relating to everybody else who is aiming for Enlightenment. This is the meaning of spiritual friendship.

Why is friendship important to us, and to our spiritual development? The poet William Blake was a great believer in friendship, like many of his time. He wrote, 'The bird a nest, the spider a web, [humans] friendship.'[75] In more modern times, we tend to value sexual-romantic love more than friendship-love.[76] This is still not the case in India, where friendship retains its traditional importance. When visiting people at home in India, I've lost track of the number of times I've been introduced to somebody's 'brother' or 'cousin', only to find out later that their *biological* family is much smaller than this.

Our friendships have a profound impact on us. The choice to spend time with this person rather than that person, over time, influences our behaviour and even our character. This is because we tend to copy the people we spend time with, especially if we seek out and value their company.

Remember the insight from anthropology in Chapter 1? We are group-dwelling mammals, and our behaviour is driven by habit and social copying. And the insight from attachment research in Chapter 2: just as our attachment figures in the first two years of life have an enormous impact on our development, so our later emotional and spiritual life is shaped by other people.

If we are friends with people who act unskilfully (this traditionally refers to things like misusing sex and drugs, or gambling), then we will tend to learn and copy their ways. If we are friends with people who act skilfully and understand how actions have consequences, if they are generous and wise, we will tend to learn and copy them too.

As well as being a flavour of Buddhism as a whole, *kalyana mitrata* or spiritual friendship is a particular flavour of the Triratna Buddhist Community. It's understood that there can be no sangha or spiritual community without spiritual friendship. Spiritual friendship is the bedrock of the sangha. And Sangha is one of the Three Jewels or ideals of Buddhism. So, in the Triratna Buddhist Community, friendship is valued and encouraged.

The Buddha said that living with people who are spiritually immature is a source of long-lasting grief. Associating with them is always painful, like associating with enemies. By contrast, associating with people who are wise is pleasant, like relatives coming together.[77] When we realize the importance of spiritual friends in our spiritual life, we may start to feel a strong sense of companionship towards them. Not something tepid, lukewarm, and half-hearted, but really warm, even loving! This is the emotional quality of *kalyana mitrata*.

The Buddhist scriptures record another story about the Buddha and one of his attendants, illustrating the importance of *kalyana mitrata*. The attendant is a young monk called Meghiya, so this is presumably before Ananda's time. Meghiya is determined to go off by himself to strive in meditation. He's found a delightful mango grove for the purpose, and he asks the Buddha for permission.

The Buddha reminds Meghiya of his role as attendant, but Meghiya insists. He argues that the Buddha has no more work to gain Enlightenment, but *he* still needs to strive. Three times he asks to be released from his role to go and meditate. In the scriptures, when the Buddha is asked three times, it is usually the cue for him to go along with whatever is being asked, no matter the consequences. He tells him, 'What can I say, Meghiya, as you are talking about striving? Do what you think it's time for.'[78]

So Meghiya goes to his mango grove and sits down to meditate. But things don't go as planned. Instead of ascending into the *dhyana*s (superconscious meditative states), Meghiya's mind is dragged through the mud of craving, hatred, and cruelty. That afternoon he goes back to the Buddha and recounts what happened. The Buddha replies that, when the heart's release is not mature, there are five things that mature it.

The first is *kalyana mitrata,* spiritual friends, spiritual companions, spiritual camaraderie. This is the importance of spiritual mentorship. It's not just the first thing on the list, it's also a *necessary* condition for the other four, which are (i) keeping the precepts, (ii) Dharmic conversations, (iii) persistent effort towards the goal, and (iv) wisdom into how things arise and pass away. With these five things in place, Meghiya will experience the heart's release.

Meghiya needs to learn the importance of *kalyana mitrata* in order to make progress. Perhaps Meghiya hasn't fully appreciated the benefit he could gain from the Buddha's company? The most natural way to get a glimpse of wisdom is through friendship with people who are more experienced. This is the sense in which *kalyana mitrata* is the whole of the spiritual life.

The great Tibetan commentator Gampopa classified four kinds of *kalyana mitra*: the ordinary human being, the bodhisattva, and archetypal figures on the level of relative and absolute truth. He points out that, when we are beginning on the path of Enlightenment, we can't even see the face of the higher teachers, so we need to start by associating with an ordinary human being. So our greatest benefactor is an ordinary human being. By associating with them, receiving the light of their teachings and shining it on the path to Enlightenment, we can learn to glimpse the faces of the higher *kalyana mitras*.[79]

With this in mind, let's examine the friendship between my teacher Sangharakshita and one of his teachers, Dhardo Rimpoche. In 1988 I had the immense good fortune to visit Rimpoche in Kalimpong. I was about to start work for the Karuna Trust, a Buddhist charity funding health and educational projects. I decided to use the last of my holidays as a student to visit some of their projects in India. One of them was a school for the children of Tibetan refugees in the foothills of the Himalayas. It had been founded by Rimpoche, so it was also an opportunity to meet a real Tibetan lama.

Dhardo Rimpoche had left his position as abbot of an important Tibetan monastery to become headmaster of this school. He chose Kalimpong as it was the main crossing point for Tibetans fleeing the Chinese. Though he was unwell and close to the end of his life, he received me with great kindness. I vividly remember him asking after my health, my accommodation, and whether I was getting the kind of food that would nourish me.

I felt deeply touched by his concern. His wrinkled, smiling face reminded me of my Nanna, my paternal grandmother, who always seemed to be looking out for us. He asked me to come back the next day. It was then that he gave me a *thangka* (cloth image) of Green Tara, which I still cherish.

During the visit, Rimpoche told me about some of the immense difficulties he had faced to set up the school, and proudly showed me a fountain pen, still in its original case, a gift from Sangharakshita. I wondered why he hadn't used the pen. He replied that it was too precious to use, and it served as a reminder of his friend. I felt touched to hear of the connection between them. Rimpoche confirmed this by saying that he regarded Sangharakshita's disciples as his own. And this was how he treated me.

Sangharakshita spoke about this friendship in public more than once. The friendship spanned the fourteen years that Sangharakshita lived in Kalimpong. It had a steady course, a gradual deepening. There were no dramatic moments. Their backgrounds were very different. Sangharakshita had been born in Tooting, South London, not far from where I grew up. He had been sick as a child, and spent his time reading books. When the Second World War broke out, he joined the British Army, ending up in India. He demobbed early and became a freelance wanderer, then ordained as a bhikkhu in the Theravadin tradition. His teacher took him to Kalimpong and told him to stay there to work for the good of Buddhism.

By contrast Rimpoche was an incarnate bodhisattva. As a child in Tibet, he had been recognized as a *tulku* – an incarnation of a previous important lama. This meant that he had been given an elaborate Tibetan Buddhist education. Afterwards he travelled to India to become the abbot of a monastery in Bodh Gaya, and acted as the Dalai Lama's cultural and religious representative in India.

Temperamentally they were also different. According to Sangharakshita, Rimpoche was kinder by nature, but of course he was a bodhisattva! Sangharakshita had to work on this aspect of his character. Both were quite reserved, not touchy-feely. It took a while for them to become friends. Sangharakshita was initially struck by Rimpoche's straightforwardness and honesty, and Rimpoche invited Sangharakshita to the opening of his Indo-Tibetan Buddhist Cultural Institute (ITBCI) School. They appreciated each other's love of the Dharma, the Buddha's teaching, and a friendship developed based on this mutual respect.

In 1956 they accepted an invitation from the Indian government to join a pilgrimage to the Buddhist holy sites. This was part of the Buddha Jayanti, celebrating the 2000th anniversary of the Buddha's Enlightenment. They were together for ten days, day and night, and this gave them the opportunity to really get to know each other.

Over the years, Sangharakshita learned quite a bit of Dharma from Rimpoche. Later, he took initiations from him. And here's the important part: Rimpoche became Sangharakshita's teacher without ceasing to be his friend. There was mutual support and cooperation.

After Rimpoche's death in 1990, Sangharakshita encouraged Triratna members to remember his message, which is of universal relevance. Rimpoche's message is encapsulated in the motto he gave his school: 'Cherish the doctrine, live united, radiate love.' It was these words that I saw painted on the side of the main building when I visited the school. 'Doctrine' here means the Buddha's teaching, and the truth it points towards. 'Live united' is self-explanatory. 'Radiate love' means spreading the friendship-love of *metta*, the attitude of *kalyana mitrata* or spiritual friendship.

Rimpoche embodied his own message. He loved the pupils of his ITBCI School. There must have been thousands of them over the years. He wanted them to grow up under the benign influence of the Dharma, as real Buddhists. And he radiated love, not in a sticky, sentimental way, but clean and wholesome, straightforward and unattached. Sangharakshita compared this love to the way sunshine shines on everything impartially. His face would light up with compassion, just as it had for me when I visited. It was a beautiful thing to see.

Rimpoche's life and message have become part of the Triratna Buddhist Community's heritage. I feel truly fortunate that he was my teacher's friend and teacher, and to have met him in person.

In the weeks and months after Rimpoche gave me the Green Tara *thangka*, I started to wonder why he had given me this particular image. Was it because of the beauty and tenderness of her smile? Was it because of the luminous jade-green colour of her skin, symbolizing the quintessence of compassion? Was it because she is regarded as a protector of travellers, and I had been a young, single adventurer?

Was it because Green Tara combines fearlessness with generosity, compassionate activity with meditative absorption? She has the reputation for being the most accessible of all the great Buddhas and bodhisattvas, and for playing tricks on her devotees! Or perhaps it was the sweetness of her mantra, *Om tare tuttare ture svaha*.

I fell in love with her beauty and tenderness, and she has sat above my shrine ever since. So this is Green Tara, one of the Buddhist figures symbolizing *kalyana mitrata* on the level of imagination. My relationship with her also suggests how *metta* transforms into devotion when it comes into contact with Buddhas and bodhisattvas. Of course it's not easy to convey this quality of devotion. On my ordination course in the Spanish mountains, I tried to communicate the felt sense of her presence through natural images:

In the sunlit breath of wind
That stirs the pine
Brightening it from within
I see you there

In the morning sun that
Glances on the rocks
Yellowing the grey
I see you there

In the steam rising from the earth
When sunlight follows
Hard on rain
I see you there

In the bright moment
When silence
Joins rest and ease
I know you are there[80]

When I look at the image of Green Tara on my shrine, I feel a direct link to Rimpoche and the wider Buddhist tradition. This is what is meant by the lineage of *kalyana mitrata*. But what of my relationship with Sangharakshita? How was it one of *kalyana mitrata*? I first met Bhante, as I came to know him, in

1985. 'Bhante' is a familiar and yet respectful way of addressing your teacher. I was nineteen and he was sixty. I was making a polite enquiry as to his suitability as my teacher. He responded similarly – polite and informative. I noticed the reserve that he spoke about in relation to his friendship with Rimpoche.

I got to know him through listening to cassettes of his lectures. I could do a passable imitation of his verbal tics, such as a deep 'Hmm?' The way he pronounced certain words, such as 'ascetic', sounded to me self-taught or foreign.

I learned the Dharma through his eyes. Later, when I was working on *Urthona*, Triratna's arts magazine, I had more personal contact with him. He was one of our patrons, and at least twice I asked him for money to help us stay afloat. We shared a love of the arts, and this came through in an interview I did with him.

Initially I was rather scared of him. I got the sense that he didn't suffer fools gladly. He was precise in how he spoke, and seemed to have a superhuman memory. In comparison with him, I felt uncomfortable. However, through my contact with him, I realized that I could ask him anything, as long as I was willing to hear a no. That's quite an important lesson for someone in their twenties.

After ordination I continued to call on him when I had a particularly knotty spiritual issue. This continued up until his death in 2018. He remained the source of my understanding of the Dharma, the spiritual guarantor of my ordination, and a helpful and inspiring *kalyana mitra*.

When the Buddha spoke of *kalyana mitrata* being the whole of the *brahmacarya*, the word *brahmacarya* literally means 'faring as a god or a brahma'. As we saw earlier, here he used it to mean something like 'the whole path towards Enlightenment'. The word is obviously related to the *brahmaviharas*, discussed in Chapter 3. When you are dwelling in *metta, karuna, mudita*, and *upekkha*, you are practising *brahmacarya*!

However, the word *brahmacarya* has another connotation. *Brahmacarya* usually implies celibacy. It is a monastic precept, one of the main differences between monks and laypeople. *Brahmacarya* means no sex. Don't even think about it. Forget the passion, just concentrate on compassion!

The Triratna Buddhist Order that Sangharakshita founded is neither monastic nor lay. It places commitment to the three jewels of the Buddha, Dharma, and Sangha as primary. Practice of the precepts is a secondary manifestation of this commitment, and lifestyle comes third, though it is still important. However, Sangharakshita encouraged single-sex activities, giving the order and movement a semi-monastic flavour. I have personally benefited from living and working with those who identify as men. With my sexual interest primarily in women, living and working with men removed some of the sexual pressure that I had felt, and allowed me to develop self-confidence in this area.

So it came as a surprise to me to learn in the late 1980s that Sangharakshita had been sexually active. At first I found it difficult to accept. I remember asking myself, 'How come he's allowed to have sex, when *brahmacarya* seems to be so important?' It didn't seem fair. I struggled to differentiate myself, to allow him to make his own choices. By the same token, I struggled to make my own life choices, in the light of the Buddha's teaching and my sense of what I needed to progress towards Enlightenment.

I'd like to acknowledge here that sexual contact with Sangharakshita stimulated pain and hurt for some. He himself made an apology and a confession that included this. Nowadays we are more sensitive to the impact of power in a sexual relationship between teacher and student. The one who has less institutional power in the relationship is likely to experience stronger impacts, especially if they receive what has happened as hurt or harm.

The issue is one of informed consent. It's very difficult for someone who has less power in the situation, and is usually younger, to really be aware of the power differential and likely impacts. They may be completely unaware of how they are projecting onto their teacher. If the relationship ends, the teacher may continue more or less as before – there's usually less emotional investment – whereas the student may experience a devastating impact on their relationship with their teacher, and a loss of belonging in their community.

And yet I did feel love towards him, as my teacher. At our last meeting, when Sangharakshita was in his nineties, something told me that I wouldn't be seeing him again. So, when I got up to leave, I went to shake his hand. Only instead of shaking it, I bent down and kissed the back of his hand. It was my way of letting him know that there was love between us, even devotion.

In June 2017, a year before his death, Sangharakshita wrote that friends had always been important to him. He affirmed the importance of *kalyana mitrata* in the spiritual life. The nature of *kalyana mitrata* is a matter for discussion, and there is always more to say on the topic. 'Meanwhile', he concluded, 'personal experience has shown me that it is better to keep one's sexual relations and one's spiritual friendships separate.'[81] I find myself nodding in agreement.

In the next chapter we visit the garden of love and ask: what would it look like without conventional religion? What are the different doorways into the garden of love? In the meantime I invite you to join me in a deeper dive into the Buddha's vision of lotuses and the arising of compassion for all beings.

Guided reflection: the Buddha's vision of lotuses

- Purpose of this activity: to see the beauty of all beings in terms of their potential for growth and development, and hence to experience love and compassion for them.
- Time: 15 minutes.

6

The Garden of Love

I went to the Garden of Love,
And saw what I never had seen:
A Chapel was built in the midst,
Where I used to play on the green.

And the gates of this Chapel were shut,
And Thou shalt not. writ over the door;
So I turn'd to the Garden of Love,
That so many sweet flowers bore.

And I saw it was filled with graves,
And tomb-stones where flowers should be:
And Priests in black gowns, were walking their rounds,
And binding with briars, my joys & desires.

William Blake[82]

Like 'The clod and the pebble' from Chapter 1, this poem is from the 'Experience' section of *Songs of Innocence and Experience*. It also contrasts innocence and experience, the two contrary states of the human soul. But here Blake expresses his sentiment without ambivalence.

In imagination, Blake returns to the garden of love where he played as a child. He is shocked to find that a chapel has been built in the middle of the green. It is a sinister building, in contrast with the garden of love in which it is built. Rather than being open and accessible to all, the gates of this chapel are firmly closed. To confirm its exclusive and austere status, 'Thou shalt not' is written over the door, symbolizing the peremptoriness and authority of the Ten Commandments.

Blake is dismayed to see how organized religion has enforced its negative, life-denying aspects. He turns again to the garden of love, a place where love would naturally be found. When he played there, in his childhood innocence, the flowers of love were plentiful. But under the influence of organized religion it has become a graveyard. It is patrolled by priests wearing black gowns, symbolizing the repressive aspects of Christianity.

Blake's natural, unfettered joys and desires, once free and innocent, are now either buried beneath mounds or bound with briars. The garden of love has become a symbol for the lifeless wasteland of repressive religion. Joy has been replaced by instruction. Natural motivations have been demonized, and love is nowhere to be seen.

Thanks to Blake, we know what the garden of love *wouldn't* look like. So what *would* it look like? Fortunately, Blake gives us some clues in the corresponding poem in the 'Innocence' section:

> The sun does arise,
> And make happy the skies.
> The merry bells ring,
> To welcome the Spring.
> The skylark and thrush,
> The birds of the bush,
> Sing louder around,

The bells cheerful sound,
While our sports shall be seen
On the Echoing Green.[83]

Here are joyful symbols of spring and childhood. We might feel delighted with a sense of freshness and vitality. In Blake's engraving, older children play with bats and balls on the green while their mothers nurse the younger ones in the shade of an oak tree. The oak on the village green is here a symbol of strength and security. The older folk sit with the mothers under the tree and laugh away the cares of age, remembering the joys of their youth.

But, before we get carried away, perhaps we need to take a step back and ask if we really need an image for love? The ancient Greeks had at least four words for love: *storge* (empathy bond), *philia* (friend bond), *eros* (romantic or sexual love), and *agape* (unconditional 'god' love). They had many images, including Eros and Aphrodite, rather than a singular image. The Christian writer C.S. Lewis describes four loves: affection, friendship, eros, and charity. He didn't seem to need an image for these. A modern relationship counsellor enumerates five 'love languages': words of affirmation (appreciation), quality time, gifts, acts of service, and physical touch.[84] He sees them as languages, so no image is necessary.

In the previous chapter we learned that we need images of beauty to nourish our imaginations. We saw how the goal of the spiritual life could be envisaged in terms of ideal beauty, and the path in terms of increasing love for that beauty. We also saw that there is no reason why this approach should not be developed within the general framework of Buddhist practice.

Could there be such an image for love? In Chapter 1 I described how we tend to think of love only in terms of being loved. It's important to emphasize the other direction, loving. For a sense of wholeness we need traffic in both directions: loving and being loved. This gives us the image of a two-way street. Definitely an image, though hardly uplifting!

I like Blake's image of the village green because it's accessible to all. However, I prefer the symbolism of a garden, as more fully embodying the beauty and richness of love. Not a road or an ascent, but a garden. In a garden, where we go matters less than what we notice. I also want to explore the different doorways through which we can enter into the garden of love. So perhaps it could be a circular, walled garden, punctuated by doorways, to symbolize how love protects and matures what grows within.

The doorways could capture the two-way flow of the street metaphor. Some of the doorways would be larger and more public, and some less obvious, or even hidden from view. Some of them were originally separate, but over the centuries traffic has worn them into one.

Beauty would be one of the doorways leading into the garden. It would be one of the doors of liberation (*vimokkha-mukkha*) mentioned in the previous chapter. Or perhaps beauty would permeate the whole garden, sharpening the senses and brightening the colours of the trees, shrubs, and flowers.

But what would the garden of love actually look and feel like? It would need to be fit for the Muses, those ancient goddesses of creativity, to live there. Which doorway shall we try first? We seem to have entered the garden by the gateway of *Beauty*, so let's turn around and contemplate this doorway first. As Rumi says, every morning we wake up empty and unsettled. Before diving into study or other tasks, we can pause. We can pick up a musical instrument and start playing, or do something else that brings beauty into the world. There are countless ways to honour life, to express devotion and to let love guide our actions.[85]

We can enact the beauty that we love. There are many ways of experiencing the deep sense of meaning, beauty, and love that we find in study, meditation, and prayer. We don't need to be precious about the ways we can act in accordance with our highest ideals and deepest values.

Next to the gateway of *Beauty* I can see a doorway with a sign that says *Power With*.

Beauty comes in like a goddess
And melts you with her eyes;
You hear music and laughter,
And from that moment
You never want to leave her side.

Righteousness comes in to the sound of a drum
And lines you up along a wall;
Because you have to, you obey,
But when his back is turned
You slip away.[86]

'Power with' is another way of describing the 'love mode' from the Introduction. As we saw there, we could follow the Buddha's teaching purely in terms of embodying the love mode. We could live in a spirit of helpfulness and tenderness towards the whole world. This is nonviolence, the most direct and important manifestation of our commitment to the three jewels.

Close to this is the doorway of *Freedom*. Love thrives on freedom; 'L'amour est l'enfant de la liberté', as the old French song says.[87] Love is the child of freedom, never that of 'power over'. For us to love, we need to be able to give and receive freely. Perhaps we can only become aware of this when our freedom is challenged. Harvey Milk, the 1970s LGBT campaigner, said, 'If you are not personally free to be yourself in that most important of human activities [...] the expression of love [...] then life loses its meaning.'[88]

Next to *Freedom*, I can see the three doorways of *Cherishing, Protecting*, and *Maturing*. You may recall these from Chapter 1. Sangharakshita suggested that, if we want to use the word 'love' to denote nonviolence, we mean a cherishing, protecting, and maturing love. This kind of love has the same effect on the spiritual being of others as the light and heat of the sun does on their physical forms.

Cherishing means treating with fondness and affection. It could include tenderness. It implies intense liking and emotional warmth. It means loving unreservedly and fully, valuing and holding dear. 'May all beings be happy and secure!' In terms of the sun, cherishing represents the absolute affirmation of another's being. It illuminates the unique qualities of the beings in the garden, and provides the warmth that gives them a love of living.

Protecting means being responsive to others' needs and protecting them when necessary. In Chapter 3, we saw how the Buddha gives the example of how a mother would protect her only child, even at the risk of her own life. The Buddha encourages us to develop this boundless heart towards *all* beings. This means that the sun protects all beings in the garden from harm, including from unskilfulness, whether their own or that of others.

Protecting provides safety and security, so these are included in this doorway. As we saw in Chapter 2, from the standpoint of evolution, humans need to cooperate to survive. Love is the biological glue that drives us to invest in the relationships that will ensure our survival. In particular, it motivates us to overcome the difficulties posed by partnership and group living, allowing us to cooperate at a level unmatched by any other species. So this is the grand and sturdy doorway of *Protecting*, which I imagine as an ancient, fortified city gate.

Maturing means supporting other beings to learn and grow. If we know how to take care of beings, they will grow. We can bring in the parable of the rain cloud from the *White Lotus Sutra*. During the rainy season, dense clouds fill the sky, and rain pours down everywhere. Moisture fertilizes all the plants equally. Every growing thing receives its share. But the plants, herbs, shrubs, and trees don't all grow in the same way. They keep their distinctive qualities, even though they are all nourished by the same cloud. This means that the sun in the garden of love provides a vision of potential and support for beings to grow in their own way.

This was the doorway that the Buddha initially came through, soon after his Enlightenment, when he had a vision of beings as lotuses. He saw the beauty and lovableness of those who had 'but little dust' in their eyes. He also saw the beauty and lovableness of *all* beings having the potential for growth and development, even the ultimate potential of Enlightenment.

So we can imagine that, adjacent to this gateway, is a lotus pond filled with blue, red, and white lotuses to symbolize the Buddha's vision. When we need refreshment from the world, we can come to this pond and be nourished by its beauty. The water will also give comfort to escape the heat of the summer sun.

Next to these is the doorway of *Wholeness*. German has a word for this: *Geborgenheit*. This is untranslatable, but it means something like security, in the sense of warmth, belonging, and communion. We touched on this in Chapter 1, where Erich Fromm described love as the mature response to the universal need for union and communion. And in Chapter 5 we heard Aristophanes' comic fairytale of the severed halves, and learned that love is our desire for and pursuit of the whole. Ladies and gentlemen (and those who don't identify as such), I give you the gateway of *Wholeness*!

Some way along the garden wall is a doorway marked *Well-being*. This includes health and joie de vivre. As we saw in Chapter 2, love increases your chances of surviving illness, your mental and physical health, your life satisfaction, and even the length of your life. It does this by bringing practical and emotional resources, so it's still about survival. Being in a supportive social network reduces your risk of dying by 50 per cent. The biggest factor here is the nature of your relationships, or love.

Joie de vivre is instantly attractive and lovable, so it's part of this doorway onto the garden of love. It's also part of what it's like to be *in* the garden of love. Love brings a freshness to your eyes, lightness to your heart, and a spring to your step.

Walking round the wall, we see a round doorway close to the ground. We need to kneel down, or even lie down, to see it. It's the height of a baby. *Touch* is essential for healthy development. We know this because babies who don't get touched don't develop cognitively, so they find it difficult to attune to the people around them. The doorway has a smooth, skin-like texture, as if it's designed to be felt with the hands rather than seen.

Now we come to a number of doorways that address our emotional and psychological needs. The first is *Openness and Emotional Warmth*, which includes closeness and affection. Openness and emotional warmth allow us to really connect with other people. They allow us to take delight in, to appreciate, and to be at one with ourselves, others, and life itself. Openness is the capacity to say a full yes to someone or something, and is the core of love. Emotional warmth is love's basic expression. It is the desire to reach out and touch, connect with, and nourish what we love.

If openness is the clear, cloudless sky above the garden, emotional warmth is the sunlight streaming through the sky, warming and nourishing the plants, animals, reptiles, insects, microbes, fish, and humans within.

Openness is also our capacity to let others be – to allow them, to let them in and receive them as they are. We can do this in a gentle, spacious way, without dominating them or bending them to our will. So this doorway is joined by a secret passage to the doorway of *Power With*. This kind of letting be is one of the greatest kindnesses that we can offer to those we love.

Next door to this is *Appreciation*. This includes such qualities as acceptance, being valued, mattering, and belonging. In any love relationship, appreciation is crucially important. We want to know that our efforts are seen, that our love and care are seen and recognized. This gives us a sense of being valued, of being accepted, of mattering and belonging.

Belonging comes in different shapes and forms. In Chapter 2 I described a profound experience of belonging. As a teenager, when I heard the opening verses of the *Heart Sutra*, I was convinced that I had heard them before. They sounded so familiar. Perhaps I'd known them before and just forgotten them. I was filled with a deep sense of coming home, of belonging to *these* people and *this* text. So, in the garden of love, the *Heart Sutra* can always be heard as a low musical hum in the background. If you listen carefully at any time, you can just make out the words, 'Form is only emptiness, emptiness only form.'

Next to this is *Dignity*. This includes the qualities or values of being taken into account, consideration, and respect. And next to this, we encounter the doorway of *Care and Support*. We'll have more to say about these two gateways in Part Two, when we turn our attention to love in Buddhist partnership.

Now comes the doorway of *Friendship*. As we saw in Chapter 5, we have an unusual situation in the modern West, compared with other parts of the world and previous eras. Romantic love tends to be emphasized, while friendship tends to be de-emphasized, or valued less. This doorway is made from wood and has a pleasing aspect; it's clear that it is used from both directions.

Next is *Eros*. I'll allow you to imagine what this doorway looks like! Are there veils hung over the gateway, and scents in the air, or is a muscular youth standing there? Whatever your fancy, *Eros* provides the obsessive element and endless motivation of falling in love. *Eros* may be only temporary, but, as Plato pointed out, it provides a strong motivation for self-improvement and the wish to contribute to life. We'll hear more about Eros in the next chapter on love and sex.

Next door is *Empathy*. This equates to being seen, heard, and understood. The famous Swiss psychiatrist Carl Gustav Jung once said, in relation to his own life experience,

> Loneliness does not come from having no people about one, but from being unable to communicate the things that seem important to oneself, or from holding certain views which others find inadmissible.[89]

Loving a person means learning the song of their heart and singing it to them when they have forgotten it. We sing it to them by empathizing with their suffering. In the past, some philosophers and scientists have debated whether we are social animals or born loners who reluctantly learn to interact with others.

This seems to depend on our understanding of human nature. The study of anthropology, primatology, and evolution tells us that humans are essentially group-dwelling social beings. However, it is the study of neuroscience that has given us a conclusive answer to this age-old question. The discovery of 'mirror neurones' in humans and primates confirms that our brains are deeply social. We are born ready to tune in to and interact with the people around us. Our brains create neural maps to make it easier for us to tune in to others. These maps allow us to imitate others, understanding their feelings and intentions – in short, empathy.[90] We'll return to explore how empathy can increase the flow of love in partnership in Chapter 8.

Forming a pair with *Empathy* is *Vulnerability*. Knowledge of life is participatory. If you're not prepared to participate, or take risks, love is unlikely to be part of your life. Risk and vulnerability are the essence of love. Marshall Rosenberg, founder of Nonviolent Communication, described this process as one of empathy and honesty. Honesty means vulnerably expressing what's in your heart to your loved ones. Telling them what's alive in you, rather than any judgements you might have of them. It means expressing *how you are*, rather than what *the other person is*. Like empathy, this kind of vulnerability is likely to be received as love. We will also return to this topic in Chapter 8.

Not far from *Empathy* and *Vulnerability*, we see people sitting cross-legged in meditation adjacent to the doorway of the *Four Flavours of Love*. These are the four *brahmavihara*s or Immeasurables of Chapter 3. As a reminder, they are *metta* (love or loving-kindness), *karuna* (compassion), *mudita* (empathic joy), and *upekkha* (equanimity). Transcendence is in the air. The doorways are constantly expanding, to symbolize how these qualities are constantly enlarging their scope. As they enlarge, they include more and more beings, ultimately all beings.

We explored the *brahmavihara*s in Chapter 3, so I won't say any more about them here except to note a peculiar aspect of *mudita*. *Mudita* allows us to join others in celebration. In fact, certain needs are best met in community, among them mourning and celebration. How easily we fall in love when we are celebrating! Our heart opens, we feel expansive and want to take home a reminder of this moment and how we feel. Could that person over there be our reminder?

Closely aligned to the *Four Flavours* is the doorway of *Meaning*. This includes values such as shared reality and truthfulness. When love is alive and moving in us, we feel confident that our life is meaningful, regardless of our outer circumstances. We feel that we are connected with something larger than ourselves. We feel the burden of isolation lift, filling us with peace and wellbeing. When love is absent, we feel bereft, and it's hard to find joy, even when we're fortunate in other aspects. We easily fall into a sense of meaninglessness, anxiety, or despair.

What to say about *Truthfulness*? It's not just Shakespeare's poetic spell, there is something *true* about love. As the Danish existentialist philosopher Søren Kierkegaard observed, 'The best defence against hypocrisy is love.' One of the fruits of love, by which it can be recognized, is that it exposes hypocrisy in all its forms. This protects the lover against falling into hypocrisy.[91]

In the same chapter, Kierkegaard points out that the only absolutely convincing evidence for love is that it is known and recognized by another person's love. Like is known and recognized by like. *It takes one to know one.* Only a person who abides in love can recognize love, and, in the same way, their love is known. This is part of what is meant by shared reality. The other part is that, if we share values or ideals with someone, this can be a doorway to love.

The next doorway is sometimes camouflaged by bushes; however, I'm pretty sure it's there. It's the doorway of *Awareness and Insight*. Love means an awareness of the being of another person. This brings to light the wisdom aspect of the first precept.[92] Our awareness of the other person will express itself in kindness, and we will want to support them to flourish. No act of kindness is too small. It's incredibly important that we act on our kind intentions. If we don't, it may be more difficult next time.

Insight will give us a profound sense of how interdependent we are. We all have the same basic needs, the same wish to thrive. We can recognize that nobody's needs get met unless everybody's needs get met. Trying to meet our needs at the expense of other people, or even the planet, is a relatively short-lived goal.

And so we come almost full circle round the walled garden of love, to the doorway of *Healing*. For some of us, this may be the first doorway we come to, rather than the last. This is *Healing* in the specific sense of healing the mood of grievance that we may have carried around for ages. It means acknowledging the deep pain that has come from experiences of being unloved. It means mourning that we didn't get the love and cherishing that we needed to be healthy and thrive. We can allow ourselves to feel the sadness that comes with this. If we go deeply into this mourning, we come across what is most precious in our lives – life-enriching love and cherishing. There will be more on this topic in Chapter 12, 'Lost Loves'.

And, of course, this list may not be complete. You may be aware of other doorways into the garden of love. Take a moment now to check for yourself.

The garden of love is an archetypal image. Once activated, an archetypal image possesses a life of its own and impinges on our attention whether we like it or not. It may insist on continuing the conversation, even when we regard it as finished. Partnership is the topic of Part Two of this book. We'll be looking at specifics, but everything that we've learned about love will be applicable to its challenges and joys.

Before moving on, I invite you to complete this activation with a guided reflection. Sit awhile with me in the garden of love, and enjoy its beauty and abundance.

Guided reflection: the garden of love

- Purpose of this activity: to visualize the garden of love in a way that works for you, and to enjoy its beauty and abundance.
- Time: 25 minutes.

Part Two

Love in Buddhist Partnership

7

Self-Love

The time will come
when, with elation,
you will greet yourself arriving
at your own door, in your own mirror
and each will smile at the other's welcome,

and say, sit here. Eat.
You will love again the stranger who was your self.
Give wine. Give bread. Give back your heart
to itself, to the stranger who has loved you

all your life, whom you ignored
for another, who knows you by heart.
Take down the love letters from the bookshelf,

the photographs, the desperate notes,
peel your own image from the mirror.
Sit. Feast on your life.

Derek Walcott[93]

I still can't read this poem without tears coming to my eyes. It holds a special significance for me. In 2009 I was going through a very painful separation from my partner of five years. What had started out as high hopes and enthusiastic love had ended in hurt and blame. Friends sent me messages of encouragement, including the exhortation to 'keep my pecker up'. Though I could acknowledge their kind intentions, none of their messages really helped. Except this one.

Walcott's poem touched me differently. There was nothing sentimental or pitying about it. Simply an emphasis on the importance of self-love through self-compassion. 'You will love again the stranger who was your self.'

When I lived in Cambridge in the 1990s I tried out all sorts of self-improvement schemes. One of them was a guided visualization involving a tree. It had a hypnotic quality to it, but the only thing that I could remember afterwards was a man with a US–English accent saying, 'Try to give yourself the love that you seek from others.' Despite agreeing with the sentiment, I found it insincere and humorous. I would say it at inopportune moments, probably when other people really needed empathy. I would say it *even though I didn't know how to do it*. There was some truth to it, but, in the absence of a method, it remained just a nice idea.

In this chapter we're going to explore a process of self-compassion based on what we've learned in Part One and on Marshall Rosenberg's Nonviolent Communication. From experience, I can say that it really works.

But first, let's address its opposite, self-hatred. Experiences of loss or suffering of any kind can be exacerbated by self-hatred. It seems surprisingly common in the West, given that we are materially better off than many other parts of the world. When Indian Buddhist friends come to live in the West, I'm used to warning them that people in the West are less happy than in India. They generally refuse to believe this. How could people who have full bellies, washing machines, wide-screen TVs, and the latest smartphones be unhappy? After about six months they start to look around them and notice that Westerners do seem to be a rather unhappy, anxious lot, suffering from low self-worth.

Depression is a common and burdensome mental disorder. Globally, an estimated 5 per cent of adults suffer from depression. More women are affected than men, and it can lead to suicide. Though it seems counterintuitive, there's evidence that people in higher-income countries are more strongly affected than those in middle- or low-income countries.[94] There are various suggestions as to why this is the case; however, low self-value or self-hatred is a common factor.

When Westerners encounter Buddhism they may become fascinated with the *anatta* (no-self) doctrine or *sunyata* (emptiness). They may interpret this doctrine as saying that there is no such thing as the self. They may think it means some kind of void, an experience of depersonalization, annihilation, or lack of identity. As the Buddhist philosopher Nagarjuna says,

> If their view of emptiness is wrong, those of little intelligence will be hurt. Like handling a snake in the wrong way, or casting a spell in the wrong way.[95]

This may reinforce a sense of self-hatred.

When he returned to the West, Sangharakshita came across a young woman who was delighted with the *anatta* doctrine. It was what had converted her to Buddhism. She kept repeating, 'There's no self, there's no me, I am not.' After a few days on retreat, she reported that she had discovered something in her meditation. She realized that she liked the no-self doctrine because she hated herself. She actually liked to feel that she wasn't there, to cancel herself out. She realized that this was an expression of her self-hatred.[96]

The Buddha explicitly rejected nihilism and associated extreme forms of ascetic practice, amounting to self-torture. He did this from the vantage point of experience. He had tried out practices such as holding his breath until he fainted or standing naked in the midday sun. Apparently he took them further than anyone else, before he realized they left him too weak to meditate. Besides, they were based on hatred of the body. Through these experiences he discovered the middle way between asceticism and hedonism, between nihilism and eternalism.

When we are suffering, we need love most, and yet we may find it difficult to give it to ourselves. To aggravate the situation, we may express our suffering to others in ways that are unlikely to elicit compassion from them – for instance by appearing to blame them for our misfortunes.

We tend to judge ourselves harshly. What would it mean to see the preciousness of all things, including ourselves? In traditional Buddhist practice, we can do this by reflecting on our death.[97] Can you sit quietly now and sense the tentativeness of life, the mortality of your body?

Sometimes, when we hear about our friends' and relations' illnesses, it can seem that we are holding on to life by a thread. Death is certain for all of us – the only thing that is uncertain is the exact hour and nature of our death. Imagine being at the end of your life, in a week's time, a month's time, a year, or a decade. It doesn't matter exactly when, for the purpose of this exercise.

Now cast your mind back over the course of your life, and bring to mind two occasions when you acted skilfully. They don't need to be grand, just whatever actions come to you. As you remember these deeds and picture yourself doing them, notice how you feel and what they mean to you. Perhaps you experience a surge of enthusiasm and gratitude to your past self for contributing to life in these ways?

When you have finished this reflection, you can reflect on it! What did you pick out from a lifetime of words and actions? Were they simple, straightforward everyday actions? Or longer-term projects like raising a family or writing a book? Did your actions bring you into deeper connection with others, as when you are there for someone in a caring, attentive way? We feel that we are really contributing when our heart is touched and the other person's heart is touched by our actions.

However, you might have found this exercise extremely difficult. Perhaps you struggled to identify occasions when you acted skilfully, or rejected the ones that came to mind as being too small, superficial, impure, or imperfect. If yes, this is a reflection of how hard we are on ourselves. We judge ourselves harshly, we have little mercy on ourselves. It's difficult to acknowledge that love and the desire to contribute to life can shine freely from our hearts. And yet it can and does.

Can we allow the flavour of acting skilfully, of contributing to life, to permeate our lives? When we bring full attention to how we have acted skilfully, we can start to see the preciousness of life, and the potential for acting skilfully grows inside us.

A simple, caring presence can permeate the moments of our life. What would it mean to live like this? Is your way of life, the path you have chosen, leading to this? On our deathbed, we're probably not going to be checking our bank balance to find out the quality of our life. We are more likely to be asking the questions that everybody else asks, 'Did I love well? Did I live fully? Did I learn to let go?'[98]

The Buddhist doctrine of *anatta* really means 'no fixed self' rather than 'no self'. It implies that there is no eternal, unchanging *atman* or soul. We need to develop a strong sense of ourselves before attempting to go beyond this. As my Buddhist teacher Sangharakshita said, 'Unless you are a healthy, growing individual – unless, as it were, you love yourself – you can't love others.' A person who doesn't truly love themselves tends to be preoccupied with themselves in a way that doesn't support the people around them.[99]

Getting to know yourself intimately is a necessary condition of an intimate relationship with someone else. Through practising the Dharma, you get to know yourself more deeply. You become familiar with your body, speech, and mind. You see how your mind works, the stories you tell yourself again and again. And through this awareness come freedom and energy.

You also cultivate love, *metta*, towards yourself, so that your awareness is permeated by warmth, by cherishing, protecting, and maturing. This is what I mean by self-love or self-compassion. You can do this by repeating phrases from the *karuna bhavana* (development of compassion), one of the guided reflections at the end of Chapter 3: 'May I be well, may I be free from suffering.' In this way, you develop loving-kindness towards yourself, with an awareness of your particular suffering.

Bear in mind that, if you focus on your suffering, you may start to feel distress and overwhelm, so it's important to focus on your thriving, your welfare. What do you need to thrive at the moment? What would give you a sense of wholeness and completeness?

Self-compassion has all the benefits of self-worth or self-esteem, without its disadvantages. If you experience a high level of self-esteem, you might start to treat the people around you as less worthy of your care and respect. The same isn't true for self-compassion. People who have developed self-compassion take responsibility for the impact of their actions on others – they just don't beat themselves up along the way.

Kristin Neff, a researcher in this area, doesn't see a difference between self-compassion and compassion for others. She defines them in the same way, as having three elements: a sense of kindness, common humanity, and mindfulness.[100] Self-kindness is contrasted with self-judgement. It means actively treating oneself with care and understanding rather than with harsh judgement. It includes the desire to alleviate one's own suffering and actively soothing and comforting oneself.

Common humanity is contrasted with isolation. It means seeing one's own experience as part of the larger human experience, rather than as something isolated or abnormal. It means recognizing that life is imperfect, characterized by *dukkha* (unsatisfactoriness), and we are too. We can say to ourselves, 'It's not just me who suffers like this.'

Mindfulness is contrasted with overidentification. You need to be aware of your suffering in order to direct compassion towards it. Mindfulness avoids the extremes of suppressing painful feelings or wallowing in them. Mindfulness allows us to *be with* painful feelings as they are. Can we turn towards our own suffering compassionately rather than trying to fix it or fade it?

As the Buddha saw when he discovered the middle way, if we are violent towards ourselves, it's difficult to be compassionate towards others. When we act in the power mode towards ourselves, it's difficult to be genuinely loving and compassionate towards others. When critical self-judgements prevent us from seeing our own beauty, we can lose connection with our life-energy.[101]

We may have been conditioned to view ourselves as objects full of shortcomings, and so end up relating violently towards ourselves. This violence can be replaced with compassion in our moment-to-moment evaluations. We need to know how to evaluate events and conditions in ways that support learning and lead to the enrichment of life. Unfortunately, we may have been trained to evaluate ourselves in ways that promote self-hatred rather than learning.

Think of the last time that you made a 'mistake'. How did you speak to yourself immediately afterwards? Did you tell yourself, 'That was stupid!' or ask, 'How could you do that?' or call yourself an idiot? These ways of talking to ourselves suggest that we are judging our actions as wrong or bad. The self-admonition implicitly assumes that we deserve to suffer for what we have done. I see this as a tragedy. Instead of benefiting from our experiences, which can show us our limitations and guide us towards growth, we get enmeshed in self-hatred.

Even if we 'learn our lesson' by judging ourselves harshly, what kind of lesson do we actually learn? To be motivated by destructive energies such as shame (as opposed to regret or remorse) or guilt, rather than a clear desire to contribute to life for ourselves and others. Shame can be a species of self-hatred, and lessons learned in reaction to shame are not free and joyful.

Even if we intend to act from kindness and sensitivity, if people sense guilt or shame behind our actions, they are less likely to appreciate what we do. In other words, there is a cost to ourselves and others, and that cost is measured in terms of a reduction in trust and cooperation between us, and a reduction in a general sense of life-energy.

One word that has enormous power to stimulate shame and guilt is the word 'should', as in 'I should have known better' or 'I shouldn't have done that.' When we use this word on ourselves, we usually resist learning, because it implies that we have no choice. When we hear any kind of demand, we tend to resist it because it threatens our need for autonomy – our strong need for choice. We have the same reaction to internal tyranny in the form of *should*.

A similar thing happens when we use the word 'must' towards ourselves, as in 'I really must do more exercise.' We keep telling ourselves what we must do, and we keep resisting it because we want autonomy. If we do submit to these demands, our actions will be devoid of life-giving energy.

When we communicate with ourselves through inner judgement, blame, and demand, it's hardly surprising that we come to see ourselves more as objects than as human beings. A basic premise of Nonviolent Communication is that, when we judge someone as bad or wrong, what we are really saying is that they aren't acting in harmony with our needs. If we are judging ourselves in this way, what we are really saying is, 'I didn't act in harmony with my own needs.' We are more likely to learn from this kind of evaluation.

So, when we notice that we aren't contributing to life in the way that we had hoped, we can evaluate ourselves in a way that inspires change in the direction we want to go in, and from a basis of self-compassion rather than self-hatred. We can train ourselves to recognize judgemental self-talk and to immediately focus our attention on the underlying needs.

For example, if we reproach ourselves with 'You idiot!', we can stop and ask, "What unmet need of mine is being expressed through this moralistic judgement? What need of mine wasn't met when I acted in this way?' When we connect to this need, we may notice a remarkable shift in our body. Instead of shame, guilt, or depression, we may experience a transformed feeling, a sweet pain that could be sadness, frustration, disappointment, fear, or grief.

Whatever the feeling is, it will be more life-connected than the guilt, shame, or depression that preceded it. Mourning is the process of fully connecting with unmet needs and their accompanying feelings. We will return to the topic of mourning in Chapter 12, 'Lost Loves'.

When it is our own actions that we are mourning, we experience a regret that helps us to learn from what we have done without stimulating self-hatred. When we are focused on what we need and value, we are naturally stimulated towards creative possibilities for how to get these met. By contrast, the moralistic judgements we use when blaming ourselves tend to reduce creativity and perpetuate self-punishment.

Once we have mourned our unmet needs, we turn our attention to self-forgiveness. Turning our attention towards the part of ourselves that chose to act in the way we now regret, we ask, 'What need of mine was I trying to meet?' We are always trying to meet needs and enrich life in some kind of way, even if we don't always succeed. When we listen empathically to ourselves, we will be able to hear the underlying need.

Self-forgiveness occurs when this empathic connection is made. We are able to recognize how our choice was an attempt to enrich life, even as we acknowledge how it didn't meet our needs. Self-compassion entails holding both parts of ourselves, the self that regrets the past action and the self that acted. Holding both empathically frees us in the direction of learning and growth, and increases our capacity to act in harmony with our needs.

Discovering that you have access to love directly through self-compassion starts to put the frustrations and disappointments of ongoing partnership into perspective. You become less dependent on your partner for approval, which is a poor substitute for real love. You can stand on your own and dare to be yourself. Since you are less tempted to give up on your self-connection in order to win love, you experience less resentment.

A healthy partnership can also play a part in our spiritual growth. It can open a channel through which love can flow. Even when this is happening, we need to remember that genuine growth comes about through inner processes, especially softening and opening our protective heart. If we're always looking to another person to do this for us, our heart will never develop this muscle for itself.

Accessing love directly through self-compassion allows us to inhabit our partnership more fully, with greater presence and empowerment. The less dependent I am on another person to do the work of love, the more freely I can see them as they are, show myself as I am, and take the risk of real intimacy. When we both let go of trying to extract love and acceptance from the other at any cost, we can see our partnership in a new light, as a field of learning and play where we can grow and transform through each other's influence.

One step in this direction is to work with resentment. How often do you do things and then feel resentful because you're telling yourself that you 'have' to do them? It's worth looking at the energy behind these actions. Are they motivated by your desire to contribute to life (a form of self-compassion), or fear, guilt, shame, or obligation? When we can see clearly how our actions contribute to life, even hard work has an element of play to it.

Here's an exercise to help us increase the amount of playful, joyful energy available to us, and to deepen our sense of self-compassion.

Firstly, write down all the things that you tell yourself you *have* to do. List any activity you dread but do anyway because you tell yourself you have no choice. My list included making a living and doing the washing up. When I realized how much of my time was spent on these two activities, it was easy to understand why I don't fully enjoy life.

Secondly, clearly acknowledge to yourself that you are doing these things because you *choose* to do them. Insert the phrase, 'I choose to...' in front of each item on your list.

Thirdly, get in touch with the intention behind your choice by completing 'I choose to...' with 'because I want...'. So I wrote, 'I choose to make a living because I want to support myself and Gesine.' I felt a strange sense of curiosity and satisfaction as I wrote this. Curiosity about my motivations and satisfaction that I'm taking care of both of us in this way. Making a living also contributes to self-empowerment, and prompts me to contribute to life in ways that I wouldn't otherwise.

Then I wrote, 'I choose to do the washing up because I want cleanliness, a sense of order, and to support whoever is cooking next. I also want to share responsibility for looking after the house.' I felt an appreciation of the time I take to do this task and how it aligns with my deeper values of mutual responsibility. I resolved to remind myself of these purposes the next time I feel bored or resentful when doing the washing up.

For these two items on my list I discovered the important values behind the choices I've made. After gaining this clarity, I'm more likely to experience these actions as a form of play, even when they involve hard work or frustrations. However, for some of the items on your list, you may uncover one or more of the following motivations.

For money: we have been trained to strive for extrinsic rewards in our society. Perhaps the chief of these is money. However, choices prompted by a desire for rewards are costly. There is an absence of the satisfaction that comes from clearly meeting a human need. Despite its obvious usefulness, making money can become an obsessive end in itself.

For approval: like money, this is an extrinsic reward. We have grown up being motivated for these rewards, and we may be addicted to getting a smile from our partner for wearing 'nice' clothes, to receiving a pat on the back, or to hearing that we are a 'good' son, lover, partner, worker, and so on. In this way, we try to buy the love of those closest to us, and deny ourselves in order to be liked.

By contrast, when we do things with the sole intention of enriching life, one's own and that of others, we find others genuinely appreciating us. Their appreciation confirms and guides us in contributing further, and yet it doesn't *replace* the satisfaction of knowing that we have chosen to use our access to resources to enrich life.

To escape punishment: if we do the washing up to escape punishment, we are likely to feel resentful about it.

To avoid shame: we may do some tasks to avoid self-judgement that we are bad or wrong or selfish. If we act purely on this impulse, we are likely to end up detesting the activity itself.

To avoid guilt: we are afraid of feeling guilty for failing to fulfil other people's expectations of us. We may even be afraid that they will withdraw love completely. There is a world of difference between this and acting out of a clear awareness of our own need to contribute to life.

To satisfy a sense of duty: when we use a language that denies choice, for example *should, have to, ought, must, can't, supposed to,* we can act out of a vague sense of guilt, duty, or obligation. This can lead to acting in ways that reduce a sense of humanity and the safety of the beings around us. Under the National Socialists, German bureaucrats sent millions of people to their deaths without feeling emotionally affected or personally responsible. They did this by communicating in *Amtssprache* (office language, or officialese), which denied their sense of choice and treated the people being sent to their deaths as so many units of production.

After examining your list of 'have tos', you may decide to stop doing some of them and recommit to others. To the extent that we act from the motivation to enrich life, we are being compassionate and loving towards ourselves.

In the next chapter we will go into the practical issues of how to say 'I love you'. We'll touch on vulnerability, honesty, empathy, gratitude, and saying and hearing a no. In the meantime, to deepen the roots of self-compassion, I invite you to join me in a guided reflection on how to learn from your limitations without losing self-respect.

Guided reflection: how to learn from your limitations without losing self-respect

- Purpose of this activity: to deepen the roots of self-compassion by holding the needs that weren't met by an action of yours, along with the needs you were trying to meet.
- Materials: you'll need something to write on.
- Time: 15 minutes.

8

How to Say 'I Love You'

> If you bring forth what is within you, what you bring forth will save you. If you do not bring forth what is within you, what you do not bring forth will destroy you.
>
> The Gospel of Thomas, one of the Gnostic Gospels

When it comes to declaring our love for our partner, we can get ourselves tangled in knots. How do we say 'I love you' in a skilful way, in line with what we've learned in Part One?

The following is a role play by Marshall Rosenberg, founder of Nonviolent Communication (NVC). It highlights two different ways of understanding love. Puppets are used: the Jackal represents language and thinking that disconnect from life, and the Giraffe represents language and thinking rooted in empathy and connection, with a specific emphasis on needs.

> Jackal: Do you love me?
>
> Giraffe: Before I can answer your question honestly, I need to get some important things clear. Are you using the word love as a feeling?
>
> Jackal: Well of course!
>
> Giraffe: Okay, well I needed to get that clear. So you mean, 'Am I feeling certain warm, cuddly, tender feelings towards you?'

Jackal: Yes!

Giraffe: Okay, I needed to get this clear, because we Giraffes do not use the word love as a feeling. It's much too important to us to get it confused with a feeling. It's a need for us. But since you use it as a feeling, okay I'm glad to know that. Would you ask the question again?

Jackal (mildly frustrated, still keen to get an answer): Do you love me?

Giraffe: When?

Jackal (now really surprised and frustrated): When?

Giraffe (trying to explain): Well, I want to be honest. I can see how important this is to you. But how can I be honest with you about what I feel toward you without reference to a specific moment? Feelings change every few seconds. Life is changing. Feelings are part of life. So I'd have to know a specific time and place to ever answer your question of how I feel.

Jackal (in a raised voice): Well, what about right now?

Giraffe (matter-of-factly): No. (Jackal looks shocked.) But try me again in a few moments.[102]

We may aspire to listen with the ears of tolerance, see through the eyes of compassion, and speak with the language of love, as Rumi exhorts.[103] However, real life in partnership tends to be more like Marshall's role play. Talking about love with your partner can be tricky territory. As the role play demonstrates, it can be difficult to answer a question such as 'Do you love me?'

By the same token, it can also be difficult to tell someone, 'I love you.' There can be uncertainty about how your message will be received. And, if you are on the receiving end of such a message, you might feel uncertain about what it means. Does it imply that your partner loves the clothes you are wearing or the last thing that you said? Do you need to keep wearing the red dress you've got on for the rest of your life? If you're brushing your teeth when your partner says, 'I love you', does it mean you need to brush your teeth when you want them to say it again? Does it mean that your partner wants you to stay just as you are now?

So it's important to express the need for love in ways that also honour our partner's needs for autonomy and freedom. Sometimes 'I love you' comes out naturally and spontaneously, and is received with gratitude. Some people really want to hear those three little words. Gesine and I have explored various alternatives for when 'I love you' seems awkward: 'You're my love', 'We belong together', 'I'm here for you', 'I'm happy to wait for you', 'I take you seriously', 'I love us', 'I love how we are together', and 'I'm glad to be alive with you.'

In *Being Me, Loving You*, Marshall Rosenberg explains that NVC really grew out of his attempt to understand the concept of love and how to manifest it. How do you actually *do* love, rather than just talk about it?[104] From this perspective, NVC is an exploration of the love mode that we heard about in the Introduction. NVC is a language and way of thinking that make it possible for couples to connect with each other and give to each other from the heart.

Marshall had come to the conclusion, as we've seen in Part One, that love is not just something we feel, but something that we manifest, something we do, something we need. It is also something that we can give. We can give of ourselves in different ways.

One way is to reveal ourselves nakedly and honestly to our partner, for no purpose other than connection. Rather than blaming, criticizing, diagnosing, or punishing your partner, you can just say, 'Here I am, and here is what I would like. This is my vulnerability at this moment.' Expressing ourselves vulnerably is a manifestation of love. We are in the territory made famous by psychologist Brené Brown in her 2011 TED talk, which has racked up 21 million views.[105]

In her research, Brown found that there was a certain group of people whose lives seemed to be blessed. It didn't matter what had happened to them in childhood, they found a way through. When she researched the characteristics these people had in common, she found that they shared what she called 'vulnerability'. According to Brown, vulnerability means two things: you're aware of the risks involved in getting close to others, and you do it anyway, because you realize how important closeness really is. As Gesine and I have seen again and again in our work with couples, vulnerability can be the difference between happiness and misery.

We want to connect with our partner, yet at the same time we don't want to get caught up in their worldview or preferred strategies for doing things. So how do we do both? We can be loud and clear about what we feel, what we need, and what we want back from our partner. And we can do this without doing two things that turn assertiveness into the power mode: criticism and coercion.

We assert ourselves without criticizing our partner – there's no implication that our partner is wrong, selfish, insensitive, and so on. We say nothing that classifies what they *are*. Rather we assert ourselves by saying what's going on inside us and what we would like them to do.

And we express this as a request rather than a demand or coercion. In partnership, this topic takes on a central importance. Our requests will be received as demands if our partner believes that they will be blamed or punished if they don't comply. Then they only see two options: to submit or to rebel. The moment our partner hears anything from our lips that sounds like a demand, or that we don't value their needs as much as ours, or that we are out to get our way, they are likely to put their energy into defensiveness and resistance. Their capacity to respond compassionately diminishes. They withdraw their cooperation, and, in turn, this makes it less likely that we are going to meet our own needs.

When our partner hears demands, it looks to them as though our love is conditional. It looks as though we are only going to love them when they do what we want. We may become locked into a battle of wills. Resources can seem to be stretched to the limit, and there seems to be no other way. However, demands are an expensive currency, and we all pay the price in terms of resentment, connection, and cooperation. The more important it is that your partner does something, the more important it is that they hear what you're asking as a request, not a demand.

So can you express your 'please' so that your partner can receive it as a gift, an opportunity to give? Can you find a way to say, 'I want to make it clear that *no* is an acceptable answer. Please only do this if you can do it willingly. If you do it out of guilt or resentment, we'll both suffer. Please only do it if it comes from your heart as a gift.' Only when no one feels like they're losing, giving in, or giving up do both partners benefit from an action.

Another way that we can give of ourselves is *receiving* our partner's words. It's a gift to receive our partner's message empathically, connecting with what's alive in *them*, making no judgement of this. It's a gift when we try to hear what's alive in them and what they would like.

With these two ways that we can give of ourselves, *honest expression* and *empathic listening*, Marshall concluded that NVC is really just a manifestation of his understanding of love. It connected him to love in a broader spiritual sense, and it's the closest thing to love that he ever experienced.

Communication allows you to relate to your partner and connect with them. And it's more than the words you speak. It includes silence, listening, and nonverbal behaviour. Although we learned how to communicate when we were growing up, partnership brings particular challenges. Developing our communication skills can bring us closer. However, without a compassionate intention – to value everyone's needs, to see people as being as real as ourselves – communication skills can seem like hollow techniques.

Nonverbal behaviour communicates a multitude of messages. There's gesture, posture, proximity, touch, tone of voice, eye contact, and facial expression. If you look away or roll your eyes when your partner is speaking, the message is clear. When you make eye contact and smile when your partner enters the room, again the message is clear.

However, not all such nonverbal behaviours are so obvious, and we're probably only aware of a small percentage of the nonverbal messages we are sending. Our partner may be picking up on a message that we didn't intend to send. This is why it's so important to separate the *impact* of a behaviour from our *intention* in acting or speaking. It's important to acknowledge both. Love can be communicated (or not) in a myriad different ways.

Love is embodied in silence as well as in speech. And there are different kinds of silence. There's the silence of giving your attention, your presence to what your partner is communicating either verbally or nonverbally. You attend to the feelings and needs behind what they are saying. This is empathic listening, empathy as attention.

Then there's the silence of becoming temporarily overwhelmed by a strong feeling. It wells up deeply within you and moves you, so that you can't speak. You remain silent until the feeling subsides. Then there's the reflective pause, when you take a moment to consider and think things through, without speaking. These two correspond to self-compassion, explored in Chapter 7. Then there's the open, peaceful silence that emerges in the depths of connection, when there is nothing more to say for the moment.

These kinds of silence are likely to be received by your partner in a loving way. However, there are other forms of silence that are unlikely to be received as love. There's the silence of withdrawal and disconnection. There's the silence of punishment, when you know that it will be painful for your partner and you do it anyway. Then there's sulking silence and hostile or frozen silence.

Loving communication doesn't necessarily mean saying everything on your mind. The Buddha recommended that we express ourselves only when it's accurate, kindly, *and* helpful to the other person to do so. When speaking to your partner, it's important to take into account *their* feelings and needs, alongside your need to be heard. It takes time, sensitivity, and effort to become aware of your own and your partner's style of communication. And, when we do express ourselves, we can do it without criticism or coercion.

Now let's look at empathic listening, the other way we can give of ourselves. As mentioned, it's a gift to receive our partner's message empathically, connecting with what's alive in them, and making no judgement of this. It's an open secret, but this kind of listening is very likely to be received as love. In the longer term, empathy leads to secure attachment (see Chapter 2) and is listed by the eminent psychologist Carl Rogers as one of his nine therapeutic conditions.[106]

Empathy has been linked to oxytocin, one of the four neurochemicals associated with love. As we saw in Chapter 2, oxytocin lowers your inhibitions by quieting the amygdala, the ancient part of your brain that assesses threats. This makes you more confident, giving you an unusual sense of calm as you take the first step in forming a relationship.

The presence of oxytocin increases a sense of bonding, trust, and empathy, and decreases stress. There is an actual correlation between levels of oxytocin in your blood stream and your ability to empathize. Conversely, the more stressed you are, the less you are able to empathize with others.

There is a strong link between empathy and intimacy. Understanding another's emotional experience, and being able to let them know that you know, leads to a deepening sense of closeness. In *I'll Meet You There: A Practical Guide to Empathy,*

Mindfulness and Communication, Gesine and I describe our experience of the various ways in which empathy can deepen sexual intimacy.

It creates bonding and trust: empathizing and being empathized with bring us closer to each other. I'm aware of Gesine's inner world, and she mine. There is a sense of heart connection, mutual care, understanding, and love. Within this emotional safety, there is a greater openness to 'feel' each other, and let the other know what we like.

Empathy increases our overall sensitivity towards each other, so we're likely to do more of what the other likes, and less of what they don't like. When we're tuned in to each other, we can enjoy the other's arousal and pleasure just as much as our own. If tensions and conflicts arise, empathy supports repair and renewal.

Overall, if you're able to sense your partner's feelings and needs, you're more likely to engage in activities that increase intimacy. So empathy is an important predictor of the survival and breakup of marriages.[107]

If our partner knows how to express themselves without criticism or coercion, we can just receive them. If our partner uses criticism, then we might need to put on our Giraffe ears! Earlier we heard that the Giraffe is a symbol of compassionate, life-enriching communication. We can put on our Giraffe ears when we want to focus on the underlying feelings and universal needs of the other person, rather than hearing criticism or blame.

When we hear, 'The problem with you is...', we can hear, 'I'm in pain and what I would like is... (please).' We hear no criticism, only unmet needs. We understand that criticism is a tragic expression of unmet needs. It's tragic because it's unlikely that they are going to get what they want, and likely to lead to tension and disconnection.

Another way to talk about empathy is presence. Do you know how to be present with your partner as intensely as if you were meditating? Presence greatly enhances the quality of connection. And, when you are present, you are open to love. As we will see in the next chapter, love entails mutual awareness and understanding. In other words, genuine presence. This is what creates the conditions for lasting love.

After the initial phase of falling in love, you may go back to a more critical stance towards your partner. Why do they leave things out on the sideboard instead of putting them away? Couldn't they tidy up their side of the bed, desk, room, or life?

How do you remain open, awake, and present to the person in front of you? Love isn't a thing to be possessed. If you cling to it or try to control it, it leaves the room. It's not a state to be achieved; it's not a destination that you can reach once and for all. It's a moment-by-moment process, a certain quality of connection between you and your partner.

If you don't feel your partner's presence, rather than blaming them or the relationship, can you intensify *your* practice of presence, maybe taking some time for self-connection? The principle is this: if you have space for yourself, you are likely to have space for your partner. When you've done your moment of self-connection, can you suggest an activity to do together, with the phones off? It doesn't matter what you do, whether it's the dishes, a walk, or eating. Being together is more important than what you're doing. Talk, listen, and appreciate each other as you engage in the activity. Enjoy each other's company. Love is an experience to be shared.

Gratitude

A special form of honest expression is appreciation or gratitude. It's special because it has a profound power to deepen partnership and be received as love. Gratitude is more than an appreciation for what you enjoy in life. It is an appreciation for life itself, even with its ups and downs. We can practise being grateful for the opportunity of life and not take it for granted. Similarly we can practise being grateful that our partner is alive and not take *them* for granted. Gratitude increases the overall energy available for life: it is life-affirming.

When you express gratitude or appreciation to your partner, it enriches both your lives. It helps you to see clearly your partner's qualities and skilful actions. It's too easy to get bogged down in the frustrations of daily life. By paying attention to your partner's qualities and skilfulness, you aren't ignoring the things you find uncomfortable, you're simply bringing the relationship back into balance.

When gratitude is in the air, you can put your difficulties into perspective and work together to find creative solutions. You can remain connected even when you strongly disagree. Can you find something that you appreciate about your partner every day? Perhaps it's the way they look at you, the clothes they choose, the care with which they prepare food or ask how you are? Awareness of the little things in daily life will gradually help you to cultivate a feeling of appreciation.

I grew up feeling resentful for being alive. I couldn't receive life as a gift – there was too much unacknowledged pain. It was only in 2008, when I led an NVC workshop on gratitude, that I realized the power of it. I just felt so human! That feeling stayed with me, and I resolved to keep a nightly gratitude diary. Eighteen years later, I'm still keeping a nightly gratitude diary. Only now, Gesine and I do it verbally, with each other, as the last thing before we go to sleep.

I've found that gratitude is juicier, the more specific you can be. Can you tell your partner what they've done to enrich your life, how you feel about it, which needs of yours have been met, and finish with a request for 'More of the same, please!'? When you choose to express your gratitude/appreciation to your partner in this way, it can help to bring them alive, and experience fully what it means to be loved.

On our side, it's important to be aware of how our partner is contributing to our welfare. This is the first step towards gratitude. Without an awareness of benefits received, we won't know when to express gratitude. We need to be alert and attentive to this, without minimizing the suffering in the world.

Practising gratitude and appreciation can bring fresh energy into our lives and help us to appreciate all beings and the planet that supports us. It can change the way we look into our partner's eyes and increase the sense of honour and love that we have for them. Cultivating gratitude naturally leads to generosity, and generosity is essential to partnership.[108] Without a free flow of resources – material, psychological/emotional, and spiritual – partnership will struggle to survive.

Gesine and I aspire to the principle 'Freely given and freely received.'

Generosity of spirit means letting go of hurts and being willing to reconnect after breakdowns. It doesn't mean forgetting or brushing them under the carpet. It means learning and letting go. Holding on to resentments is like holding you and your partner's heart hostage. Learning and letting go give love a fresh chance.

Psychologist John Gottman and his associates have studied long-term relationships for more than forty years. They found that they could predict with 90 per cent accuracy what was going to happen to a relationship over the next three years. With accuracy like this, who needs a crystal ball? They examined a couple's physiology and behaviour during a discussion about something that they didn't agree on.[109]

They found that there was a clear difference between couples whose relationship lasted and those whose relationship fell apart. For the couples that lasted, the ratio of appreciation to things they didn't enjoy was 5:1. For those whose relationship fell apart, the ratio was roughly 1:1. What would it take to stay at 5:1 with your partner? Intense *metta* practice?

If you don't put energy into your intimate relationship, it's likely to deteriorate. Couples who focus on children or work may gradually learn to ignore each other. If this starts to happen, there are things you can do to remedy it. Gottman invites us to look out for the warning signs, which he calls the 'Four Horsemen of the Apocalypse'. They are: contempt, criticism, defensiveness, and stonewalling.

Contempt is probably the most powerful predictor of the end of a long-term relationship. Contempt includes direct insults, sarcasm, or one partner assuming that they are better than the other. An air of superiority is the best predictor of divorce. As we saw above with Marshall Rosenberg, criticism is also a sign that the relationship is going nowhere. So is defensiveness, when you respond to your partner's 'complaint' with righteous indignation, or as if you are the innocent victim. If you behave in this way, it looks like you're not taking responsibility for your part in the situation. The fourth horseman is stonewalling or emotional withdrawal. People who do this don't give their usual nonverbal cues to the speaker – they look away or down and stop responding.

Criticism and defensiveness are found in all relationships. The difference is that people who are skilled in communication will notice a loss of trust and connection and make an attempt to repair it. This is where empathy comes in. They do some self-empathy as preparation, to the point where they can reach out to their partner and acknowledge what's going on for *them*. Of course this attempt has to be received by their partner for it to be effective. There needs to be willingness on both sides: on the one side to reach out and attempt a repair, on the other to accept the attempt.

Acceptance and rejection

Another area in which we can learn to give and receive love is acceptance and rejection. Most of us long for acceptance and regard it as essential for partnership. We learn about the pain of rejection at an early age, whether or not we had loving caregivers. We want a partnership that is a safe refuge from the rejection that we may have experienced as a child, and may continue to experience in the adult world.

Gesine and I have both worked on self-acceptance, so that we're not dependent on one another to meet this need. Self-acceptance implies coming to terms with yourself, what you want from life, and any limitations. At the same time, we seek acceptance from each other. This doesn't mean that we accept each other as we are. It means that we acknowledge what's important to each other *without necessarily agreeing*. This is acceptance with integrity: acknowledging what your partner needs at the moment, without necessarily agreeing with their worldview or their favourite strategies.

It's different from trying to change your partner so that you don't get triggered any more. It may be difficult to accept that you can't change your partner. You can change yourself, not another person. Did you get into the partnership hoping that your partner would change or improve? This is a recipe for profound disappointment. Your partner may change over time, but that's their own choice and initiative. You can love them and empathize with them, and this is like the sunshine and rain that will help them to flourish. But how they change is up to them. You may grow together or apart. You can also inspire them to change by the changes you make in your own behaviour, but nagging or trying to control them will only create resistance.

In the next chapter we're delving into the shadow side of love. In the meantime, I invite you to dwell in gratitude, for life in general and your partner in particular.

Guided reflection: dwelling in gratitude

- Purpose of this activity: to dwell in gratitude for the opportunity of life and for your partner's presence.
- Time: 15 minutes.

9

The Shadow Side of Love

Falling in love again
Never wanted to.
What am I to do?
I can't help it.[110]

The poor thing can't help it. Marlene Dietrich and most of us think that our bodies will do the job for us. However, we have responsibility for love, and especially for emotional and sexual fidelity in a long-term relationship. When we find someone other than our partner attractive, we can restrain ourselves from daydreaming about them as a partner. We can guard the gates of the senses.

You might wonder what would happen if you told that person they were beautiful. You have given yourself permission to cross this boundary, even though you are in a committed relationship. Perhaps you think, 'What harm can it do?' But your hormones can take over, and every close conversation creates a bond.

What else can we do, from a Buddhist perspective? In the eighth century CE, the Buddhist poet-monk Shantideva wrote *The Bodhicaryavatara* for a settled monastic audience. His treatment for falling in love might sound harsh to modern ears. In his chapter on 'The perfection of meditative absorption' he recommends reflecting on the *asubha* or relatively unlovely aspects of the person we are in love with.

Earlier, Shantideva has pointed out that beings are impermanent, and you can't hold on to them. When you're in love, you can't meditate with or without them, and you're tormented by longing. You lose awareness, positive emotion, and a sense of responsibility. Your own body will one day rot away. The same is true for people who are dear to you. He resolves to dwell alone in the forest to meditate.

If this isn't enough, he encourages us to reflect on how intense emotions of craving and hatred bring suffering on us, in this and future lives, because they lead us to act unskilfully. You may have experienced the highest bliss when you embraced your lover, but now imagine them as a corpse. They are nothing but bones. Why don't you still want to cuddle them? The face you adored is now being stripped by vultures. Why do you recoil? Why don't you protect it from others, as you did before? Would you worship this corpse with garlands, sandalwood, and jewellery?

And now it gets very personal, as Shantideva plays on the theme of purity and impurity. Your beloved produced shit, but you wanted none of it. Those in love, he proclaims, are entranced by filth. You have no passion for what is foul, so why do you embrace another, a 'cage of bones bound by sinew, smeared with slime and flesh'? He goes on, 'You have plenty of filth of your own. Satisfy yourself with that! Glutton for crap! Forget (them), that other pouch of filth!'[111]

What is the emotional impact of reading these words? Horror, disgust, or humour? This kind of reflection can have unintended consequences. It can become a stick to beat ourselves with, stimulating self-hatred or hatred of the body. It could even increase our hatred towards other people.

If neither guarding the gates of the senses nor reflecting on unloveliness appeals, what can you do? A relatively straightforward step is to acknowledge the unsatisfactory aspects of your experience. When you're in love, 'It's got to be per-er-er-er-er-er-fect', in the words of the song by Fairground Attraction.[112] Anything that can help to break this spell will bring your feet down to the ground.

Perhaps you're a morning person and they are an evening person. Perhaps they have some habits that you don't appreciate. Perhaps they don't always look as charming as when you first met them. Whatever it is, without straining for it, may help to give you a more balanced, realistic picture of them.

If we don't take these steps for ourselves, we may experience something much more painful and even destructive. We may fall out of love. This is also an opportunity for practice. We can reflect that our experience of falling out of love is a part of what it means to be truly human and give birth to a genuine compassion for ourselves, our lover, and all beings. We may find healing through self-compassion to the point where we are able to empathize with the 'good reasons' why our lover does what they do – the needs they are trying to meet when they act.

When we are able to acknowledge these needs, without necessarily agreeing with our lover's worldview or the way they lead their life, we rehumanize them and ourselves. We have done the work of forgiveness and reconciliation – no further steps are needed.

Possessiveness and jealousy

Also concealed in the shadow side of love are possessiveness and jealousy. These can lead us to act in profoundly unskilful ways, including taking another person's life. In the Western literary canon we have Shakespeare's *Othello*, a study of the 'green-eyed god' of jealousy. Jealousy gets its power from combining greed for one object with hatred for whoever or whatever would take it away. Hatred is revealed as the reflex of frustrated greed, and combines with it in jealousy for extra power.

In Buddhist psychology there is a single term (*irsya*) for jealousy and envy. Envy is what you feel in relation to something you don't have but would like to have. Jealousy, as we've seen, is what you feel in relation to something or someone that you regard as in your possession.[113]

Jealousy is most often associated with relationships, particularly sexual relationships. It can begin in childhood, especially if you've been an only child and you're suddenly ousted from the nest by a younger sibling. It can arise from a lack of self-value. If you don't value yourself, if you don't love yourself, you're likely to become emotionally dependent on someone else's love for your emotional security.

So, instead of your value being in your own control, you can only get it from someone else's regard. If there is any threat of that person transferring their regard to someone else, it threatens your *whole* value as a person. You risk losing your self-value. If they leave, it may feel as though they'll take your identity with them.

So jealousy is the fear of almost being destroyed, and it can lead to murder. By contrast, to need affection, companionship, and warmth is healthy and skilful. These needs can lead us to make friends as well as lovers, and can lead us to community or sangha.

Perhaps the first step in dealing with possessiveness and jealousy is simply acknowledging the reality in front of you. Sometimes your partner will not say, do, or feel the thing you want them to. They have a will of their own, and this doesn't always coincide with who you want them to be. It can be deeply painful to discover that they are unwilling or unable to change to meet your expectations.

It's worth remembering that there's nothing wrong with them, or the world – they just don't meet your needs at the moment. Or, more precisely, they aren't supporting you to meet your needs in the way you would prefer. Perhaps you haven't yet fully acknowledged the first noble truth of Buddhism, that there is an unsatisfactory aspect to experience. You might unconsciously assume that, if you just try hard enough, you can make your partner into the person you want them to be.

Perhaps you want them to be more focused on you and the partnership, and less focused on work or other people. Perhaps you start off encouraging them, and, when this doesn't seem to be effective, you resort to subtle manipulation, then bribery, then domination. It's only when we are able to acknowledge the differences between us that we are able to meet each other as separate individuals with our own feelings and needs. This is essential to forming meaningful relationships with respect and dignity at their core, rather than control.

Acknowledging the reality in front of you means seeing clearly and responding in freedom. In finding your freedom, you free your partner to grow and develop in their own way, rather than in your image.

To look at it from a Buddhist perspective, we don't really understand what love is, so we suffer when we lose it. It's very important to distinguish between what we might call immature or possessive love and mature or true love. Immature, possessive love says, 'I love you and I want you to make me happy.' We're back to 'The clod and the pebble' of Chapter 1:

> Love seeketh only self to please,
> To bind another to its delight,
> Joys in another's loss of ease,
> And builds a Hell in Heaven's despite.[114]

When we fall in love in this way, we take away each other's freedom, create bondage, build a prison. By contrast, mature or true love says, 'I love you and I want *you* to be happy. If that includes me, let's celebrate! If it doesn't, in any case, I wish you health and happiness.'

Mature love helps both partners to be free, to break all sorts of bondages. A mature person doesn't fall in love, they rise in love. Only immature people fall. They stumble and fall down in love. They were just managing to stand, and now they cannot manage and they have fallen down. They were waiting for it and hoping for it. They don't have the strength and integrity to stand alone.

A mature person has the strength and integrity to stand alone. And, when they give love, they give it without any strings attached. When two mature people are in love, they are together and yet alone. They are fully together. At the same time, they help each other to become more free. There's no push and pull, no attempt to dominate, only freedom and love.

This leaves both partners free to reflect. You might reflect, 'I don't see how I'm going to get my needs met in this partnership. Now, there are eight billion people on this planet, so perhaps I need to start somewhere else.' Again it could be, 'My partner is trying to enrich their life the best they know how, given their background and experience. I will see if we can grow together around and through these difficulties and differences.'

You can choose to acknowledge the reality in front of you, rather than pouring your energy into pretending. When you take this step, you may find that your quality of life increases, and you inspire others to do the same.

We tend to think that the more we grasp and cling, the more we care. But the more we grasp and cling – the more we try to *own* experiences, people, things – the more we will suffer. This is because we are seeking ultimate safety and security where we won't find it. From a Buddhist perspective, if we want safety and security we need to turn to the unconditional love that is an aspect of Enlightenment.

As we saw in Chapter 6, 'The Garden of Love', true love thrives on freedom. We need to be able to give and receive love freely. There is no element of coercion. 'If you love someone, set them free', as Sting sang in the 1980s.[115] Or, paraphrasing Zen teacher Thich Nhat Hanh, 'Love in such a way that the person you love feels free.'[116]

Are you capable of allowing the other person to be free? This might depend on your capacity to be alone. The capacity to be alone is not different from the capacity to love. It may seem paradoxical, but it isn't. It's an existential truth. Only if you are capable of being alone are you capable of sharing, of connecting at the deepest level with another person, without possessing them, without becoming dependent on them, without using them, without reducing them to an object, and without becoming addicted to them.

If you are capable of being alone, of enjoying your own company, you can allow the other person to be totally free, because you know that, if they leave, you will still find happiness. Your happiness cannot be taken away by the other person, because it wasn't given to you by them in the first place.

At the same time, safety and security are important in long-term romantic partnerships. When you kiss your partner on the lips, you're really asking them a kind of question. It's something like, 'Do you still love me? Have you managed to hold on to the lacerating tail of love? Have you managed to tend to your wounds?' – the ones that inevitably appear when you're vulnerable to each other. 'Is my name still safe in your mouth?'

And the answer you're looking for isn't in words, which can be faked, but in the touch of their lips. You can tell if they want you, if they are distracted, if they are hurt and don't want to talk about it. Alongside this, you're responding to that very same question coming from your lover's lips: 'Do you still love me? Am I safe with you?'

Part of our conditioning as human beings is that we see ourselves as the centre of our world, even, in some cases, the centre of the universe! So our relationship with others tends to be self-referential. We may think of ourselves as loving and affectionate. However, we may only be aware of others to the extent that they satisfy our needs. We make this kind of assessment of them and then attribute our assessment *to* them, as a quality *of* them. As William Blake says,

> What is it men in women do require?
> The lineaments of Gratified Desire.
> What is it women do in men require?
> The lineaments of Gratified Desire.[117]

Blake uses the word 'Desire' to mean life-serving needs. He cites the case of people who identify as heterosexual men and women. I wonder if this also applies to people who don't identify in this way or have a different sexual orientation?

When we assess someone as likely to help us meet our needs, we say that they are a friend or lover, good, kind, helpful, and so on. If we assess that someone is unlikely to help us meet our needs, we say that they are an enemy, bad, wrong, unkind, and so on. So we're only aware of the person to the extent that they might support us to meet our needs. As we relate to people subjectively in this way, they become objects to us.

This is especially true for our nearest and dearest. Parents and children, partners and siblings very rarely know each other. They know their own reactions to one another, and attribute these reactions *to* the other person. So they think that they know them, whilst not really knowing them at all. They only know their own projected met and unmet needs. The longer you live with someone, the less likely you are to know them. Is there any truth to this?

What is one partner to another? If someone is fortunate, their partner is a wonderful sensation of warmth and comfort, being cherished and belonging. That is what their partner *is*.

They may not know their partner as a person. And this is how it continues for most of us, most of the time.

This is why there are so many misunderstandings between partners, so many disappointments. They are at cross-purposes, because they don't really know each other. They don't really know what the other needs to flourish, so they aren't really able to love them. Instead, what we have is pseudo-communication between projections, like two blindfolded ice-skaters earnestly trying to locate each other. As they flounder about on the ice, they struggle to embrace or land blows in return for supposed hurts.

When we begin to recognize another person's humanity, we take a significant step away from our self-referential conditioning. It's the step from relating to them as *objects* (that may or may not help us to meet our needs) to treating them as *persons*, with their own feelings and needs. It means recognizing that their world, with its joys and sorrows, is just as important to them as ours is to us.

As we recognize others as full persons, they become subjects in their own right. This step requires imagination, to experience life 'as if' from their point of view. It also requires courage, because we may find recognizing someone else's existence as equal to our own deeply threatening.

We may experience it as threatening the validity of our experience of life. It suggests a closeness of connection like the bond between parent and child. It goes against the grain of our conditioning, and so it takes effort. But the rewards are rich, because it can also give rise to love.

Without mutual knowledge and understanding, love is unlikely to flower. If we are able to develop mutual awareness and understanding, even mutual love, then we shall also know what the other person needs. This is different from what we think would be good for them. It means knowing what they need to flourish, whether or not it will benefit us. We will then know how to support them, how to contribute to their life.

We can look at our partner, simply take them in and acknowledge their existence. We can see the marks of joy and pain in their face, their gestures, and respect the fullness of their life experience. As we saw in the previous chapter, we can listen to them, really listen to them, not just the words, but their vocabulary, intonation, and volume. This is what gives their words colour and meaning.

From this we can sense what is important to them, what is in their heart. And, as we witness this, we can trust their sincerity, that they are doing the best they know how at the moment. Even if we find their expression confused or lacking congruence, we can allow them the space to unravel their meaning and let clarity emerge.

Imagine your partner is upset and says, 'You put your work and Buddhist practice before our partnership. I'm number three in your priorities. When was the last time we had any quality time together?' You might be tempted to react with, 'You're so needy. It's a sign of spiritual immaturity. When are you going to learn to enjoy your own company? Besides, what about all the time we *do* spend together?'

And, if you react in this way, what do you imagine comes next? Raised voices, escalating tension, hurt, rejection, anger, pulling away, and distance. So what is the alternative? As we saw in Chapter 7, you could take a moment to do some self-connection. Your self-talk might go like this: 'I feel hurt and angry when my partner talks to me like this. I'd like the understanding that I *do* care for our partnership, and, at the same time, I care about other things as well. I find it painful when I hear them talking about quality time. As far as I'm concerned, every moment we spend together is quality time.'

When you've taken a moment to self-connect, you might choose to ask them, 'Are you feeling hurt and angry because you're longing for mutual care for our partnership?' If they say yes to this, you might follow up with, 'Do you want to know that you matter, that we belong together, that you're safe in our love?' And if they say yes to this, you might ask, 'Do you want understanding for how precious it is when we spend time together without distractions?'

As we saw, responding in this way doesn't mean that you agree with your partner's view of the partnership or their preferred strategies. In empathy, we simply acknowledge what they need and how they feel about it. We can allow people to change, not holding on to a fixed view about who they are or who we want them to be. We can support them by being receptive to them, seeing what they really need.

In his commentary on the Buddha's noble eightfold path, Sangharakshita equates love with awareness. He says, 'Love [is] awareness of their being.'[118] It is clear that the practice of mindfulness of others is not the cool and detached observation that it is sometimes mistaken for, but a warm and loving awareness that brings us closer to other people.

It may be difficult to get a sense of how you could be an individual, enjoying your freedom and autonomy, and at the same time part of a thriving intimate partnership. The Buddha offers a vivid image in the *Sedaka Sutta: The Bamboo Acrobat*.

He tells the story of two acrobats, the Master and his female assistant Medakathalika.[119]

They are performing for the local villagers. The Master climbs his bamboo pole. Once he is on top, he invites Medakathalika to climb the pole and stand on his shoulders. As she does so, the Master offers her some words of encouragement:

> You look after me, my dear Medakathalika, and I'll look after you. If we look after each other and protect each other, we'll be able to perform our routine, receive some donations, and safely climb down the pole again.
>
> But Medakathalika has other ideas. She says:
>
> No, Master, that's not going to work. You look after yourself, and I will look after myself. If each of us looks after ourselves and protects ourselves, we'll be able to perform our routine, receive some donations, and safely climb down the pole. That's the way to do it!

In ancient Indian society, masters of any trade or profession were regarded with great respect, even devotion. Nevertheless, in this case the Buddha finds himself in agreement with the assistant. He comments: 'Just as Medakathalika, the assistant, said to her Master, "I will look after myself", so I encourage you monks to practise mindfulness.' He goes on to say, 'You can also practise mindfulness by saying, "I will look after others." Looking after oneself, one looks after others. Looking after others, one looks after oneself.'

The Buddha declares, 'We can do this by practising mindfulness, by developing it over time. We can do this with patience, nonviolence, loving-kindness, and care.' So the Buddha encourages us to develop awareness of our body, feelings, and thoughts with the focused attention of an acrobat balancing on a bamboo pole. One momentary lapse of concentration and we tumble to the ground!

It is an image of intense inner awareness and concentration, almost a matter of life and death. But there are two people involved, and, for their safety, they rely on each other's practice of mindfulness.

The Buddha suggests that ultimately we are responsible for our own balance, and it would be foolish to neglect this when directing our attention to others. And yet, others are directly impacted by how we do this. So there is individual *and* mutual responsibility. No matter how much we love our partner, we can't take away their pain, make them happy, or enlighten them. Each of us practises the Dharma for ourselves. Even if we travel together, we also travel alone. And yet, 'Looking after oneself, one looks after others. Looking after others, one looks after oneself.'

In the next chapter we will go where angels fear to tread. In the meantime, I invite you to join me in a guided reflection on the place of jealousy in your relationship.

Guided reflection: reflecting on jealousy

- Purpose of this activity: to reflect on the place of jealousy in your relationship. Where does it arise? How could you respond skilfully?

- Time: 15 minutes.

10

Love and Sex

She walks in beauty, like the night
Of cloudless climes and starry skies;
And all that's best of dark and bright
Meet in her aspect and her eyes.

Lord Byron[120]

Who would be foolish enough to write a chapter on love and sex? We'll return to sexual orientation and gender identification in the next chapter. In this chapter we'll be looking at the connection between love and sexual activity, in the context of romantic partnership. So let's get to know each other more closely. There will be different moods. We'll start off with a serious reflection on sexual ethics, get diverted by the role of laughter, and conclude with sex as an addiction. Are you ready for the ride?

From an evolutionary perspective, the sex drive compels humans and other beings to have sex and perpetuate their genes. This also perpetuates their species. The massive pleasure associated with sexual stimulation and orgasm motivates us to seek it out again and again, whatever the odds.

First, let's look at what constitutes sexual misconduct. According to the Buddhist tradition, it comprises rape, abduction, and adultery. These are regarded as unskilful because they are expressions of craving and violence. The ancient texts assume that it is men who carry out these acts against women. Sadly, this is still the case today – the vast majority of these acts are carried out by men. However, what is written here would also apply to women.[121]

In the case of rape and abduction, the violence is against the person who is targeted, and their parents or guardians if they are a minor. In the case of adultery, the violence is against the other partner, inasmuch as their domestic life is disrupted. But this traditional formulation doesn't include sexual violence against men, or those who don't identify as male or female. It also doesn't include various sexual behaviours that I would regard as unskilful. It's worth investigating this precept thoroughly, as it can be a basis for confession and regret. Here are some principles to consider.

Apart from rape, abduction, and adultery, I consider the following as forms of sexual misconduct:

Sex with a minor: for most people over the age of eighteen, sex with those under eighteen is sexual misconduct. Children only gradually become aware of their own sexuality and choices. As adults, we need to respect and protect this.

Sexual harassment: there's a lack of respect (first precept), and 'taking the not given' (second precept).

Prostitution is more of a grey area. However, it's likely to involve sexual misconduct, whether we're sex workers or customers. When we mix sex with other forms of power, such as money, the potential for objectification and coercion increases.

S&M (sado-masochism) may be unskilful, even if it's consensual, because there is usually an element of violence and craving that can make it addictive.

Masturbation and porn: being curious about our bodies and

other people's bodies is natural and healthy. Yet both have the potential to become addictive.

One-night stands are unlikely to support contentment.

Non-monogamy could be unskilful. As I know from personal experience (see Chapter 11), there is a potential for one partner to get hurt. What agreements do you have with your partner, either spoken or unspoken? And is it really possible to pay full attention to each other, with multiple partners? Or is the longing for multiple partners motivated by craving or addiction to excitement?

The traditional formulation of the Buddhist precepts is 'I undertake the training principle to abstain from...' So it's formulated in terms of things to refrain from. We can also formulate the precept regarding sexual behaviour positively, as *santusti* or contentment. This is more likely to support us in making amends. It is something we can *do*, and, without a plan for changing our behaviour, we are likely to repeat the same old patterns.

For a single person, contentment might mean being content with your single status, at least for the time being. For someone in a settled or long-term relationship, it means being content with your partner. Not just a passive acceptance of the status quo, but a positive state of freedom from using sex to satisfy needs in a neurotic manner, which is compulsive or without awareness. We'll return to the subject of addiction later in this chapter.

Sex activity could be relatively skilful when it takes place between mutually consenting adults in a committed relationship, on the basis of love and respect. This is most likely to support contentment. Or we can be celibate, making a positive choice in this area. A committed relationship can support *santusti* because we are no longer on the market, looking for our next fling or partner. When we find someone other than our partner attractive, we can restrain our minds from wandering into a daydream about what it would be like to have them as our partner. We can guard the gates of the senses.

We may have learned to watch our mind when we are meditating. However, can we watch our mind when we find someone attractive? Can we watch the scenario playing out in our mind without acting on it? In this way, we can guard against acting out of greed, hatred, and ignorance, and cultivate the self-restraint of contentment. We can learn to control our sex drive.

My partner and I have an agreement that gives us clarity in this area. We have agreed that, if we want to have sexual contact with another person, we will finish our partnership first. This clarity makes it easier for us to develop contentment in relation to each other.

If we can restrain from acting unskilfully and cultivate contentment in this area, perhaps we can relax and enjoy sexual activity as one of life's pleasures, like food, rest, fresh air, or laughter, held in love and wholeness.

I've heard it said that laughter is the best aphrodisiac. So I decided to look into the research to see if there is any truth to it. What is the number one characteristic that US women look for when they are placing an advert on an online dating site? Millionnaire? Muscular build? Neither. It's VGSOH or 'very good sense of humour'. A good sense of humour is one of the most sought-after characteristics in a romantic partner.[122]

A sense of humour is associated with being outgoing ('extrovert') and warmth. Displaying social skills and warmth through humour is an effective mating strategy because these traits are highly valued in long-term relationships by both men and women. There is another school of thought that humour is valued as a sign of intelligence in a potential partner. The current research finds little correlation.[123]

The benefits of regular laughter are well-known. We all know that being able to laugh with our partner is necessary for a healthy relationship. We can ask, 'What's funny here?' and 'Will we still be laughing at Christmas?' Laughter comes from playing with each other, finding out what we both enjoy. It's flirting with the connection. The shared release of endorphins and serotonin during laughter and playful communication triggers pleasant feelings. These create a bond of goodwill, like sexual activity itself, which works as a buffer against the inevitable disagreements that arise.

We all find different things funny, whether it's a look, a wry comment, a catchy punchline, a sophisticated pun, or slapstick. Why not laugh about sex itself? There's no two ways about it, sex is funny, tragic, both, or neither.

When I was in my late twenties, I was walking north from King's Cross station in London. As I passed through an area of relatively poor housing, a woman in her forties approached me holding a cigarette, which she raised to her lips. 'Excuse me, Sir,' she said in a posh voice, 'do you have a light?' I said, 'No, sorry, I don't smoke.' Then she looked at me intently and said, 'Business?' 'I'm sorry, Madam,' I replied, 'I don't mix business with pleasure.'[124]

Some facts about laughter. Laughter is anatomically mediated by the epiglottis constricting the larynx. Children laugh approximately 300 times a day, adults 10–15 times a day.

What happened, people? You don't stop laughing because you grow older. You grow older because you stop laughing.

I've done some original research on the connection between laughter and sexual activity, as part of my standup comedy routine. I invite members of the audience to tickle themselves, then ask, 'How much fun was that?' The answer is, invariably, not much. Then I ask them to get someone else to tickle them. This works much better. I conclude, 'So it's more fun when someone else tickles your fancy than when you do it yourself!'

I heard that 'Women give sex to get love. Men give love to get sex.' Is there any truth to this? What about people who don't identify as male or female?

Why do some people regard sex as a spiritual experience? Because giving is receiving and receiving is giving. And nobody really knows who is who and what is what, because, in reality, both are giving and receiving. Who can say?

Making love with a long-term partner is a bit of a lottery. It all depends on complex factors such as the closeness of the full moon and both of you being in the mood at the same time. One night I was feeling confident, so I asked my partner, 'Have we hit the jackpot?' 'No, sorry,' she said, 'I'm too tired. It's a rollover.'

Isn't there something humorous about the tangles we get into? As my Buddhist teacher Sangharakshita once said, 'A sexual relationship is like a lobster pot – easy to get into and difficult to get out of.'[125]

And what of the impact of sexual activity on your meditation practice? I was on retreat once and heard a reporting-in from one of the community members. He said that regular sex was like taking a shotgun to the cabbage of your meditation practice. There's only a smoking stalk left in the ground! Is this true for you?

My partner asked me to include at least one belly laugh in this chapter. I looked down at my stomach and noticed some middle-age spread, but I couldn't find an actual paunchline. She told me that it was below the belt. I looked again, but I still couldn't find one.

My partner asked me, 'What's it like having a willy?'

I said, 'It's difficult to answer – I've never not had one, so I have nothing to compare it with.'

'Tell me anyway', she said.

I said, 'It's like being chained to a ravenous wild animal. It's like being in a supermarket and seeing someone you fancy down the aisle. You carry on with your shopping, but you try to coincide with them, to catch a glimpse of their face or body. After a while, you're so mesmerized by them that you're just following them around with your tongue hanging out, and you don't care who can see. It's like that.'

'I see', said my partner, in a serious tone.

'Now that I've got you,' I said, 'what do you think about this chapter on love and sex? Is there anything you'd like to add?'

'Well, I'm acutely aware of people's suffering in this area, especially women. And I don't like to talk about sex or having sex. I prefer to talk about "making love" to emphasize the relational aspect, rather than the physical act. Sex is something you can buy – it's about stimulation and release. Whereas making love has different connotations – it's about the quality of loving connection.'

I asked her, 'Would it give you dignity and respect to talk about making love?'

'Yes, there's so much emphasis on the physical body, physical attractiveness, that it's difficult to stay connected to myself as a person relating to another person.'

'I see. Do you want to be seen as a whole person, rather than a body, even a body that I find attractive?'

'Yes, I want you to want the whole of me. Making love with a partner takes place in the context of your relationship as a whole. If your partnership is loving and promotes growth, so will your lovemaking. It's not just a physical release, but sharing love and pleasure, the expression of a rich and full life.'

My partner added, 'You also haven't talked about the physical, erotic aspect of love and sexual attraction. What it feels like in your body. When I feel attracted to you, I can feel my cheeks going red. And I have butterflies or nervousness in my stomach. I feel physically attracted to you. I like your smell and the taste of your skin.'

Can you feel the sap rising? If you're young and healthy, you're likely to engage in sexual activity on your own or with others. The needs connected to this kind of sexual activity are touch, closeness, and release. Difficulties can arise when we try to meet other needs as well. We may not be aware that we are trying to meet needs such as security, warmth, belonging, dignity, or being valued, and we may not communicate these needs to our partner. So these needs may lurk under the bed, by which I mean they are not acknowledged and not talked about.

The biggest test is what happens when a relationship breaks up. If your partner tells you, 'I've found someone else', you may feel a sense of grief and loss. However, if you can accept their decision, then you've probably kept a sense of awareness, choice, and self-responsibility. But, if you can't meditate for three months, there may have been less awareness. The question is, can you remain happy, or at least content, whatever storms may come?

In Chapter 5, we saw that it's wise to keep our sexual relations and our spiritual friendships separate. We also touched on the issue of consent, which can be fraught in relationships involving a power differential. The Buddha didn't teach about sexual consent in the way it's currently understood. Nowadays, we tend to emphasize the importance of verbal consent, and take this as our benchmark. For instance, sex without affirmative consent is defined as assault on US college campuses.

The texts of the Pali Canon didn't define ethical sex in these terms. As we've seen in previous chapters, they promoted celibacy as the most realistic path to Awakening. Therefore, in the monastic rule book (*Vinaya*), sexual ethics is discussed solely in terms of celibacy. Sexual transgression is defined primarily in terms of penetration by a penis, and other forms of sexual harm aren't considered.

The *Vinaya* also presents a different understanding of consent, based on inner affective states rather than verbal permission. This is very delicate territory and goes against our current understanding. Personally, I'm deeply reluctant to accept that someone can be held responsible for enjoying an act that is initiated through force. It goes against my understanding of where the responsibility lies. However, the *Vinaya* account does deepen our understanding of consent in one important way: by bringing out the fact that consent is dynamic, affective, and rooted in the body. This is a different level from verbal permission.

Such an understanding of consent can address those situations where a person in an unequal power relationship says yes, or tacitly gives in, because they fear something worse will happen if they don't. Levels of compliance may change over time. According to this understanding, someone who verbally consents, but doesn't psychologically accept the encounter, intend for it to happen, or fully embrace their physical response, would not be considered a consenting sexual agent.

Buddhist ethics is primarily an ethics of intention, or more accurately volition (*cetana*). Unskilful actions are motivated by greed, hatred, and ignorance. Skilful actions are motivated by generosity, love, and awareness. A Buddhist teacher may not intend harm in having sex with a student. They may even feel loving-kindness towards them. However, the karmic consequences will be determined by the volition they have acted on.

If this volition includes an element of ignorance – for instance of the likely consequences of their action in the context of an unequal power relationship – then the act will lead to suffering for themselves and others. How much more so if they deliberately use their position to coerce someone into sex.

I am deeply sceptical of claims that some teachers are motivated by 'crazy wisdom' when the teachers in question seem to have ignored basic Buddhist ethics. Sex is a great leveller – we all know how seductive it can be. We seek to reward ourselves in different ways, and, for some people, this means sexual activity and orgasm with someone we find attractive.

Sex can bring fun and playfulness into a long-term relationship. It can also bring conflict, for instance when one partner wants sex more often than the other, or sex of a different kind. Consent is important here. It's such an important topic that we'll return to it and give it more space in Chapter 14, when we consider saying and hearing a no.

I'm well aware of the potential for sex to become addictive. I spoke to a friend of mine, a fellow Triratna Order member who identifies as a gay man. He holds space for members of Sex and Love Addicts Anonymous (SLAA), a twelve-step programme. I asked him: when does sex become an addiction? He told me that it varies from person to person. However, the main sign is that we end up doing things that we don't want to do.

'It's when you feel driven to do things that are against your values', he said. 'Things that risk your current relationships and way of life. We all have an addictive urge to some extent. The trouble is, if you suppress it in one area, it comes up in another. It's a bit like Whack-a-Mole.'

He continued, 'Sex addiction is not necessarily about quantity – having lots of sex. It's about the quality of the interaction. If the quality of the interaction is destructive, against the person's values, then I would say it's an addiction.'

I asked him, 'When did you notice that *you* were addicted?'

'Well, I didn't realize, although I described myself as "the boy who couldn't say no". I ended up getting into situations that I didn't really want to be in. It was only when I was 30 or 31 and I heard the words "sex addiction" that I even saw it as a problem. When I knew that there was something called sex addiction, I realized that it was something I was doing. I went to a twelve-step meeting and found that I identified with the stories that I heard from the people there. As they were talking, I remembered all the times I hadn't been able to say no.'

'In the preamble to twelve-step programmes it reads, "We admitted that we were powerless over sex and love addiction – that our lives had become unmanageable." Later it says words to the effect that "We felt powerless to make wise choices in relation to sex and love. We were enslaved, captive to sex and love... Looking for love in all the wrong places, we became true addicts." That really hit home.'[126]

He continued, 'I came to understand that I was trying to meet my needs neurotically – needs for connection and control. How do we have a healthy relationship to our sexual urges, rather than cutting them off? You can cut substances such as alcohol out of your life completely, but you can't cut your sexual urges out in the same way.'

'Paradoxically,' he said, 'I used sex to avoid intimacy. By intimacy, I mean "into-me-see", so I'm talking about the connection and closeness that comes from being vulnerable with someone. I had a series of flings, rather than a long-term relationship, because I was afraid of someone really seeing me. I was always falling for guys who were unavailable. Addiction really is a tragic expression of unmet needs, as Marshall Rosenberg said.'

'Addiction is a very hopeful but deluded state. It's not really looking at the reality of the situation. You go back to the same thing again and again, hoping it will give you nourishment, or at least the kick it once did. But it doesn't. As

Albert Einstein supposedly said, "Insanity is doing the same thing over and over again, but expecting different results."'[127]

'The opposite of addiction, surprisingly, is *connection*. If I see myself as separate, then I go into fear. I'm a tiny ego threatened by an (almost) infinite universe. Whereas, if I'm plugged in, if I realize my interconnectedness with all things and all beings, then I won't experience that kind of scarcity mentality.'

'Addicts are ripe for self-transformation, as they've hit rock bottom. So they're willing to put work into it. And that's what the twelve-step programme is all about – finding a true connection with the way things are, experiencing interconnectedness. I wouldn't have come across the Dharma if I hadn't had this addictive way of dealing with things – so in a way it's a blessing in disguise. I discovered something that I didn't even know I was looking for!'

I nodded in agreement, 'We're all addicted to something. For most of us, it isn't Enlightenment. So what would you say to someone who is wondering if they're addicted to sex and love?'

He replied, 'Do they want to stop? If they don't really want to stop, or change their behaviour, then they won't. Shame can complicate things, but it can also motivate you to stop. You need to be in the right place, to really feel the suffering involved, otherwise you'll just keep doing it. And underneath, you may find that it's difficult for you to really receive love – that's the connection between sex and love.'

I thanked him for his insights.

Sangharakshita formulated a tantric version of the five precepts that presents them energetically, in terms of how we use our energy. The first precept is 'Do not obstruct the energy of any other person', and the second is 'Do not drain the energy of others. Give freely of your own energy.' The third precept is 'Do not misuse energy.' So this broadens out the precept from sexual misconduct to energy in general.[128]

I don't want to become a pious Buddhist, 'mindful', alienated, constantly blocking my energy. We need pleasure. We need to find ways to express our energy that leave us feeling happy, bright, and positive, rather than bringing us down. Maybe having a loving playfight with our partner will bring us closer to Enlightenment? This comes back to finding the beauty that we explored in Chapter 5.

And, with this, we might be coming to the end of the chapter. One last joke. How do you know when it's time to stop? It's when your partner looks you in the eyes and says, 'You're getting a bit heavy, could you come to my side?'

In the next chapter we're going to explore different experiences of loving and being loved. In the meantime, I invite you to join me in reflecting on this chapter. When did you use your sexual energy less than skilfully? What could you have done differently?

Guided reflection: reflecting on the chapter

- Purpose of this activity: to reflect on this chapter. In particular, when did you use your sexual energy less than skilfully? What could you have done differently?

- Time: 15 minutes.

11

Different Strokes

> Love takes off the masks that we fear we cannot live without and know we cannot live within. I use the word 'love' here not merely in the personal sense but as a state of being, or a state of grace – not in the infantile American sense of being made happy but in the tough and universal sense of quest and daring and growth.
>
> James Baldwin[129]

Baldwin was born in Harlem in 1924 and grew up as a Black man in a society deeply entrenched in racism. He had relationships with both men and women, despite living at a time and in a place where homophobia was pervasive, especially within the Black community. While Baldwin could be described as bisexual, he rejected labels relating to sexual orientation. He found them limiting and noted how their meanings can change over time. In the years leading up to his death, Baldwin expressed the belief that love transcends sex and gender, emphasizing that it is the individual, rather than their gender, that we truly fall in love with.[130]

He argued that people create categories to feel secure. For instance, white people invented the category of 'Black people' to define their own identity. The concepts of 'white' and 'black' are arbitrary and unreliable. 'You can't tell a Black man by the colour of his skin', he explained to one interviewer.[131]

Through literature, he realized that his experiences were part of a shared human condition, rather than something entirely personal:

> You think that no one else has ever suffered the way you have suffered. Then you read something or hear something, and you realize that your suffering does not isolate you. Your suffering is your bridge to others. Many people have suffered before you. Many people are suffering around you, and they always will. What you can do is to bring a little light into that suffering, so that the person can begin to comprehend it, and begin to live with it, and begin to change it, to change the situation.[132]

This is what Buddhists call compassion.

In the quotation at the head of this chapter, Baldwin was writing in 1963 about the 'Negro problem'. His evocation of love as an antidote to personal, ethnic, and cultural estrangement is as relevant today as when it was written. Baldwin is a remarkable figure – a voice of difference calling us back to our common humanity.

In 1948 he left America for France to escape the fate of being identified as a 'Negro'. In Europe he found liberation, being seen as American more than Black. He also encountered Gallic racism, mainly directed towards North Africans, whose skin colour could barely be distinguished from that of the French.

Baldwin realized that identities help us to locate ourselves in the world, but can also trap us:

> We take our shape within and against that cage of reality bequeathed us at our birth; and yet it is precisely through

> our dependence on this reality that we are most endlessly betrayed.[133]

So long as we cling to identity, he warned, it is meaningless to speak of a 'new' society, as the function of such identities is to convince those given inferior status of the reality of that decree. In other words, we can become bound by the nature of our categorization.

Throughout his work there runs a tension between embracing Black identity as a refuge from racism and recognizing that a 'new' society can only be built by transcending such identities. This tension can be creative rather than destructive. As we saw in Chapter 7, we need a strong sense of ourselves before attempting to transcend the ways we identify. Unless we're healthy, growing individuals, unless we love ourselves, we can't love others. In the same way, we need a healthy sense of our racial, sexual, gender, and cultural identities before we can transcend them.

Locating your identity can be a starting point to build an effective sense of agency. You can take your experience of exclusion from the mainstream of society, and the trauma involved, and transform it into an effective and dignified sense of self. This allows you to move in the direction of self-determination. The risk is that we take such identities as ultimately real. At the same time, we all need a sense of community, and identity gives us this. Who and whatever we identify with, we can take our traumatic memories and heal them. This is the topic of the next chapter, 'Lost Loves'.

In this chapter, I want to explore experiences of inclusion and exclusion at a public level by considering 'different strokes' – different ways of experiencing and expressing love, in particular LGBTQ+ and polyamory. I have a couple of jokes left over from the previous chapter. I've been asking around my friends to find out what LGBTQ+ stands for. I've heard a few suggestions, but so far no one has given me a straight answer. I saw two guys wearing matching outfits so I asked them if they were gay. They promptly arrested me!

In every human society the love between two individuals is seen as a public issue. Each society has its own rules for who to love, for how long, when and where. As soon as you fall in love or partner up, you are likely to encounter these rules as a torrent of opinion on the character and appearance of your chosen mate, the acceptability of your choice, the length of time to wait before any ritualistic celebration, and so on.

If you defy these rules, you will experience the disapproval of your family or group. In some countries, being openly gay can lead to a visit from the police, violence, prosecution, and/or death.

Humans have evolved to dedicate the vast majority of their cognitive brain power to observing, analyzing, and memorizing the lives of others. This is because, as we saw in Chapter 2, our social network (who we love) is key to our survival. If we understand the relations between everybody in our group, it means that we will know who is a potential partner, when we can improve our status, who is an enemy or ally, and who has skills that we might need. Who we choose to love, whether it's friends, family, or lovers, *is* a public issue. And every society has evolved its own norms and rituals around the experience of love.

But first, is romantic love a human universal? Given what we've seen in previous chapters, you might think so. However, it took a ground-breaking ethnographic study by two social anthropologists in 1992 to confirm the presence of romantic love in all cultures. They researched the topic in 166 countries across the world, and found evidence that romantic love for a sexual partner is a constant in all societies.[134]

This doesn't mean that romantic love appears in the same guise in all of them. How we display our romantic love to the wider world is constrained by tradition and culture. Where we grow up also affects how we define love. In Arab Muslim culture, for a man to fall in love with a woman is to risk being out of control. Falling in love is regarded as an evil because it shifts the balance of power from male to female. In Bedouin culture, marriage is seen as a matter for the men of the family to decide, so any hint of passion is discouraged, as it risks leading to a partnership outside of established social control.

Cultures view love differently. Collectivist cultures such as those of Brazil, Russia, Central Africa, China, and many Arab Muslim countries view passionate love as negative, as following the heart rather than contributing to society. Individualistic cultures such as those in the West view passionate romantic love as freedom and the ultimate expression of the individual.

Another factor is the status of women. In societies where the status of women is relatively high and the norm is the nuclear family, romantic love is widely accepted and valued as the basis of marriage. In societies where women have low status and extended families are the norm, romantic love is actively suppressed and regarded as an unacceptable basis for marriage. Romantic love is based on a sense of uniqueness and a meeting of equals. Where women are seen as inferior to men, this cannot be encouraged. In a heterosexual nuclear family, there is a greater need for a strong bond between the man and the woman. In an extended family, the need is not so great, as there are other people around to call upon.

Society's rules about love shift over time as political, religious, and economic conditions change. Jane Austen documented love and marriage among the middle and upper classes of eighteenth-century England. My partner Gesine is fascinated by her books and the films made of them – it was one of the reasons she was keen to live in England! For a woman in these times, love wasn't an individual affair but a collective one.

Courtship followed a strict ritual. First moves were only allowed by the woman, who would invite a potential suitor to 'call'. The couple spoke in a place where they could be observed, then walked out together, accompanied by a chaperone. Only when mutual 'strength of feeling' was confirmed would the couple be allowed to meet alone.

We may laugh at the stuffiness and rigidity of these rituals, but our modern experiences of love are still bound by rules. Instead of being based on ritual, modern love in the UK is based on the authenticity of our emotions. Emotion must be the driver of our choices, rather than considerations of wealth or status. Anyone who marries for wealth or status is likely to be called a gold-digger or worse.

By contrast, marriage rules in India relate to caste and religion. Bollywood films depict wild romances, often associated with outlaws, hidden away in beautiful landscapes. The main theme is the gap between this fantasy and the audience's reality, where a partner is vetted by family and religious figures. Despite the influence of Western attitudes in other areas of life, the rules around intercaste and interfaith marriages remain strong. Indeed, marriage may turn out to be the last bastion of the caste system.

Social, religious, and cultural rules around love are ultimately about control. They are there to make sure that identities are maintained. Romantic love threatens this process of group identification because it is powerful and unknowable. It motivates people to undergo amazing trials and tribulations in order to be with their beloved. And so those in power fear it, as it threatens to divide group loyalties.

So what does the Buddhist tradition say about these societal rules on love? As we saw in Part One, the primary act of the Buddhist life is going for refuge to the three jewels of Buddha, Dharma, and Sangha. Our ethical behaviour is an expression of this, and the lifestyle we choose is an expression of our ethical observance.

When it comes to love, who you love is regarded as an ethically neutral matter. How you behave towards them can be either skilful or unskilful, depending on the state of mind or volition with which you act. It's not about *who* you love, but about *how* you treat them. To explain this, my teacher Sangharakshita pointed to the traditional Theravadin distinction between conventional and natural morality (*pannati-sila* and *pakati-sila*).

Conventional morality is the morality of the group, class, or caste, and its purpose is to maintain the norms and identity of that group. These social observances are rooted in neither skilful nor unskilful states of mind, so they are of no karmic significance.

By contrast, natural morality is the expression of a truly human state, our capacity for wisdom and love. It arises from a sense of solidarity with all life, and has karmic consequences. The ethical criterion is psychological – does this action arise from greed, hatred, and ignorance, or from generosity, love, and wisdom?

Natural morality supports the growth and development of the individual and the emergence of a genuine spiritual community. It encourages us to recognize that actions have consequences – for ourselves, for others, and for the environment – and to take responsibility for those consequences. Natural morality is formulated in the five precepts, which offer a blueprint for truly human actions and states of mind. They do not come as commandments from a god, or from the group, but emerge from our potential to develop and our deep yearning to do so. Natural morality is the foundation of human life, whether individual or collective.

In many situations, conventional and natural morality coincide. For instance, stealing goes against both. At the same time, most people, most of the time, are moral for reasons of social conformity, or conventional morality. So what do we do when they seem in conflict?

It's a question of being sensitive. We can be sensitive to other people's conventional morality, provided it doesn't go against natural morality. The same goes for laws. Law is an attempt in each society to enforce both conventional and natural morality. However, there are some laws that go against natural morality, and we may take a stand against these laws, and even break them, in order to stay true to ourselves.[135] As I said in my previous book *The Burning House*, I suggest only doing this after prolonged reflection and consultation with your spiritual friends, as it will put us at odds with the society in which we live.[136]

We may think that we have come a long way in the UK since Oscar Wilde spoke in court of 'the love that dare not speak its name'. However, as the 2018 Stonewall report 'LGBT in Britain: home and communities' clarifies, only 46 per cent of LGBT people feel able to be open about their sexuality with their family. A third of LGBT people of faith aren't open with anyone in their faith community about their sexuality, and 35 per cent of LGBT people have hidden their sexual identity at work through fear of discrimination. Almost one in five have experienced negative comments or behaviour from co-workers.

At university, 28 per cent of LGBT students were excluded by other students because of their sexual identity. The number of LGBT people who have experienced hate crime in any year has risen 78 per cent since 2013.[137] If these were the facts of your life, how open would you be about your love life?

And what about the seventy-two countries where homosexuality is still illegal? Governments often turn a blind eye to attacks on LGBTQ+ people (the Q stands for Queer and the + stands for others who don't identify with these labels). Some countries, such as Chechnya, have state-sponsored campaigns targeting gay men, who are abducted, tortured, and even killed. In nine countries, including Pakistan, Qatar, the UAE, Nigeria, Somalia, and Iran, having sex with someone of the same sex is punishable by death. While this punishment isn't always enforced, it leaves LGBTQ+ people open to harassment and blackmail.

In these circumstances, it is critical to avoid your love life becoming a matter of public knowledge. You may even deny your sexuality publicly in order to stay safe. The name of the game is visibility management – constantly reassessing how open to be about your sexuality. This is something that the heterosexual population is unlikely to consider.

I've loved several men over the course of my life. I still get a frisson of excitement and satisfaction in writing that. At the boys' public school I attended, 'gay' was one of the most common terms of abuse, along with 'wanker' and 'prick'. I had a crush on a first-former with an angelic face, but was careful to make sure neither he nor anyone else found out.

When I was sixteen one of my best friends was a forty-year-old bisexual ex-priest. He told me how he had been thrown out of the Anglican Church for being named in the trial of a male prostitute. From that point onwards, they regarded him as a bit of a loose cannon! He was scared about what would happen if some people at his current church in Croydon found out.

This was the 1980s. He took me once to the only openly gay pub in Croydon. It was a Friday night, and I was still in the suit I wore for school, minus the house tie. A young 'master' from the school came through the door, glanced around, and recognized me. I still remember the look of horror on his face. I also chose not to speak to him, in order to protect both of us.

Even in Buddhist countries, homosexuality has been regarded as sexual misconduct. However, there are no scriptures in the Pali Canon condemning homosexuality. Sadly, some people who identify as LGBTQ+ still feel guilty about not observing matters of conventional morality, especially where society attaches great importance to these. They may feel as if they have done something 'wrong', when they have only gone against custom and convention. Only matters of natural morality have any direct connection to the question of karma. Are we really behaving ethically, or just respecting the prejudices of the group in which we find ourselves?

As we've seen, acting ethically is a matter of acting on and developing skilful mental states. The precepts of natural morality restrain us from acting on the basis of greed, hatred, and ignorance, and help us to act on the basis of love, generosity, and wisdom. This is what Buddhism regards as skilful and unskilful. If we do act against natural morality, against our ethical principles, we may feel *beneficial regret*, which is directly related to valuing the ethical principle we have gone against, and supports us to make amends.

Perhaps it's worth taking a step back to understand why Buddhism regards sexual orientation and gender as a matter of conventional rather than natural morality. In the previous chapter we explored the third precept, the principle of abstention from sexual misconduct. It can be stated positively as: 'With stillness, simplicity, and contentment, I purify my body.' It's important to understand this precept in the context of traditional Buddhist cosmology.[138]

The universe is seen as having three horizontal layers, the higher layers being more refined, blissful, and luminous than the lower. The lowest of these planes is the *kamaloka*, or world of sensuous desire. This comprises the six realms of the Tibetan wheel of life: the hell realm, the hungry ghosts, the angry gods, animals, humans, and *deva*s (lower gods). Above this is the *rupaloka* or plane of archetypal form, which comprises the gods who attend brahmas (great gods), and nonreturners – beings who are so far along the road to Enlightenment that they will no longer be reborn in the *kamaloka*. The third and highest plane, the *arupaloka* or formless realm, is inhabited by brahmas themselves, and even greater gods.

Now, here's the thing: even in the *rupaloka* there is no sexual dimorphism, or separation into male and female. Inhabitants of this plane, from the human point of view, are androgynous. Sexual dimorphism is only found in the *kamaloka*, including our human realm.

From this cosmological perspective, the Dharma life is a progression from lower to higher planes. This means progressing from a state of biological and psychological sexual dimorphism to a state of spiritual androgyny. A state of sexual dimorphism is a state of polarization, tension, and projection, so it is also a state of discontent. The state of spiritual androgyny, by contrast, is a state of harmony, relaxation, and contentment.

Observance of the third precept isn't just about abstaining from the various forms of sexual misconduct. It's also about developing stillness, simplicity, and contentment. For most of us, the bridge will be meditation. When we are truly meditating, we temporarily transcend our state of sexual dimorphism. We cease to identify as male or female. As we enter the *dhyana*s or states of meditative absorption, we ascend to the *rupaloka* or even the *arupaloka*, becoming, for a time, a *deva* or a brahma. This is the origin of the word *brahmacarya*, which means faring or living as a brahma.

Full-time meditators have always known that meditation

and celibacy go hand in hand. This is why single-sex situations can be supportive, because they give us some respite from sexual polarization and allow us to experience what it's like simply to be human. If you want to experience contentment, to be free from sexual polarization, you could try loosening your identification as a man or a woman, in an exclusive or absolute sense. After all, according to traditional Buddhist teaching, you have been both many times, in previous existences. You may even have been a *deva*, an androgynous being.

To the extent that we relax this identification, we will act less like the highly polarized angry gods. Male angry gods are fierce, aggressive, and ugly, rather like the orcs in *The Lord of the Rings*. Female angry gods are voluptuous, seductive, and very beautiful, rather like 1950s Hollywood starlets. This doesn't mean that we can ignore genuine differences between men and women, which might lead to a relatively colourless unisexuality.

What we need is transformation and progression rather than negation and evasion. The Dharma life consists in relaxing an identification with a particular psycho-physical gender, so that it becomes relative and provisional, then no identification at all. This will allow us to understand the basis of the third precept more deeply and help us to practise it with confidence.

Polyamory

Monogamy is the socially acceptable face of romantic love, in the majority of countries. However, is it really the only option?

What is the basis of couple exclusivity? We know that most of our primate cousins fear non-exclusivity: males want access to fertile females, and females want to make sure that all the male's resources – food, protection, education – are directed towards her offspring.

This 'mate guarding' leads to jealousy in humans, and the demonization of adultery. It becomes a moral and legal issue. Our love is meant for the one, rather than the many. Our love is regarded as a precious commodity, the sharing of which diminishes its value to the recipient. This zero-sum view of romantic relationships is deeply ingrained in Western society. It's based on the belief that a lover should be entitled to all of their partner's love, and that love is finite – you can only love one person fully.[139]

In Christianity, marriage is a sacrament, a ritual performed in the eyes of God. Karl Marx critiqued capitalism as the bourgeoisie controlling the means of production at the expense of the working class. The same could be said of Christianity and other religions, as they attempt to control the means of producing babies – the next generation.

In Buddhist countries, the marriage ceremony is a blessing rather than a sacrament, and divorce is common and socially accepted. Monogamy is not compulsory, and polygamy is not regarded as sexual misconduct in any sense. Acting on the basis of greed, hatred, or ignorance is a matter of natural morality. Whether you have one partner, two, or four, is a matter of conventional morality.[140]

And yet in the West, polyamory is usually viewed as deviant. Apparently we can love many children, friends, and pets, but only feel the excited flutterings or devotion of romantic love in relation to one person. However, there are people who practise polyamory, a form of consensual non-monogamy (CNM), and who enjoy the freedom of loving and being loved by more than one partner. They believe in the saying, 'If you love, love openly', where each person is acknowledged and valued.

Open communication and agreements become very important. The key here is consent. A friend of mine was writing a book on the subject and asked me to share some insights from Nonviolent Communication. Now, I don't claim to have extensive experience of CNM. I've found myself loving more than one person at various times in my life, but this hasn't usually included a sexual element.

The one time I maintained a sexual relationship with two people was a while ago. My then partner told me emphatically that she wanted me to be free to sleep with other women. She had spent time in a polyamorous community in Portugal, and this was almost an article of faith to her. I took up her invitation and started an intermittent relationship with another woman. Though it brought richness to my life to love two people, I struggled to organize my diary and my heart to keep the connection with both.

When we eventually separated, it came out that my 'main' partner had felt jealous about the second woman. What she really wanted was for me to feel free to love other women, and *still choose to love her exclusively*. I guess it would have met her needs for being loved and valued in a free way.

Despite my mixed experience, I was happy to oblige my friend and shared some pearls of wisdom! None of what I said applies exclusively to polyamorists. However, the more people involved, the more important is effective and compassionate communication. I suggested how to prepare for a difficult conversation with your partner(s): do some self-empathy or get empathy from a friend, and make time for the conversation. When you're in the conversation, find out if touch helps to keep the connection, empathize, remember what is unlikely to be received as empathy (advice, diagnosing, etc.), say how you are rather than what you think the other person is, identify and express your needs, and make specific requests for how to meet them. You can find the full interview in *A World beyond Monogamy: How People Make Polyamory and Open Relationships Work and What We Can All Learn from Them.*[141]

To end the chapter, I'd like to return to James Baldwin's hopeful and sonorous words:

> Identity would seem to be the garment with which one covers the nakedness of the self: in which case, it is best that the garment be loose, a little like the robes of the desert, through which one's nakedness can always be felt, and, sometimes, discerned. This trust in one's nakedness is all that gives one the power to change one's robes.[142]

In the next chapter we delve into mourning and healing traumatic memories related to lost loves. In the meantime, I invite you to join me in reflecting on the themes of gender identity and sexual orientation.

Guided reflection: exploring themes of gender identity and sexual orientation

- Purpose of this activity: to bring greater awareness to the choices we've made relating to gender identity and sexual orientation.

- Time: 20 minutes.

12

Lost Loves

I hold it true, whate'er befall;
I feel it, when I sorrow most;
'Tis better to have loved and lost
Than never to have loved at all.

Alfred Lord Tennyson[143]

Can I tell you about my most profound experience of lost love? I was in love with a woman for eight years. During all that time, she'd been in a relationship with another man. After about five years, I thought I'd moved on. I'd even had another partner for two years. But, deep down, the feelings hadn't faded.

After eight years, I finally wanted to be whole again. So I wished for my soul to return. But nothing happened, there was no movement. I realized that, if I wanted my soul to come home, I would have to go and get him. So I vividly imagined going round to the street where she lived, where my soul had been camped out for the past eight years. When I arrived, he was standing outside her front door. The words of Paul Simon's 'Graceland' came to me:

Losing love
Is like a window in your heart
Everybody sees you're blown apart
Everybody sees the wind blow.[144]

My soul was in his early thirties, and he looked like he hadn't slept for years. I guessed that he'd never been inside. After a while, I told him of my longing for wholeness, and asked him to come home. He didn't answer, but looked even sadder. I asked him why. He reminded me of a puja (Buddhist devotional ritual) from a few years previously. She'd been there. I'd kept my eyes closed so as not to get distracted.

At a certain point during a mantra, I had opened my eyes and seen a luminous column of energy above her head, stretching up to the ceiling. I remember telling myself, 'That looks like a thirty-foot-high goddess to me. How are you going to integrate that?' From this recollection, I got a sense of how I might empathize with my soul, to establish trust and connection.

I asked him, 'Are you longing for a connection with beauty and wonder? Are you desperate for a sense of completeness?' He nodded. I was tempted to tell him that the situation was hopeless and that he might as well give up, but I kept my mouth shut and waited until I was ready to empathize with him again.

I asked, 'Is it difficult to imagine experiencing a sense of completeness anywhere else?' He nodded again, then looked down at his feet. I could tell that he was really in touch with his pain, so I asked, 'Are you grieving for the loss of your hopes and dreams?' He told me, 'I've wasted eight years. Life and love.' We stood together, joined in grief for lost hopes and dreams.

Much later, I asked him, 'Are you desperate for warmth and love?' He replied, 'Yes, but at the moment I'd settle for warmth.' 'Would you like to come home with me? I've been working on emotional warmth and empathy since you left.'

He nodded and followed me. At first he continued to look sad, but, as we went on, his mood lifted and he started to look relieved.

The poem at the head of this chapter comes from Tennyson's *In Memoriam A. H. H.*, published anonymously in 1850, the same year that Tennyson became poet laureate. The poem was born of a profound, life-altering grief, and took seventeen years to complete. 'A. H. H.' stands for Arthur Henry Hallam, Tennyson's closest friend, who died suddenly in 1833, at the tender age of twenty-two. Hallam wasn't just a friend to Tennyson, he was also an inspiration for art and literature.

Hallam's death shattered Tennyson's world. The poem details a three-year journey of mourning. The lines quoted come from the first year. Through the poem, Tennyson learned to live with his profound sense of loss, and found hope in love itself as a miracle.

No book on love would be complete without a chapter on grief for lost loves. We're unlikely to go through life without losing love at some stage. Can we mourn and heal these traumatic memories? It's worth exploring, because anxiety, trauma, and overwhelm may be blocking our ability to fully love and be loved. More broadly, most of us need healing as part of our spiritual life. When we recognize this, we can direct our spiritual practice towards healing our body, heart, and mind.

The Buddha was known as a healer as well as a teacher. In the well-known story of Kisa Gotami, the villagers tell Kisa to go to the Buddha with her dead baby, because, if anyone can heal it, he can. As it turns out, he isn't able to bring Kisa's baby back to life, but he *is* able to set her on a path to healing.

A wise spiritual teacher can help us to address the pain and conflict in our life, instead of turning away or ignoring it. This can lead to inner integration, harmony, and healing. Without this healing, we may find that our meditation stays superficial, or we are unable to integrate our meditative experiences into our lives.

Perhaps we come to the Dharma hoping to escape from our sorrows, the difficult areas of life. Perhaps we hoped to attain wisdom and compassion and be free of conflict. We might be disappointed when we relax our minds and find that all the unfinished business of our heart and body comes rushing back.

Genuine maturity means discovering the depth of our sorrow, our grief from the past, unfulfilled longings, and the pains that live in our body, stored up during the course of our life.

Unhealed pain, rage, and childhood trauma can become powerful unconscious forces in our life. Until we can bring awareness and understanding to these sorrows, we may find ourselves acting out their life-disconnected patterns of greed, hatred, and ignorance, over and over again.

Grief and mourning are aspects of love and compassion. Grief is all the love you want to give, and don't know how. All that unspent love gathers in the corners of your eyes, as a lump in your throat, a pain in your chest. It's important to acknowledge losses when we feel them. We might think that we're being 'good' Buddhists by toughing it out when something ends, saying, 'I can handle it, I'm not attached.' However, for our mental and emotional health we need to acknowledge our feelings.

Even the Buddha missed his two chief disciples, Sariputta

and Mogellana, after their deaths. He's recorded as saying, 'There is a void in the Sangha where they were for many years.'[145] Grief and mourning are part of how we respond to suffering. We are capable of acknowledging our own suffering and that of others. We can resonate with it, without getting overwhelmed.

One of the Sanskrit terms for compassion (*anukampa*) literally means 'trembling with', so we can tremble with suffering, ours or that of others. We can experience our pain as an aspect of our interconnectedness. Compassion is an integral aspect of the bodhisattva path. As we saw in Chapter 4, a bodhisattva is an ideal Buddhist, who is swept up by compassion and longs to rescue all beings from samsara.

So how do we do it? How do we mourn and heal our love losses? How do we lift ourselves out of the paralyzing helplessness and depression of incomplete mourning? If we know how to mourn, we're much less likely to get depressed.

I've come to understand grief and mourning as human needs, just like celebrating. I see them as two sides of the same coin. We mourn when our life isn't being enriched. We celebrate when it is. As William Blake wrote:

It is right it should be so;
Man was made for joy and woe;
And when this we rightly know,
Thro' the world we safely go.

Joy and woe are woven fine,
A clothing for the soul divine;
Under every grief and pine,
Runs a joy with silken twine.[146]

When we acknowledge both joy and woe, we can go safely through the world, because we will be safe within ourselves.

We tend to think of grief as something reserved for bereavement, the loss of life. But of course we can also feel it in relation to lost loves and lost dreams. Like celebration, grief is best done in the company of other people. It's a collective need, bringing us in touch with our common humanity. If we don't have community in our grief, it can feel doubly painful and isolating. Rituals are important here, because they bring this collective aspect.

Grief tends to come in waves, as it's a process rather than a one-time event. And, when the waves rise up, we need a safe space where all feelings are welcome. As the Sufi poet Hafiz says, it's best to stay with our grief for a moment rather than giving up on it. We usually regard loneliness as an enemy. It's not something that we choose to invite in. It's restless with the desire to escape our situation and find something or someone to keep us company. When we sit with it, even for a moment, we can begin to make friends with it, and we notice our habitual fear decreasing.[147]

We can look for the remedy inside the pain, as the Sufi poets suggest. Rumi encourages us not to run away from our grief, but to 'look for the remedy inside the pain'. His argument is that the soft beauty of the rose is associated with the sharpness of a thorn, and rubies come from stones.[148]

Instead of giving up on our feelings of loneliness and grief, Hafiz suggests that we let them in. They are like a sharp knife, cutting us into pieces in preparation for cooking. Once we're in the pot, the experience will season us, giving us a flavour that nothing else can. If you prefer to be fermented rather than cooked, it will turn you from a dull-brown liquid into a life-giving elixir.

Hafiz offers these everyday examples of how one thing transforms into another. Just like these processes, grief can be transformed into something else, with time, effort, and suitable conditions. The secret of loss is in the longing. Longing can make our eyes soft with love, our voice tender, and give us clarity about what is paramount.

Though we try to push it away and fill the space where it could appear, this kind of longing is what is keeping us alive. If we but knew it, it's our connection with life. It's how life is moving through us at the moment. It is a truly human experience. If we can pay attention to it over time, longing can give us compassion for ourselves and others, and a direction we haven't yet known.

When we're in grief, some things don't help. These include being told, or telling yourself, 'Perhaps it's time you moved on' or 'You'll get over it. There's plenty more fish in the sea.' We need to learn how to mourn our losses. If we can stay with this process, it can become healing and integrating. As Hafiz suggests, if we go deeply into mourning, we discover what is most significant in our lives. If we want to fully inhabit our life and love, we first need to grieve for the loves we have lost.

There are steps in this process. They always start with listening to the story we are telling ourselves about what happened. When we lose love, so much of our energy is trapped in thinking that we can't really start anywhere else. The story includes any judging and blaming of ourselves and others.

It might include denial: 'This can't be happening to me!' It might include anger: 'How could they do this to me? Nobody treats me this way!' It might include bargaining: 'If they come back, I won't behave like that again.' It might include depression: 'My love life is a failure. I'll never have love in my life.'

At some point we need to separate our thinking from what actually happened. So the second step in the process is observing what you saw or heard. Here's an example: 'I noticed that by the end of June they had stopped returning my calls.' Or: 'I moved out of the house we bought together on 2 June.'

As you recall these specifics, notice how you feel in your body. This is the third step in the process. We need to embody our grief physically, as a bodily experience, in order to find the ruby within it. You might be feeling anxious or depressed, heavy or fearful.

The fourth step is exploring the significance of your loss. What does it mean to you now? You can do this by delving behind or underneath the physical sensations in your body. What's behind or underneath your fear? What are you longing for? When we connect to the significance of our loss, what we are longing for, we can acknowledge this with the awareness that others also long for this. This step helps us to acknowledge when our heart is shutting down, and allows us to stay open.

Conversely, when we experience any pleasure or tenderness, we can cherish it and rejoice, then make a wish that others also experience it. In these ways, we can share the burden of our heart, and the lightness and joy. It's a direct way of bringing whatever we experience onto the path of Awakening.

In the previous chapter we heard how spiritual progress is an ascent, a journey upwards towards the light. However, if we're not careful we may leave everyone else behind – our partner, family, friends, and neighbours. We have 'escaped' but their suffering continues. The journey to Enlightenment for the benefit of all beings – cultivating the bodhicitta – is more likely to take us down rather than up.

Instead of transcending suffering, we begin to fully inhabit it. We explore insecurity and pain, without pushing them away. Rather than trying to fix suffering, we let it be. We descend into the depths, and, as we descend, we notice that we are surrounded by millions of other beings. They have become our companions in Awakening. At the bottom we find love, healing, and interconnectedness. We can rest here.

When you are fully connected with your deepest longing, sense again how you feel in your body. This is the fifth step. A transformed feeling is a sign that you are really connected with the deepest wellspring and inspiration of your life. It's also important to keep a bodily reference as we go through the process, to mark the changes in our psycho-physical organism.

If you go looking for this kind of compassionate sadness, you won't find it. It won't show up under a microscope. All you'll find is a kind of tenderness, tinged with sadness. The story has dropped away – you're not blaming anybody any more, least of all yourself. It feels natural, human. It's been called the genuine heart of sadness, holding the sadness and pain of samsara without losing sight of Awakening.

The sixth and final step of mourning and healing is imagining a next step. The purpose of this is to complete and ground the process. You can take this step by imagining doing something to acknowledge and honour your loss. What could it be? Perhaps talking about your grief with a close friend? Or creating a ritual by yourself or with others? What helps you to honour the loss congruently?

If we follow these steps today and over time, we can begin to transform our anxiety and depression into genuine, heartfelt mourning.

Of course you don't need to break up with your partner in order to experience a sense of loss. If you love someone long-term, you get to see them change, and this sometimes means mourning the person they used to be. Perhaps they are too exhausted to be that person any longer. Perhaps they've grown out of being that person, or never ended up growing into them. We want the person we love to get their spark back when it goes out.

However, it's not our responsibility to hold our partner accountable for the person they used to be. Our job is to self-empathize, to connect with our own mourning, and then to travel with our partner, honouring who and what emerges along the way. Sometimes their flame will shine brightly. Sometimes it will just be a flicker, and it may take a while for our eyes to adjust.

I started this chapter with a personal story of soul reclamation. I'd like to finish with an archetypal myth from the Mediterranean. In ancient times, the Orphic mysteries were popular initiation cults dotted around the region. At their centre was the figure of Orpheus, shown in innumerable paintings and mosaics holding a lyre, surrounded by animals. It was said that his music could tame them. There seemed to be no limits to the power of his songs.

In Virgil's classic retelling, the singer dares to descend to the Underworld to rescue his recently deceased wife – Eurydice.[149] She had the misfortune to be fatally bitten by a snake as she escaped from being raped. Orpheus descends and charms the King of Death and innumerable ghosts, pacifying their terrors with his songs. Anyone else would have died immediately, on entering the cold, dark halls of the Underworld. But he has to obey one rule, if he wants to reclaim his wife. She must walk behind him as he leaves, and he *must not look back*. He only has to walk ahead of her and not look back to make her his again.

But what does he do? On the threshold of the Underworld, when Orpheus is already in the realms of the upper air, a sudden mad desire seizes his heart. He must see her. He stops, turns, and looks back upon Eurydice. But she is still within the doorway of the Underworld, and with his frenzied look he breaks the bond. Three times a crash of thunder falls, and Eurydice cries out, 'Orpheus, what ruin have you brought upon us? The fates recall me and dark sleep overcomes my swimming eyes. Farewell! I am borne away. My arms no longer reach out to touch you. I am yours no more!'

And, as she speaks, she vanishes suddenly, like smoke dissolving into empty air. She vanishes from his sight, and, though he clutches at vain shadows, and longs to speak to her, she comes no more.

He weeps for seven months, on a cliff by the sea, in cold caves, among old oaks, all the while singing of his grief. His singing could have moved a heart of stone. Alone he wanders, mourning lost Eurydice. He never loves again. The Bacchae punish him for this, in their midnight frenzy. They feel scorned by him, tear him limb from limb, and scatter his remains over fields. His head finds its way into a river, and, as it drifts downstream, finds a voice to cry out, 'Eurydice. Ah! Poor Eurydice!' His cry is taken up and echoed by the river banks.

In Rilke's retelling of the story, Orpheus becomes a teacher through his grief. He teaches all creatures to listen. He holds the circle of life, the flow of spirit, the changes in the seasons, the return of spring. Orpheus becomes a symbol of renewal and regeneration.[150]

In the next chapter we're going to find out what it means to grow together in partnership. As preparation, I invite you to go deeper into the process of mourning and healing lost loves.

Guided reflection: steps to mourning and healing

- Purpose of this activity: to go deeper into the process of mourning and healing a lost love.
- Tools: a notepad and pencil (optional).
- Time: 15 minutes.

13

Growing Together

Let me not to the marriage of true minds
Admit impediments; love is not love
Which alters when it alteration finds,
Or bends with the remover to remove.
O no, it is an ever fixèd mark
That looks on tempests and is never shaken;
It is the star to every wand'ring bark
Whose worth's unknown, although his height be taken.
Love's not Time's fool, though rosy lips and cheeks
Within his bending sickle's compass come;
Love alters not with his brief hours and weeks,
But bears it out even to the edge of doom.
  If this be error and upon me proved,
  I never writ, nor no man ever loved.

William Shakespeare[151]

Shakespeare is writing of love as an eternal ideal. His argument is simple: if it changes, it isn't really love. We can recognize love by the fact that it weathers all storms. He's willing to bet his lifetime experience and creative output on this. As I read the poem out loud, a memory arises of a visit to the Asian Art Museum in San Francisco. Wandering through the Buddhist collection, I came across a golden *rupa* (statue) of a male figure locked in ecstatic love-making with their female consort. The figure was called Guhyasamaja, which means 'Hidden union'. It was the quality of the connection between them that struck me, the compassionate, rapt expression on their faces.[152]

I read from the label that this statue represented the union of wisdom and compassion. The male represents compassion, as the more active aspect, and the female represents wisdom, the more receptive. Buddhists don't see these figures in sexual terms – the figures arouse devotion rather than sexual feelings. But I didn't care what it *meant* – I had fallen in love with it.

This was a heart response. Even when I looked down at their interlocking groins, I didn't feel sexually stimulated. I felt a warmth in my heart and my whole body. Fast forward to today, and I find myself holding my partner in my arms, close to my chest. Could I hold them with that same passionate, compassionate energy? Could I hold them and all beings to my heart? How deep could it go? A thousand kisses deep?

The Buddha himself was a homeless wanderer and encouraged his disciples to 'go forth' from home. Buddhism later flourished as a settled monastic tradition. Nowadays, many people who have a serious interest in following the Buddha's teaching want to practise within a partnership. How can partnership and Dharma practice be mutually enlivening? How can partners grow together, even if one of them is not committed to the Dharma life?

As we saw in Chapter 5, in the Triratna Buddhist Order we have the clarity that commitment to going for refuge to the three jewels is primary. Acting ethically and following the precepts is secondary. Lifestyle comes third, though it's still important. Many Order members have chosen or stayed in a partnership, living out their full-time spiritual commitment in this setting.

I'm one of them. Why? It's something to do with love. I need emotional warmth and closeness to thrive. Touch is also very important for me. Perhaps I didn't get enough of it as a child. Despite this choice, I still find it challenging to dance on the edge between passion and compassion.

Every day I encounter the koan of how to express my commitment to the three jewels while also being committed to partnership. There's nothing easy about it. Sometimes I feel as if I'm being pulled between two planets that both want my full attention. Sometimes things flow and I can hear the music of the spheres!

But what happens when one partner wants to grow and the other doesn't? Perhaps the other is quite happy just as they are, thank you very much! How do you resolve this kind of conflict in the spirit of freedom, mutuality, and equity? Even if only one partner is committed to the three jewels, it can enrich the relationship. That's if both partners respect their differences and are committed to each other's spiritual welfare. Attending to your partner and working on your communication can be part of your Dharma practice and enhance your spiritual development.

One of the core teachings of the Buddha is that everything is impermanent. Everything is in a state of flux. The same is true of partnership. Even if it feels like magic one moment, you can't hold on to it. You can only live and appreciate it fully while it is here and then move on to the next moment, the next day.

If you dwell in the past, reliving past glories, you may find yourself unable to appreciate what is in the present. If you dwell in the future, the same will happen. Instead, you can change and grow together. Can you appreciate the infinite subtlety and mystery of human communication? This will help you and the relationship to stay fresh.

Perhaps we can learn to 'kiss the joy as it flies', to use William Blake's immortal phrase. To appreciate our experience rather than appropriate it. To relish whatever closeness and love we may feel in partnership with a keen awareness of its impermanence. From a certain point of view, this can make the moment even more beautiful, knowing that it is fleeting, like a bubble on a stream, or the previous moment of a ball of foam. In this way, we can blend insight into reality with our everyday experience of partnership.

More prosaically, we can grow together. Loving and being loved help us to grow. They are like the sunshine and rain that we need to flourish. If those we love could have seen us before they met us, they would be able to see the difference they have made to our lives. All of us need to be free to grow and change. If we try to fix ourselves or our partner in one mould forever, we're going to create suffering. The challenge in partnership is to learn how to move along together.

Of the couples who come through our doors for mediation and counselling, it's the ones who regard partnership as an opportunity for learning and growth who get more from the sessions. I've also noticed that these couples are more likely to be together in six months' time. I would even say that this kind of growth orientation is a sign of a healthy partnership.[153]

Love is not a thing that you either have or lack. It's not a possession. As we've seen in earlier chapters, it's a fundamental need, and a quality that can be expanded towards all beings. Developing love towards all beings is embodied in our love for those closest to us, and in compassionate action towards suffering. Our greater, more expansive love needs to be experienced in relation to the beings around us.

Growing together means supporting each other to grow and develop. It means being spiritual friends (*kalyana mitra*s) to each other. We explored this fundamental aspect of the Buddha's teaching in Chapter 5. We saw that spiritual friendship is the *whole* of the spiritual life. But is spiritual friendship really compatible with romantic partnership?

As we saw in Chapter 9, sexual/romantic relationships tend to be exclusive and possessive. When sexual relationships come to an end, unskilful emotions can be released and recrimination is common. These are the opposite of spiritual friendship, and would seem to have been in the background all the time. Ultimately, sex is based on grasping and craving for gratification. We may be able to conduct our sexual relationship with consideration and dignity, and even have friendly feelings towards our partner. But, if it comes to an end, what is our reaction likely to be? Depending on our answer to this question, it might be unlikely that we can have a sexual relationship with someone and be spiritual friends with them.

In a sexual relationship, if you give your partner something, it's usually in order to get something greater in return. In other words, it's a reciprocal relationship. Whereas, in spiritual friendship, you give something for the sake of your friend, unconditionally, with no expectation of return. Giving and receiving freely is closer to the state of egolessness, or *sunyata*, that is the goal of the Buddhist life.

In partnership we inevitably bump up against each other in small and large ways. My partner Gesine loves potatoes, which are part of her German heritage. I struggle to digest them in certain forms. When we're shopping and cooking, how do we find consent, something that works for both of us? Again, Gesine loves redecorating our house. I love reading and writing. How do we give each other space to flourish? There are no easy answers, and, if we don't address our frustrations when they are relatively small, they can build up and add to the stress of the partnership.

Is there a way to respect and honour each other's needs, without giving up on our own? We've both grown through this kind of enquiry, and learned more about each other. Partnership is a powerful opportunity to learn about who you are and act accordingly. Your partner may act as a mirror to you, reflecting back your own mental states. It can feel deeply uncomfortable to see your own anxieties, annoyances, and resentments mirrored in your partner's face and voice.

Do you know how to take responsibility for your feelings and needs, and to actively communicate these to your partner? Can you let go of trying to control the situation and any attempt to maintain a certain self-image? Do you know how to be disarmingly honest about your limitations? It takes ongoing work and awareness for this level of trust to develop. Each partner needs to reveal vulnerably what they are discovering about themselves day by day. And each partner needs to listen to the other and receive what they are revealing with an open heart. This doesn't happen all at once – it develops over time.

Your partner is like a mirror held up in front of you. Through their eyes you can see both shadow and light. Couples often come to our Nonviolent Communication workshops. At a certain point, we ask people to bring to mind a difficult moment, when they could have done with deeper self-connection. Sometimes people say, 'No, I can't think of a moment when I've struggled. It's all fine.' If I'm feeling mischievous, I say, 'Shall we ask your partner?'

It always gets a laugh, because we know intuitively that other people have a different view of us, and may struggle with our inconsistencies or limitations. Even acknowledging difficulties can go a long way towards addressing them. You could try saying, 'Hmm, I hadn't thought about that. I don't know. Could we explore it together?'

In a partnership you quickly learn that you aren't always going to get what you want. Or, if you do, there will be a price to pay later, in terms of resentment and a reduced willingness to collaborate. We need to take two people into account. We may have unrealistic expectations that create suffering. For instance, expecting that you will both enjoy the same activities and friends.

If your partner takes up a new activity, say working in a community orchard or playing chess, you may interpret this as an expression of their desire to get away from you or an indication that you are growing apart. In this way, your interpretation creates suffering. When you stay with what is happening, without interpretation, you are unlikely to exacerbate the pain of the situation.

Again, if you don't really commit to the partnership, you're unlikely to have the energy and determination to work through difficulties and bring the relationship to life. Human beings and relationships are infinitely subtle and complex, so there is no end to what you can learn about yourself, your partner, and love. This is what I mean by growing together.

My teacher Sangharakshita once said, 'Unless your work is your meditation, your meditation is not meditation.'[154] We could say something similar about partnership, 'If your partnership is not part of your Dharma practice, then Dharma practice lacks integrity.' If we really wish to be transformed by the Buddha's teaching, we can break down the barriers between partnership and practice. We can bring our cultivation of awareness and love to our partnership, and consider whether the conditions we live in are conducive to the welfare of all beings.

You might decide to leave the partnership – the subject of the next chapter – or challenge your partner on their behaviour. Or you might decide to redouble your efforts to practise within the situation. We both shape and are shaped by our environment. We're here to help each other along, to go to sleep each night with gratitude for the day on our lips and wake up each morning with respect saying, 'Good morning, my love.'

Out of interest, I searched the early Buddhist scriptures for examples of couples. One example is Visakha and Punna Mantaniputta. Visakha was one of the foremost lay disciples of the Buddha. She was known for her deep devotion to the Dharma and her generosity. Punna became an enlightened monk.[155] Then there's Nakula's father and mother. They have been faithful to each other for many years, even in their thoughts. They express the wish to be reborn together. The Buddha comments that the way to be reborn together is to be in tune with each other in confidence/trust, ethics, generosity, and wisdom. If they follow the Dharma, they will be reborn in a god realm.[156]

But my favourite is the story of King Pasenadi and Queen Mallika. On one occasion, King Pasenadi went with Queen Mallika to the upper palace. As the two of them were sitting there, the king asked, 'Mallika, is there anyone dearer to you than yourself?' Queen Mallika replied, 'Your Majesty, there is no one dearer to me than myself. And you sire, is it the same for you?' The king replied, 'It's the same for me. There is no one dearer to me than myself.'

When this conversation had sunk in, the king descended from the palace, went to where the Buddha was staying, and told him about the conversation. The Buddha confirmed their insight in a verse:

Searching in all directions
with your awareness,
you find no one dearer
  than yourself.
In the same way, others
are thickly dear to themselves.
So you shouldn't hurt others
  if you love yourself.[157]

Remarkably, the king and queen had seen through the illusion of their royal status. They'd had what we might call an empathic realization. The dearest person in the universe is... themselves. By the same token, other people are dearest to themselves. So, if you love yourself, you will also love others and avoid harming them. This is the ethics of empathy, reflectively comparing our experience with that of others and acting on this reflection.[158]

Knowing yourself is essential for a fulfilling long-term relationship. If you are unable to stand on your own two feet, you may wear your partner down. We need a degree of emotional and spiritual maturity in order to enter into a relationship of mutuality. Many of us don't know ourselves, and this can create tension. If we are open to it, we can learn as we go along. However, sometimes we need to acknowledge our limitations and start again in a different place.

As the *Karaniya Metta Sutta* (see Chapter 3) says, are you capable? Have you developed your abilities as a partner? Do you know how to work on yourself? Do you know what you want from life? Are you in touch with your values and inspiration? Do you have an awareness and care for the feelings and needs of others?

We need to become a healthy, happy human being. We can't really skip this step, and, if we try, we will encounter far more serious difficulties down the line. For some people, partnership is key. Of course it may be more, if we encourage each other to grow together towards Enlightenment. The relationship may provide the context for psychological and spiritual development. Or not. As we've seen again and again, there is nothing sacred about partnership, or any institution. It is our intentions or volitions that are skilful or not. If we act from generosity, love, and awareness, happiness will follow us as the cart wheel follows the hoof of the ox. If we act from their opposites, suffering will follow just as surely.

Compared to traditional ideas about marriage, partnership suggests mutuality, equity (equal valuing), and freedom of choice. We could even name these as the values of partnership. In any case, these values are aspects of the love mode, as distinct from the power mode. They are Dharmic values. They are more in line with Reality than their opposites. So, if you can relate in the spirit of mutuality, equity, and freedom of choice, you will be bringing the Dharma alive in your daily life and relationships.

I was the middle of three children, with an older brother and a younger sister. Everything had to be shared three ways, or there was trouble! We all got very accurate at dividing chocolate or cake into three pieces, then allowing the other two to choose. We believed in equality, because this was the only way we were going to get our fair share. Equality tends to mean that each person gets the same amount of whatever resource is available.

This doesn't work so well for partnerships, because there are many resources that can't be neatly split in two. Time, for instance, or children, or energy. What is important is that each partner is fully valued and that their wellbeing and spiritual development are fully considered and supported. The word I use for this is 'equity'.

In our partnership, Gesine and I value somewhat different things. Gesine likes to have money in her pocket to spend when she's out, and likes to renovate the house. I like to have space to write, do chi kung, and meditate. Giving me more money doesn't increase my wellbeing. Giving Gesine more time and space wouldn't necessarily increase her wellbeing either – she likes to keep busy.

Our challenge is to take into account each other's wellbeing, as well as the wellbeing of the partnership. This involves a willingness to look deeply at the needs on the table. It's easy to get stuck in our preferred strategies, especially when they seem to be limited, like time or money.

Gesine likes a sense of abundance and choice. Renovating the house gives her a sense of beauty, order, and empowerment. I love to have the space to be creative and reflect – this gives me learning, growth, freedom, and peace of mind. When we're discussing how to use our resources, we try to remember that conflicts take place not at the level of needs, but at the level of strategies.

Partnerships flourish when there is a mutual flow of giving and receiving. Receiving is also a form of giving, of generosity. Whatever you give, give it freely, without expecting something in return. Can you support your partner without keeping a tally of who owes what? Of course we want a spirit of mutuality, but be careful about keeping the score. Keeping the score makes it difficult to give or receive freely. We're calculating how many 'points' our partner just scored, rather than appreciating their loving intention to contribute to our life.

When you feel that the partnership is out of balance, do you know how to look within yourself as well as at your partner? Are you being generous towards yourself as well as towards them? Do you know how to stop doing the washing up *before* resentment kicks in? Do you know how to tell your partner that you've had enough of doing the laundry, and you'd like a change? Could they do it for the next month?

When there is a lack of mutuality, or when partners get stuck in particular roles, the quality of partnership reduces. Giving and receiving are two sides of the same coin of mutuality. The coin shines brightly when we support their dynamic interplay.

Sometimes, when we hear how we can freely contribute to our partner's wellbeing, our feelings shift towards supporting them. Gesine supports me to find space to write. I support her to have the financial resources for house renovation. I also support her to take the lead, when she wants to, in couple mediation or leading workshops on her own. There isn't a fixed timetable to giving and receiving freely. When it comes to vexed issues such as the washing up, the agreement is that we will stop doing it as soon as we start to feel resentful. Or preferably the moment before this. It's a dance, and, as we move in time with each other, we listen to each other's feelings and needs.

Sometimes sensitivities can lead to a sense of lovelessness. We may have grown up with the idea that we can heal our sense of lovelessness by loving more generously. We may have heard that the way to be loved is first to love. In the context of friendship, if you want to *have* a friend, then *be* a friend. There is a profound truth to this. At the same time, there is another equally powerful truth: we can't give what we don't have. We cannot give what we cannot receive. We can only give love richly if we are able to receive it, to soak it up and be nourished by it. If our feeling of lovelessness makes it difficult to let love in, how much do we have to give?

Who is to say that letting love in is any less valuable than giving love? The key to loving is to become more permeable to love, to let it all the way in, so that it can live and breathe in us. Only if our pores are open can we experience great love flowing freely into us and through us. Receiving love might be scarier than we thought.

Receiving and giving are the in-breath and out-breath of love. Knowing that we are loved can free us to love, to care for others as they are, allowing them to flourish as only they know how. This relates to the cherishing, protecting, and maturing aspects of love that we touched on in Chapter 1. When we are immersed in the stream of love, we can see that love is not something I give or am given. It is more like an element we can tap into, a cloud of longing, a force of nature. We can open to this, with awareness.

This can help you to feel tender towards the pain of others who feel distant from these qualities. You can see that, behind their anger and fear, they are desperate to know love, to feel a sense of belonging and the security that comes from this.

In the next chapter we will look at what happens when we trip over each other's baggage and the pain becomes overwhelming. Or one or both partners change or find themselves going in different directions. How can we stay connected to the love mode, even as we grow apart? In the meantime, I invite you to join me in reflecting on the secret union of Guhyasamaja.

Guided reflection: the secret union of Guhyasamaja

- Purpose of this activity: to reflect on the secret union of Guhyasamaja. What is the quality of connection between Guhyasamaja and his consort?
- Tools: a notepad and pencil (optional).
- Time: 15 minutes.

14

Growing Apart

Well, I remember, I remember, don't worry, how
  could I ever forget?
It's the first time, the last time we ever met
But I know the reason why you keep your silence up,
  no, you don't fool me
Well, the hurt doesn't show, but the pain still grows
It's no stranger to you and me

Phil Collins[159]

Once I co-led a Nonviolent Communication training for Catholic marriage-guidance counsellors in Freiburg, Germany. I found them to be pleasant and socially minded people, and was impressed by the quality of their listening. However, it gradually became clear that they were focused on keeping marriages together. Because of their belief in the sacredness of marriage in the eyes of God, it was very difficult for them to support couples who were growing apart.

What happens if there's no exit from a life situation? The lava that remains in a volcano after an eruption cools and forms a hard 'plug' in the top of the crater. New lava may build up pressure from beneath, but the solid stone plug blocks its escape. Overwhelming pressure within a solid, confined space eventually creates the conditions for an explosion. By contrast, when Gesine and I mediate between couples, we support their capacity to really hear each other, and the outcome remains open. There is no plug in the top of the crater, so explosions are less likely.

Partnership is based on consent. We come together by mutual consent, rather than for any considerations of power. Trust and betrayal are two sides of the same coin. If we try to rule out betrayal, broken promises, and the possibility of the partnership coming to an end, we are also moving away from the love mode and towards the power mode.

As we saw in Chapter 9, true love says, 'I love you and I want you to be happy. If that includes me, let's celebrate! If it doesn't, in any case I wish you health and happiness.' This leaves us free to reflect on whether the partnership is still serving us. Perhaps it's become clear that we are unlikely to get some of our needs met in this particular context. We can reflect, 'There are eight billion people on the planet. Maybe I need to start again somewhere else.'

Partnership is a consensual institution. We come together and separate by consent. We need an off-boarding mechanism as well as an on-boarding one. Where would we find such a mechanism? Recently, I've heard of 'conscious uncoupling', but I prefer 'Giraffe divorce' – a phrase I've heard in the Nonviolent Communication community. As already mentioned, 'Giraffe' symbolizes life-connected thinking and communication, as giraffes have a broad overview of the situation and large hearts.

When we like something or an experience, we try to pull it towards ourselves and incorporate it into our sense of self. The same is true when we fall in love with someone. We want to pull them towards us, and we don't want them to change. However, for various reasons, we do change. We may change in different ways or at different rates. Changing in a way that heightens the difference between you doesn't necessarily mean that you're being disloyal, or that the two of you are growing apart.

Even if you are more different than you once were, you can still appreciate and respect each other. Increased differences do not need to lead to increased distance between partners. If you can embrace and respect change, it adds texture and richness to the relationship.

For partnership to grow and thrive, each person needs to feel free to change. It's okay to change your mind, to want different things. Relating authentically means being curious about who your partner is today, rather than holding on to an image of who they were yesterday. It means asking, 'Who are you in this moment?'

How you change can be unpredictable. The same goes for your partner. What can keep you together is a confidence and trust that each of you wishes the other well, and this includes progressing spiritually. With this confidence and trust, you may experience change as a sense of freshness, the unfolding of human potential. As you mature, you realize that change is a vital force to keep your partnership alive. This insight into Reality finds its natural expression in love towards all beings. Your partnership can be rooted in an experience of unbounded love.

Yet partners can grow apart when they don't invest time and energy into growing together. They may no longer have the same interests or want the same things. Signs that partners within a couple are growing apart may include lack of attention, intimacy, connection, trust, and empathy.

We all come into our partnerships with baggage from the past. We can either trip over each other's baggage or unpack it together. There's nothing like partnership to show us where we are frozen, where we struggle to connect, where we are afraid or unwilling to accept things as they are. Nothing can trigger us so quickly and deeply. So partnership is a litmus test of our wholeness and spiritual maturity.

When we freeze in the presence of our partner, it's usually because their triggering has activated our own. We cannot tolerate the intensity, so we 'shut down' our system in order to avoid further pain. I need to know how to hold myself and my triggers in awareness and kindness. If I can handle my triggers, I am more likely to be able to handle my partner's.

Learning how to love and be loved doesn't mean we will never be triggered again. It means that we gain some freedom. This freedom develops through a process of understanding and unfolding, which gives us some space – when we are triggered – to notice what is happening to us and why. So we're not quite so quick to react automatically. We can find out where we are hurting inside, and direct love or self-compassion in this direction.

If I can face what is hard in myself and give it self-compassion, I'm more likely to be able to face what is painful in my partner. Then I can offer genuine kindness and empathy when they need it. If we can learn to speak about these experiences, it will also help us to notice when one or both of us get triggered. These conversations can help partnership become deeper and more intimate.

Through making peace with what my partner triggers in me, as well as their triggers, I can become more accepting of both of us. This can be a profound way to bring more love and understanding into the world. This is the secret meaning of partnership. Learning to surf the turbulent waves of partnership can allow us to become more patient, more understanding, and more open-hearted. We can become a clearer channel through which love can flow.

Authentic, loving presence means witnessing and respecting differences without seeking to minimize them. It also means feeling the pain of not being able to fully share my world with my partner. Yet, again and again, the longing for love, closeness, belonging, and touch arises anew. Personal, embodied love can be an expression of greater love, giving it a place on this earth.

Many people have grown up defining love as denying yourself and doing for others. At a young age, they learned, 'If you love somebody, you do what they ask.' I would like to offer a different definition. Could we define love as honestly expressing our feelings and needs, and empathically receiving our partner's feelings and needs? Honestly expressing our own needs rather than making demands: 'Here I am, and here's what would make my life more wonderful.' Receiving our partner empathically doesn't mean that we must agree or comply, just accurately receive what they express as a gift of life. How does this definition of love sound to you?

If you're struggling to get on together, you can look at how you communicate with each other. Between what is said and not meant, and what is meant and not said, much of love is lost. Communication can be a delicate and fragile business.

Misunderstandings and unspoken feelings can create distance, even if partners care for each other. Sometimes words are spoken without awareness of the likely consequences, and received as hurtful. Sometimes feelings and needs that are deeply felt are left unexpressed, and this can create a void, a silence that echoes with regrets. The words we choose and the words we withhold carry immense power.

In the context of partnership, where emotions are often heightened, the gap between intention and impact can lead to a reduction in affection and connection. Our challenge is to express ourselves fully, with maximum care for the other, and be prepared to receive our partner fully too.

There are various topics that Gesine and I regularly explore with the couples who come for mediation and coaching. These include how to give feedback to each other, and saying and hearing a no.

There's an old saying that, if you want to go fast, go alone. But if you want to go far, go with others. Geese provide a perfect example on their long migrations. As each bird flaps its wings, it creates an uplift for the bird immediately following. Flying in V formation adds at least 71 per cent greater flying range than one bird flying on its own could achieve.

They take it in turns to fly point, the most demanding role. Sometimes geese honk from behind to encourage those in front to keep up their speed.[160] My question is, what do you say when you honk from behind? How do you give feedback to your partner?

If it's quick feedback, for instance on a meal they have just cooked, you could tell them one thing you enjoyed and one thing you would have liked differently: 'I really enjoyed how you combined hoisin sauce with miso and vinegar to create a sweet and sour taste. I would have liked the parsnips to be more evenly cooked.'

If it's something more serious or longer-lasting, you might want to use values-based feedback. Basically there are two types of feedback. The first, which we are all familiar with, focuses on what's wrong with the person or their behaviour. This includes judgements of them as 'incompetent', 'lazy', 'careless', or 'selfish', and judgements of their behaviour as 'inappropriate', 'patronizing', or 'narcissistic'.

The second type of feedback is what we call values-based feedback. This involves setting the scene with your partner, including establishing rapport with them, allowing enough time for 'fallout', and choosing a safe place if you guess that it may be hard for them to hear. Make sure that you acquaint yourself with the facts beforehand, and in the conversation be as specific as you can. Tell your partner what needs or values of yours are on the table in relation to your observations. Check with them how this sounds, what sense are they making of your comments. If they are triggered, they have probably heard something other than what you meant. Make a suggestion as to what they could do differently next time. Be prepared for mutual exploration. Try to see things from their point of view, without necessarily agreeing with it.

If you're feeling courageous, you can even invite feedback from your partner with these four questions:

1. Would you be willing to tell me one thing that I do as your partner that makes life less wonderful for you?
2. How do you feel about that?

3. What needs of yours are not getting met?
4. What can I do to enrich your life?

As we saw in Chapter 10, sex can bring fun and playfulness into a long-term relationship. It can also bring conflict, if one partner wants sex more often than the other, or sex of a different kind. Consent is important here. Respecting the other person's no shows care and consideration that they matter more than as a means of physical gratification. If your partner says no when you're wanting sex, one thing you can do is ask them to let you know when they are in the mood.

Another way in which consent shows up is when a partner wants to stop whatever sexual activity is going on at the moment. Maybe things have heated up or gone in a direction where they don't feel comfortable any more. You can try checking with them, 'Where was the last place you felt comfortable?' and go back to that point. The willingness to be flexible shows respect and consideration for your partner.

Even if we work on our communication, we may still feel bitterly disappointed in relation to the partnership, as we were hoping to do some healing – perhaps healing the trauma of childhood separation. As we saw in Chapter 2, we may want our partner to give us the secure attachment that we haven't had elsewhere in our lives. Of course, this may never have been realistic. Trust isn't black and white. It's not indivisible but graduated. And it's wise to trust people only to the extent that they are integrated in both a worldly and a spiritual sense.

Growing apart sometimes leads to deep hurt, hatred, and even violence, especially if one partner has made a unilateral decision to end the partnership. Obviously the priority is safety, both physically and emotionally. Developing self-compassion can support this. Ill-will or hatred leads to suffering for everyone, so it's important to cultivate loving-kindness towards your ex-partner as well. You can put them in the fourth stage of one of the *metta* practices at the end of Chapter 3. If none of this works, you could try transforming your enemy image.

Part of the process of labelling and pigeonholing your partner is to create a hostile or enemy image of them. It's the mental equivalent of a visual caricature used for target practice. Relating to the image rather than the person makes it easier to dehumanize them and justify violence towards them. Here's an exercise to help us transform these kinds of hostile or enemy images. It has the capacity to reduce violence in the world and allow us to reclaim our human dignity.

Come into your heart, sensing what you are feeling right now. Is it light or heavy, expansive or contracted? And, underneath this, what are you longing for? What is your heart's wish? When you're ready, recall a specific time when you felt separate from your partner. Notice when and where you were, and what happened in the moments just before you felt separate.

Using all of your senses, create a rich first-person experience, picturing the scene in your imagination. Notice and allow your physical sensations and emotions. Write down your judgements of your partner, identifying the feeling and need underlying each judgement. For instance, if you judge your partner to be 'selfish', are you feeling disappointed, hurt, and angry, because you are longing for mutuality, care, and respect?

How are you now? Give yourself permission to feel what you feel. What needs of yours are alive at this moment? Savour your needs.

Recall the situation. Can you guess what your partner might have been saying yes to? What was in their heart? What need(s) could they have been trying to meet when they did what they did? From their point of view, what was their life-serving intention?

Savour this need within you, its importance to you and everyone. Consider the idea that, 'Just like me, this person was doing the best they could to meet their needs. If they knew a way to meet their needs with less cost, they would have chosen that.'

How are you now? Give yourself permission to feel it. What needs are alive at this moment? Can you savour them? If you notice judgements of your partner coming up again, let go of this step and return to the previous step of self-compassion. It's hard to have empathy for your partner when you are needing it for yourself.

To complete and ground this exercise, what is one step that you can take, right now, to serve the needs that you have identified, both your own and your partner's? If you need longer to do this exercise, or more support, you can listen to the guided reflection at the end of the chapter.

If you've worked on your communication issues, done some healing, transformed your enemy images, and yet you still seem to be growing apart, you could take an inventory of your partnership. Here's a list of ten questions to help you do this, individually or together – you can score each one on a scale from 'very much' to 'not at all'.

1. Do you have new experiences with your partner?
2. With your partner, do you feel a greater awareness of things?
3. Does your partner support your ability to accomplish new things?
4. Does your partner expand your view of yourself?
5. Do they help you expand your own capabilities?
6. Bring to mind your partner's skills, abilities, and talents. Do they balance out some of the areas where you sense your limitations?
7. Have they helped you to see a larger perspective on life?
8. To what extent has being with your partner resulted in you learning new things?
9. How much does your partner increase your overall knowledge?
10. Have you grown and matured as a result of being with your partner?[161]

The higher you've scored on these questions, the chances are that you have a happier and more sustainable relationship. The lower you've scored on these questions, the chances are that your partnership is not creating opportunities for you to grow and develop. Sharing your experiences with your partner might be a way to change this.

Alternatively, you might choose to seek help. Deeper issues from childhood might need more attention than the other partner can give at the moment. Gesine and I get regular partnership supervision from another Nonviolent Communication trainer. This also supports us in our work with other couples. When Gesine and I realize that we've come to an impasse in our communication, one of us will say, 'Could we come back to this with Sylvia?' As Sylvia is fond of reminding us, 'You don't do your own open-heart surgery.'

Even working on communication issues with someone else's support may not be enough to restore trust and connection. Perhaps you thought that the partnership was going to be forever, and now you appear to be growing apart and moving in different directions.

Sometimes you grow apart from someone you've been an intimate partner with. You may no longer sense their support for how you wish to grow. If they appear to offer you a choice between your growth and the partnership, you may choose to grow. Can you imagine completing a separation or divorce in a kindly and amicable way? It is possible. My partner Gesine and her ex-husband are still friends, still keep in touch to care for their adult boys, still meet at family reunions. During the divorce, which was over ten years ago now, I was deeply impressed with how her ex-husband dealt with Gesine's departure from the family. He remained friendly, cooperative, and generous throughout.

Recently Gesine asked him if he had any feelings of hurt left over from that time. He said no, not hurt, just sadness. And he acknowledged that Gesine had found what she was looking for with me – a loving partnership with opportunities for learning and to contribute to life.

Communicating compassionately during a separation can help to stave off the long-lasting harm that people experience with escalating interpersonal conflict. The key is to work towards a resolution without violence or coercion, and focus on a quality of dialogue that is most likely to generate mutual understanding.

When a separation has a high degree of conflict, it can have devastating financial and emotional consequences. This is especially true when children are caught between two 'warring' parents. As we saw in Chapter 2, children look to their parents to care for them and provide a sense of security. When separating parents express their dislike for each other's actions, this can undermine the child's relationship with the parent being judged. Blaming and criticizing can lead to an erosion of connection, trust, and self-value.

Even when partners disagree, they can try to understand where the other is coming from. They can acknowledge the feelings and needs, and move towards mutually agreeable solutions. This allows all parties to understand, heal, grow, and move forward in their lives in a healthy way.

The first thing to bear in mind is that partnership or marriage is a vehicle for meeting needs. People choose to be in partnership for various reasons. These include love, belonging, honouring traditions, connection, security, shared reality, meaning, support, and intimacy.

Similarly, people choose to separate or divorce to meet needs. They may have lost confidence or even hope that they will be able to meet their needs in the context of partnership. Trust may have been lost. Misunderstandings and conflicts may have led to one or both partners feeling pain around the other. One or both partners may have concluded that the partnership is no longer working for them.

It's important to bear in mind that some separations may not involve conflict, but rather a recognition that each partner wants something different from life and is going in a different direction. In these cases, it's more likely that the transition can occur in a kindly and amicable way.

Even when conflicts do arise, they don't take place at the level of needs. Needs are universal, so they don't refer to a specific person, location, or time. It's the strategies we identify with that can be in conflict with our partner's. When we can separate our needs from our strategies, and feel motivated to contribute to the partnership, we can connect to our partner on the level of feelings and needs.

This works best when there is a heartfelt willingness on both sides to understand – not necessarily agree with – each other, and to be vulnerable in sharing what is really alive in us. Once we understand each other on this level, we can explore strategies that meet everybody's needs – our partner's and our own.

Another key to having difficult conversations around separation is to build a healthy support system. Separation or divorce can be regarded as a failure, something shameful, to be kept hidden from public view. In part, this may come from moralistic thinking, that partnership or marriage is the 'right' thing to do. In part it may come from a belief that we should be able to resolve our own problems (self-empowerment), or that we don't air our dirty laundry in public (dignity).

However, this may be counterproductive. Firstly, we are unlikely to be able to see the situation objectively. Secondly, both parties are likely to be desperate for empathy and understanding, without having the resources to offer them. Everybody is trying to breathe, but there is a lack of oxygen (empathy) in the room. So having a healthy support system in place during times of transition can be extremely beneficial.

When we reach out to our wider community, we may find people who are willing to listen to us without bringing in their own judgements of the situation. There may even be people we both trust to support a difficult conversation. It's never too late to start building a healthy support system. The earlier we start, the easier it will be. It's incredibly difficult to put a system in place when we are already in crisis. The best time to start was years ago. The second best time is now![162]

When separation is inevitable, I recommend that you create a ritual to finalize your Giraffe divorce. It could include the following elements: *acknowledging* the impact of your actions on your partner; *taking responsibility* for things you regret or that you could have done differently; *mourning* needs that weren't met for you; *celebrating* the needs you met together; and *wishing each other well* going forwards.

So we come to the end of this chapter and nearly to the end of this book. In the Conclusion we come full circle, bringing together love in Buddhist practice and partnership. In the meantime, I invite you to regain a portion of your humanity by transforming your enemy images.

Guided reflection: transforming enemy images

- Purpose of this activity: to help you reconnect with your humanity by transforming hostile or enemy images you may have of your partner.

- Time: 15 minutes.

15

Final Thoughts: Towards a Culture of Love

> Love is as strong as death. It burns like a blazing fire, like a mighty flame. Many waters cannot quench love; rivers cannot sweep it away. If one were to give all the wealth of one's house for love, it would be utterly scorned.
>
> Paraphrased from the Song of Solomon 8:6 and 8:7

In the romantic consumer culture of the West, love is seen as an elusive visitor, appearing from an unknown place, delighting us with its presence, creating a momentary magical transformation, then disappearing as quickly as it came. It's a butterfly that alights on the path in front of us on a gusty day. It spreads its wings to reveal a vision of splendour before being swept away.

There are whole industries to help us capture this particular butterfly, to make it stay for more than a moment. These industries help us to be suitably dressed, groomed, successful, intelligent, and creative, so that we can attract the butterfly. By contrast, Buddhism teaches that the experience of love is a flower of practice. It is something that can be developed through consistent application of awareness of ourselves and others. Through developing loving-kindness, we see that feelings of warmth and empathy come from being open and receptive to other people, whoever they are.

In these final thoughts we come full circle, bringing together love in Buddhist partnership and practice to create a culture of love. What brings them together is the practice of love – opening our heart to our partner, the people around us, and ultimately all beings.

When we feel the urge to practise the Dharma more deeply, we can easily see partnership as competing with this. And yet, by the same token, spiritual development is not a thing. It's a process, and we can engage with this process whether or not we are relating to another person as our partner.

To follow the Buddha's teachings, commitment to the three jewels of the Buddha, Dharma, and Sangha is our primary concern. Second comes how we express this ethically. Our particular lifestyle comes third, as an expression of the first two. If we keep this clarity, we can see that it is possible to practise in any situation, and acknowledge that some situations may be more supportive than others.

This book began with the words of the Buddha: 'Not by hatred are hatreds ever pacified here (in the world). They are pacified by love. This is the eternal law.' We saw that we could describe the Buddha's teaching purely in terms of the love mode rather than the power mode. The love mode is a spirit of helpfulness and tenderness towards the whole world. Love is also the principle of nonviolence, the most direct and important manifestation of going for refuge to the three jewels.

Our social systems sanction punishment and reward, guilt and shame, duty and obligation. They seek to make violence against the group's 'enemies' enjoyable. They establish education systems that teach obedience to authority. They sanction 'prejudicial thinking' that values people differently based on skin colour, caste, class, race, religion, gender identity, sexual orientation, physical and intellectual ability, and so on. These systems tend to value human beings over other species and ecosystems, so they are directly responsible for the climate and ecological emergencies.

The world is not a level playing field when it comes to the distribution of resources. The forces of greed, hatred, and delusion have taken on a life of their own. In order to counteract them, we need to work together. As Dr Martin Luther King famously told an anti-war symposium, those of us in the party for peace must be as organized as the party for war. In a decade when peace activists were telling us to 'Make love not war', Dr King proclaimed love to be the only effective way to end injustice and bring peace:

> Sooner or later all the people of the world will have to discover a way to live together in peace [...] If this is to be achieved, [humanity] must evolve for all human conflict a method which rejects revenge, aggression and retaliation. The foundation of such a method is love.[163]

The Buddha's teachings on love provide such a basis for social relations. Transforming the world involves transforming our minds, and vice versa.

What would a culture of love look like? We have some clues from the image of the garden of love in Chapter 6. In these final thoughts, I want to bring out a different point. Doing the work of love is all about taking action. What kind of garden we grow depends on what we plant. If we plant a mango seed and water it, we get a mango tree. If we plant an apple seed, we'll get an apple tree – though if we want an edible apple we'll need to graft the seedling onto hardier stock.

On the one hand, if we keep doing what we have always done, we'll keep getting the same results. On the other hand, if we can awaken and make conscious choices in how we respond to the circumstances of our life, this will create our future circumstances. We may struggle to change our outer circumstances, but we can change our inner attitude, our intentions, and this is enough to transform our life. Even in the most painful external situations, we can choose compassion and understanding rather than greed, hatred, and delusion.

In Chapter 4 we came across the blessing of the bodhicitta, the will to Enlightenment for all beings. Some people write about Buddhism as if it's a path that leads up a mountain or even into the sky. From the perspective of love, it is a path that goes down towards the centre of the earth. Instead of transcending all suffering, we move towards turbulence and confusion. We sidle up to them. We slip into them, however we can.

We explore insecurity and pain, without pushing them away. Even if it takes years or lifetimes, we allow them to be as they are. We move down and down, at our own pace, towards the centre of the earth. As we descend, we notice that billions of beings are moving with us. They are our companions on the journey to Awakening.

At the bottom of our journey we discover the soothing balm of bodhicitta – the Awakening Heart/Mind. Right down at the centre of the earth, we discover the love that will not die, the love that alone can pacify the hatreds of the world.

If we consciously cultivate love, the bodhicitta can emerge in a more consistent way. Joy can arise from being in love's presence. We can recognize the energy of aliveness as blissful, or, as William Blake says, 'eternal delight'. Love or passion flowing unobstructedly is experienced as bliss. When bliss flows through our veins, it flows out of us as radiant love.

The *Itivuttaka*, one of the earliest Buddhist texts, proclaims:

> Just as the radiance of all the stars does not equal a sixteenth part of the moon's radiance, but the moon's radiance surpasses them and shines forth, bright and brilliant, even so, whatever grounds there are for making merit productive of a future birth, all these do not equal a sixteenth part of the mind-release of loving-kindness.[164]

This is the incandescent power of love. It's not a sentimental emotion, a warm and gooey feeling towards another. It's not possessive, but opens up to giving and receiving freely. In love, the lover has potential to go beyond themselves, to transcend their limited sense of self.

This kind of love is unsentimental in that it seeks to know the other and how to support their welfare. Love is creative because it seeks to refresh itself. Love is determined because it includes the qualities of patience and forbearance. Love is kinetic because it is always moving towards what is beloved. Love is passionate longing for what is beloved, prepared to sacrifice itself and go to the limits of its strength.

You cannot manufacture this kind of love. You can't fake it; you can't coax or argue it into existence. Love is not a technique, it is more like an art that subsumes technique. To love is to suffer an ordeal, to taste the most refined of sensations, to delight and wonder in beauty, richness, and wholeness. Moreover, love is to be destroyed and made new, recreated in a place of both passion and serenity.

Love is a blessing. Love is utter estrangement and suddenly finding yourself reborn in your true home. Love is a mirror in which you see your beloved for the first time, allowing you to assimilate their beautiful qualities. Love promises insight. It is not complete until it has taken us beyond ourselves, beyond exclusive partnership, to a profound love for all beings.

We are always relating to something. In developing a wise and compassionate relationship to all things, we find the capacity to honour them. Maturing spiritually involves an acceptance of life in relationship. If we are willing to relate to all things in life, we enter into a gracious spirit of practice that values life *as* life.

Each of our actions is fresh; all of our encounters are significant and related to the whole of our spiritual life. How we relate to the difficulties and problems that we encounter in our partnership is a measure of our practice. This means attending to the quality of *all* our relationships – not just the one we have with our romantic partner, but those with our family, our sexuality, our community, all humans, other species, political and economic systems, and the earth's biosphere.

Our relationship to each being and action becomes an expression of the Dharma. If we bring care and compassion to these, we can honour our interconnectedness. Nothing is outside of our spiritual life.

This care and compassion can manifest as the quality of simple presence. Simplicity is the way we open to everyday wonder. This is the ordinary mystery of waking up in the morning next to someone. When our heart feels gratitude for the gift of life, we can just be ourselves, and allow our partner to be themselves. It can bring a great sense of peace with the universe. We don't need to fix anything, simply opening in love and understanding to the joy and suffering of the world. We find that we have the power to heal ourselves naturally, and through healing ourselves we can support others to heal. Our sanity and compassion extend to the world around us.

Thirteenth-century Japanese Zen master Ehei Dōgen believed that Enlightenment is just intimacy with all things.[165] This includes the air we breathe, the earth below us, our partner, where we sleep, the lives of others. Perhaps this Enlightenment of intimacy is the same as love. It is somewhat mysterious. We don't know exactly what it is, but we can tell when it's present or absent. It is only here in the present. Past loves are a memory. Future love is fantasy. There is only one place where love and Awakening can be found, and that is in the present.

If we find ourselves displaced into the past or the future, things seem distant, hurried, or 'never enough'. The only place where we can genuinely love our partner or the world is in the here and now. This is the intimacy of the timeless present. It connects us to one another, allows us to belong and experience what it means to love and be loved. In this experience we can move out of our sense of separateness, of contraction, of a limited view of ourselves.

What keeps us from this intimacy, this love? It's usually some kind of expectation, hope, thought, or fantasy. It's the same expectation that keeps us from Awakening. When the heart is free from this expectation, true love and intimacy can emerge. Awakening occurs in the midst of all things as a love that touches and includes everything. We experience a freedom and fearlessness to enter every realm. Rather than remove ourselves from life, we rest at the very centre of it. We are intimate with all things.

Our capacity for intimacy is based on a deep respect, a presence that can allow what is inside us and others to emerge. It is the spirit of the Gnostic Gospels, quoted at the head of Chapter 8:

> If you bring forth what is within you, what you bring forth will save you. If you do not bring forth what is within you, what you do not bring forth will destroy you.

When we recognize the uniqueness of each moment, each impression, each person in front of us, we discover a beauty and grace that make all things significant. Life may be tentative and impermanent, but it is also precious. This brings an ease and sense of cherishing to our heart. It can lead to a genuine joie de vivre. We feel a sense of wholeness in our body. We recognize that we're supposed to be here, just as much as all life. We're not some random product of an impersonal evolutionary process. We belong, just as much as the trees and the sun.

This can lead to healing and grace. Could our lives be a blessing for our partner, those around us, and all things? When we're intimate with ourselves, we are able to bless everything around us, and be blessed in turn. Can we bless whatever is in front of us, whatever we touch? Can we bless, honour, and listen with respect to our partner, and all beings, so that they feel like they are having a conversation with their closest friend? Practising the Dharma comes down to the intimacy of each moment. This is where our practice is fulfilled.

To commit to Enlightenment means caring for whoever we encounter, however difficult or beautiful, holding them in our heart. Like the great bodhisattvas of the past, we can return to the world, entering the marketplace with 'bliss-bestowing hands'. Everyone we encounter will partake in our Enlightenment. And we can say to them, 'May all blessings be yours, may all gods protect you, may all blessings be yours.'

To conclude, I would like to invoke the figure of Amitabha, known as the Buddha of love. He is deep ruby red in colour, the colour of blood, the colour of love and compassion. For us, he represents the end of the path of love. He brings together passion and compassion. With joy, we can recognize that our love is a reflection of Amitabha's love.

He is totally approachable, like the setting sun. Sunset is a kind of miracle. You can look directly into the face of the all-powerful sun and it will do you no harm. As it disappears into the West at the end of the day, it allows anyone to approach.

Amitabha's spiritual power is warmth and gentleness. He is the colour of rubies, like Kurukulla, whom we met in an earlier chapter. He is the colour of fascination, the colour of emotional arousal. Through Amitabha, all our emotional energies are gently led towards Enlightenment. Through his influence, possessive passion is transmuted into discriminating wisdom.

The wisdom of Amitabha sees the uniqueness of all phenomena. A passionate lover wants to be with their beloved, the seemingly irreplaceable object of their love. They are highly aware of what makes their partner unique – their particular mannerisms and tone of voice. All these are special and lovable because they are characteristics of the beloved.

In a similar way, Amitabha's discriminating wisdom sees and loves the minute characteristics of things. The only difference is that Amitabha's love is nondual. It introduces no concept of self and other. So it doesn't make its loving attention into a basis for possessive love.

Even though partner-love can be far from ideal, it can still be nourishing and part of the supportive conditions for practice. And, in this way, we can come to experience what Dante calls, in the last line of *The Divine Comedy*, 'the love that moves the sun and the other stars'.[166]

How deep could it go? At least a thousand kisses deep.

Guided reflection: evoking Amitabha and the bodhicitta

- Purpose of this activity: to help us connect with Amitabha's nondual love and develop the Awakening Heart/Mind towards all beings.

- Time: 20 minutes.

Notes

Introduction

1 *Dhammapada: The Way of Truth*, trans. Sangharakshita, Windhorse Publications, Cambridge 2001, chapter 1, verse 5.
2 Plato, *Symposium*, available at https://classics.mit.edu/Plato/symposium.html, accessed on 12 March 2026.
3 L. Cohen, 'Hallelujah', Sony Music Publishing.
4 L. Cohen, 'A thousand kisses deep', Sony Music Publishing.
5 G.V. Catullus, *Carmina*, poem 5, available at http://data.perseus.org/citations/urn:cts:latinLit:phi0472.phi001.perseus-lat1:5, accessed on 13 March 2026.
6 *Dhammapada*, chapter 1, verse 5.
7 Yeshe Tsogyal, *The Life and Liberation of Padmasambhava*, Dharma Publishing, Emeryville, CA 1978, p.380.
8 Sangharakshita, 'Mind reactive, mind creative', in *The Complete Works*, vol.6: *The Essential Sangharakshita*, Windhorse Publications, Cambridge 2024, pp.167–73 (167).
9 J. Frederick Arment, *The Elements of Peace: How Nonviolence Works*, McFarland & Company, Inc., Publishers, Jefferson, NC 2012, p.232.

Chapter 1

10 Paracelsus, *Four Treatises of Theophrastus Von Hohenheim Called Paracelsus*, ed. H.E. Sigerist, The Johns Hopkins Press, Baltimore, MD 1941. Quoted in E. Fromm, *The Art of Loving*, Thorsons, London 1995. Paracelsus (1493–1541) was a Swiss physician, alchemist, theologian, and philosopher. He emphasized the value of observation in combination with received wisdom.

11 Sangharakshita, *The Ten Pillars of Buddhism*, Windhorse Publications, Birmingham 1994, pp.57–8.

12 Metta Sutta, in Sutta Nipata 1:8.

13 Metta Sutta.

14 Thich Nhat Hanh, *Peace Is Every Step: The Path of Mindfulness in Everyday Life*, Rider, London 1991, p.78.

15 B. Kato, Y. Tamura, and K. Miyasaka, with revisions by W.E. Soothill, W. Schiffer, and P.P. Del Campana, *The Threefold Lotus Sutra*, Kosei Publishing Co., Tokyo 1990, pp.126–8.

16 W. Blake, 'The clod and the pebble', in *Songs of Innocence and of Experience* (1794), Oxford University Press, Oxford 1970, plate 32.

17 Thomas à Kempis, *The Imitation of Christ*, book 3, chapter 5, p.47, available at https://www.gutenberg.org/files/1653/1653-h/1653-h.htm#chap42, accessed on 1 June 2026.

18 Maradhitu Sutta, in Samyutta Nikaya 4:25.

19 Asvaghosa, *Buddhacarita, or Acts of the Buddha*, trans. E.H. Johnston, Motilal Banarsidass, Delhi 1992, book 13, 'Defeat of Mara'.

20 The Rolling Stones, 'You can't always get what you want', a song written by Mick Jagger and Keith Richards from the 1969 album *Let It Bleed*.

21 J. Keats, 'Bright star! would I were steadfast as thou art', in *The Complete Poems*, ed. John Barnard, 2nd ed., Penguin Books, London 1977, p.452.

22 P.B. Shelley, 'A defence of poetry', in *English Essays: From Sir Philip Sidney to Macaulay*, ed. Charles W. Eliot, P.F. Collier & Son, New York 1909, available at https://www.gutenberg.org/files/5428/5428-h/5428-h.htm, accessed on 1 June 2026.

23 W. Blake, 'Eternity', in *The Complete Poetry & Prose of William Blake*, ed. David V. Erdman, University of California Press, Berkeley and Los Angeles, CA 1982, p.470.

24 W. Blake, 'Proverbs of hell', from *The Marriage of Heaven and Hell*, in *The Works of William Blake*, Wordsworth Editions, Ware 1994, pp.181–3.

Chapter 2

25 B. Brown, *The Gifts of Imperfection: Let Go of Who You Think You're Supposed to Be and Embrace Who You Are*, Hazelden Publishing, Center City, MN 2020, p.36 (bold typeface in the original).

26 A.C. Conan Doyle, 'The adventure of the Abbey Grange', *The Strand* magazine, September 1904 issue, republished in *The Return of Sherlock Holmes*, George Newnes Ltd, London 1905, p.270.

27 A. Machin, *Why We Love: The New Science behind Our Closest Relationships*, Weidenfeld and Nicolson, London 2022.

28 The Eagles, 'Victim of love' from the album *Hotel California*, Asylum Records 1976. Songwriters: Don Henley, Glenn Lewis Frey, Don Felder, and John David Souther. Lyrics © Cass County Music, Red Cloud Music, Fingers Music.

29 E. Burunat, 'Love is a physiological motivation (like hunger, thirst, sleep or sex)', *Medical Hypotheses* 129 (2019), DOI: 10.1016/j.mehy.2019.05.011.

30 J. Foster, 'Fatherhood and the meaning of children: an ethnographic study among Puerto Rican partners of adolescent mothers', *Journal of Midwifery and Women's Health* 49 (2004), pp.118–25.

31 *Puja: The Triratna Book of Buddhist Devotional Texts*, Windhorse Publications, Cambridge 2008, p.24.

Chapter 3

32 Metta Sutta, in Sutta Nipata 1:8.

33 Itivuttaka 27.

34 *Anguttara Nikaya* 5:342. Buddhaghosa, *The Path of Purification* (*Visuddhimagga*), trans. Bhikkhu Ñāṇamoli, Buddhist Publication Society, Colombo 2010, pp.4–6.

35 Vessantara, *The Heart: The Art of Meditation*, Windhorse Publications, Cambridge 2006.

36 Sangharakshita, *Living with Kindness: The Buddha's Teaching on Metta*, 2nd ed., Windhorse Publications, Cambridge 2008, p.45.

37 G.P. Malalasekera, *Dictionary of Pali Proper Names*, Asian Educational Services, New Delhi 1938.

38 C. Lofsness, 'An interview with William Stafford', *The Iowa Review* 3:3 (summer 1972), pp.92–106, reprinted as 'Dreams to have: an interview with Cynthia Lofsness', in *Writing the Australian Crawl: Views on the Writer's Vocation*, University of Michigan Press, Ann Arbor, MI 1978, pp.85–113 (104).

39 Culagosingha Sutta, in Majjhima Nikaya 31.

40 O. Klimecki, S. Leiberg, C. Lamm, and T. Singer, 'Functional neural plasticity and associated changes in positive affect after compassion training', *Cerebral Cortex* 23:7 (July 2013), pp.1552–61.

41 *Puja: The Triratna Book of Buddhist Devotional Texts*, p.21.

42 O. Wilde, *De Profundis*, available at https://www.gutenberg.org/files/921/921-h/921-h.htm, accessed on 1 June 2026.

43 Shantigarbha, *The Burning House: A Buddhist Response to the Climate and Ecological Emergency*, Windhorse Publications, Cambridge 2021, pp.65–75.

Chapter 4

44 L. Gomez and P. Harrison, *The Teaching of Vimalakirti*, Mangalam Press, Berkeley, CA 2022, p.71. This is a new translation of a recently rediscovered Sanskrit version of the text from the Potala library, Lhasa.

45 *Ibid.*, p.69.

46 Sangharakshita, *Creative Symbols of Tantric Buddhism*, Windhorse Publications, Cambridge 2002.

47 'I put a spell on you' performed by Hal Mooney and Nina Simone. Written by Screamin' Jay Hawkins. A UMe/Verve Records Release © 2023 UMe/Verve Label Group, a division of UMG Recordings, Inc.

48 Sangharakshita, *Creative Symbols of Tantric Buddhism*.

49 I haven't been able to find a reliable source for this quotation, so I've described it as attributed to Shams.

50 T. Merton, *Thoughts in Solitude*, Burns & Oates Ltd, London 1987, p.55.

51 Sangharakshita, *The Psychology of Spiritual Development*, talk available at https://www.freebuddhistaudio.com/audio/details?num=41, accessed on 13 March 2026.

52 *Pabbaja Sutta: The Going Forth*, in *Sutta Nipata* 3:1, available at http://www.accesstoinsight.org/tipitaka/kn/snp/snp.3.01.than.html, accessed on 20 March 2026.

53 *Sela Sutta*, in *Sutta Nipata* 3:7, available at https://www.dhammatalks.org/suttas/KN/StNp/StNp3_7.html, accessed on 20 March 2026.

Chapter 5

54 Sangharakshita, 'The veil of stars', verse CVIII, reprinted in *Complete Poems 1941–1994*, Windhorse Publications, Cambridge 1995, p.434.

55 Plato, *The Symposium*, 189–93, in *Plato: Lysis, Symposium, Gorgias*, with an English translation by W.R.M. Lamb, (Loeb Classical Library, Plato vol.3), Harvard University Press, Cambridge, MA 1996.

56 *Ibid.*, 210e6–211b5.

57 Sangharakshita, *The Religion of Art*, Windhorse Publications, Glasgow 1988, p.39.

58 *Lotuses of the Mahayana*, ed. K.J. Saunders (Wisdom of the East Series), L. Murray, London 1924, p.11.

59 Digha Nikaya 3:34–5.

60 Metta Sutta: Goodwill, in Samyutta Nikaya 46:54.

61 C. Marlowe, *Tamburlaine the Great*, part II, scene 4.

62 I. Kant, *Critique of the Power of Judgment*, trans. P. Guyer and E. Matthews, Cambridge University Press, Cambridge 2000, chapter 9.

63 *Ibid.*

64 Sangharakshita, 'Green Tara and the fourth laksana', available at https://www.sangharakshita.org/articles/green-tara-and-the-fourth-laksana, accessed on 16 March 2026.

65 *Kamada Sutta: Kamada's Lament*, in *Samyutta Nikaya* 2:6, available at http://www.accesstoinsight.org/tipitaka/sn/sn02/sn02.006.olen.html, accessed on 16 March 2026.

66 Sangharakshita, *The Religion of Art*, pp.54–5.

67 Sangharakshita, 'Forty years on: the six distinctive emphases of the FWBO', in *The Complete Works*, vol.12: *A New Buddhist*

Movement II, Windhorse Publications, Cambridge 2021, pp.663–73 (672–3).

68 W. Wordsworth, 'Lines composed a few miles above Tintern Abbey, on revisiting the banks of the Wye during a tour. July 13, 1798', in *William Wordsworth: Selected Poems*, Penguin, London 2004, p.61.

69 Sangharakshita, 'The journey to Il Convento', in *The Complete Works*, vol.26: *Aphorisms, the Arts, and Late Writings*, Windhorse Publications, Cambridge 2022, pp.261–80 (271).

70 Ariyapariyesana Sutta, in Majjhima Nikaya 26.

71 Sangharakshita, 'The veil of stars', p.434.

72 Upaddha Sutta, in Samyutta Nikaya 45:2.

73 T.W. Rhys Davids and W. Stede, *Pali–English Dictionary*, Pali Text Society, London 1992.

74 Dharmachari Subhuti and Subhamati, *Buddhism and Friendship*, Windhorse Publications, Cambridge 2004.

75 Blake, 'Proverbs of hell', p.181.

76 See Chapter 2, 'The Science of Love'.

77 *Dhammapada*, chapter 15, verse 207.

78 *Udana* 4:1.

79 Gampopa, *The Jewel Ornament of Liberation: The Wish-Fulfilling Gem of the Noble Teaching*, trans. Khenpo Konchog Gyaltsen, Snow Lion, New York 1998, pp.69–75.

80 Shantigarbha, 'Goddess', in *Guhyaloka Sonnets and Other Poems*, Urthona Editions, Cambridge 1996, p.15.

81 Sangharakshita, 'A complex personality: a note', available at https://www.sangharakshita.org/articles/a-complex-personality-a-note, accessed on 20 March 2026.

Chapter 6

82 W. Blake, 'The garden of love', in *The Complete Poems*, ed. Alicia Ostriker, Penguin Books, London 1977, p.127.

83 W. Blake, 'The echoing green', in *The Complete Poems*, p.105.

84 G.D. Chapman, *The Five Love Languages: How to Express Heartfelt Commitment to Your Mate*, Northfield Publishing, Chicago, IL 1992.

85 Jalal al-Din Rumi, *Rumi: The Book of Love: Poems of Ecstasy and Longing*, trans. Coleman Barks, HarperCollins, New York 2003, p.123.
86 Shantigarbha, 'Beauty and righteousness', in *Guhyaloka Sonnets and Other Poems*, p.12.
87 Quoted in Fromm, *The Art of Loving*, p.22.
88 H. Milk, *An Archive of Hope: Harvey Milk's Speeches and Writings*, University of California Press, Berkeley, CA 2013, p.214.
89 C.G. Jung, *Memories, Dreams, Reflections: An Autobiography*, Fontana Press, London 1995, p.356.
90 L. Carr, M. Iacoboni, M.-C. Dubeau, J.C. Mazziotta, and G.L. Lenzi, 'Neural mechanisms of empathy in humans: a relay from neural systems for imitation to limbic areas', *Proceedings of the National Academy of Sciences* 100:9 (2003), pp.5497–502.
91 S. Kierkegaard, *Works of Love*, trans. H. and E. Hong, HarperPerennial, London 2009, p.32.
92 Sangharakshita, *Vision and Transformation: An Introduction to the Buddha's Noble Eightfold Path*, Windhorse Publications, Glasgow 1990, p.70.

Chapter 7

93 D. Walcott, 'Love after love', in *Collected Poems 1948–1984*, Faber & Faber, London 1992, p.328.
94 R.C. Kessler and E.J. Bromet, 'The epidemiology of depression across cultures', *Annual Review of Public Health* 34 (2013), pp.119–38, DOI: 10.1146/annurev-publhealth-031912–114409.
95 Nagarjuna, *Mulamadhyamaka-karika* (*Fundamental Verses on the Middle Way*), trans. Stephen Batchelor, available at https://www.wisdomlib.org/buddhism/book/mulamadhyamaka-karika-english/d/doc79738.html, accessed on 16 March 2026.
96 Sangharakshita tells the story more concretely in *The Complete Works*, vol.13: *Eastern and Western Traditions*, Windhorse Publications, Cambridge 2019, pp.395–6 (in 'The FWBO and Protestant Buddhism'), and *The Complete Works*, vol.16: *Mahayana Myths and Stories*, Windhorse Publications, Cambridge 2017, pp.200–1 (in 'The drama of cosmic Enlightenment'), and more abstractly in *The Complete*

Works, vol.17: *Wisdom Teachings of the Mahayana*, Windhorse Publications, Cambridge 2023, pp.625, 629–30 (in 'Know your mind').

97 J. Kornfield, *A Path with Heart: The Classic Guide through the Perils and Promises of Spiritual Life*, Rider Books, London 2002, pp.13–15.

98 *Ibid.*, p.15.

99 Sangharakshita, seminar on *The Buddha* by Trevor Ling (1976). Quoted in Sangharakshita, 'Peace is a fire' (section on friendship), reprinted in Sangharakshita, *Aphorisms, the Arts, and Late Writings*, p.27.

100 K.D. Neff, 'Self-compassion: an alternative conceptualization of a healthy attitude towards oneself', *Self and Identity* 2 (2003), pp.85–101.

101 M.B. Rosenberg, *Nonviolent Communication: A Language of Life*, Puddledancer Press, Encinitas, CA 2015, chapter 9, 'Connecting compassionately with ourselves'.

Chapter 8

102 M.B. Rosenberg, 'Do you love me?', training video clip available at https://www.youtube.com/watch?v=otynMEeMStg, accessed on 17 March 2026. Transcribed and edited by the author.

103 M. Yousuf, M.A. Qadri, and H. Osmanov, 'Mevlana Rumi: a 13th century scholar's teachings to foster tolerance, peace and harmony', *International Journal of Education, Culture and Society* 4:4 (2019), pp.71–5, DOI: 10.11648/j.ijecs.20190404.13.

104 M.B. Rosenberg, *Being Me, Loving You: A Practical Guide to Extraordinary Relationships*, Puddledancer Press, Encinitas, CA 2005, pp.61–3.

105 B. Brown, 'The power of vulnerability', TED talk, available at https://www.youtube.com/watch?v=iCvmsMzlF7o, accessed on 17 March 2026.

106 C.R. Rogers, 'The necessary and sufficient conditions of therapeutic personality change', *Journal of Consulting Psychology* 21 (1957), pp.95–103. See also C.R. Rogers, 'A theory of therapy, personality, and interpersonal relationships as developed in the

client-centered framework', in *Psychology: A Study of a Science*, vol.3: *Formulations of the Person and the Social Context*, ed. S. Koch, McGraw Hill, New York 1959, pp.184–256.

107 Shantigarbha, *I'll Meet You There: A Practical Guide to Empathy, Mindfulness and Communication*, Windhorse Publications, Cambridge 2018, pp.39–41. See the notes there for references to the research on empathy.

108 G.W. Lewandowski Jr, *Stronger Than You Think: The 10 Blind-spots that Undermine Your Relationship... and How to See Past Them*, Orion, London 2021, chapter 10.

109 'Will you still be sending me a Valentine?' John Gottman interviewed by Alison George in *New Scientist*, 29 April 2006, pp.38–9. For the Gottmans' work, see https://www.gottman.com/couples/.

Chapter 9

110 'Falling in love again (can't help it)' is the English-language name for a German song composed by Friedrich Hollaender. The song was originally performed in the 1930 film *Der Blaue Engel* by Marlene Dietrich. The English lyrics were written by Sammy Lerner.

111 Shantideva, *The Bodhicaryavatara*, trans. K. Crosby and A. Skilton, Oxford University Press, Oxford 1996, pp.75–105, chapter 8, verses 52–3.

112 Fairground Attraction, 'Perfect'. Songwriters: M. Edward and C. Nevin. Lyrics © Mca Music Ltd.

113 Sangharakshita, *Know Your Mind: The Psychological Dimension of Ethics in Buddhism*, Windhorse Publications, Birmingham 1998, pp.215–17.

114 Blake, *Songs of Innocence and of Experience*, plate 32.

115 Sting, 'If you love somebody set them free' from the album *The Dream of the Blue Turtles*, A&M Records, 1985.

116 T. Nhat Hanh, *True Love: A Practice for Awakening the Heart*, Shambhala Publications, Boulder, CO 2004, p.4.

117 From Blake, 'The question answerer'd', in *The Complete Poems*, p.162.

118 Sangharakshita, 'The Buddha's noble eightfold path', in *The Complete Works*, vol.1: *A Survey of Buddhism; The Buddha's Noble Eightfold Path*, Windhorse Publications, Cambridge 2018, p.521.

119 *Sedaka Sutta: The Bamboo Acrobat*, in *Samyutta Nikaya* 47:19, with amendments by the author, available at http://www.accesstoinsight.org/tipitaka/sn/sn47/sn47.019.olen.html, accessed on 17 March 2026.

Chapter 10

120 G.G. Byron, 'She walks in beauty', in *The Major Works*, ed. Jerome J. McGann, Oxford University Press, Oxford 2000, p.288.

121 According to the US Department of Justice's *Violence against Women Report* from 2002, an estimated 91 per cent of victims of rape and sexual assault are female and 9 per cent male. Nearly 99 per cent of perpetrators are male. This statistic does not report those who do not identify in these gender boxes.

122 This research was done with people who identify as heterosexual men and women. I wonder if it also applies to those who identify as LGBTQ+ and nonbinary? See E.R. Bressler and S. Balshine, 'The influence of humor on desirability', *Evolution and Human Behaviour* 27:1 (2006), pp.29–39.

123 J.A. Hall, 'Sexual selection and humor in courtship: a case for warmth and extroversion', *Evolutionary Psychology* 13:3 (2015), DOI: 10.1177/1474704915598918.

124 This is a classic example of what the French call *esprit de l'escalier*, or staircase wit. Actually my friend Vajrananda suggested responding in this way, when I told him of the incident. In reality, I just shook my head.

125 Sangharakshita, *A Stream of Stars: Reflections and Aphorisms*, Windhorse Publications, Glasgow 1998, p.47.

126 The Augustine Fellowship, *Sex and Love Addicts Anonymous*, 1st ed., Fellowship-Wide Services Inc., Boston, MA 1986 (summary).

127 Another fake quote! After our talk I checked this quote out and found that the real author was Rita Mae Brown, civil-rights

campaigner and feminist author. R.M. Brown, *Sudden Death*, Bantam Books, New York 1983, p.68.

128 The fourth precept is 'Use for any given purpose the energy appropriate to that purpose, not one which is inappropriate.' And the fifth precept is 'Do not allow energy to become turbid. Keep it clear and bright.' Sangharakshita, 'Sayings, poems, reflections: excerpts', reprinted in *Aphorisms, the Arts, and Late Writings*, p.8.

Chapter 11

129 J. Baldwin, *The Fire Next Time*, Penguin Classics, London 2024, p.71.

130 'Here be dragons' (1985), in J. Baldwin, *The Price of the Ticket: Collected Nonfiction 1948–1985*, Beacon Press, Boston, MA 1985, p.685, and 'To crush a serpent' (first published in *Playboy*, January 1987), reprinted in J. Baldwin, *The Cross of Redemption: Uncollected Writings*, Pantheon Books, New York 2010, pp.158–65.

131 'James Baldwin and Nikki Giovanni, "A conversation": full broadcast video' (parts I and II), available at https://www.youtube.com/watch?v=jnoeXVALpXI, accessed on 1 June 2026.

132 *Ibid.*

133 'Everybody's protest novel', in Baldwin, *The Price of the Ticket*, p.31.

134 W.R. Jankowiak and E.F. Fischer, 'A cross-cultural perspective on romantic love', *Ethnology* 31:2 (1992), pp.149–55.

135 'Sangharakshita in conversation – 2. Morality', Sangharakshita interviewed by Subhuti, available at https://vimeo.com/28841675, accessed on 18 March 2026.

136 Shantigarbha, *The Burning House*, chapter 14.

137 'LGBT in Britain: home and communities', 2018 Stonewall report, available at https://www.stonewall.org.uk/resources/lgbt-britain-home-and-communities-2018, accessed on 18 March 2026.

138 Sangharakshita, 'The ten pillars of Buddhism', in *The Complete Works*, vol.2: *The Three Jewels I*, Windhorse Publications, Cambridge 2019, pp.370–3.

139 T.J. Burleigh, A.N. Rubel, and D.V. Meegan, 'Wanting "the whole loaf": zero-sum thinking about love is associated with prejudice against consensual non-monogamists', *Psychology and Sexuality* 8 (2017), pp.24–40.
140 Sangharakshita, 'Altruism and individualism in the spiritual life', in *The Complete Works*, vol.4: *The Bodhisattva Ideal,* Windhorse Publications, Cambridge 2019, pp.84–117 (108–10).
141 J. Kent, *A World beyond Monogamy: How People Make Polyamory and Open Relationships Work and What We Can All Learn from Them*, Luminastra Press LLC, Portland, OR 2021.
142 'The devil finds work' (1976), in Baldwin, *The Price of the Ticket*, p.612.

Chapter 12

143 A. Tennyson, *In Memoriam A. H. H.*, S4N Books, Glenshaw, PA 2017, canto 27, lines 13–16.
144 P. Simon, 'Graceland' © BMG Rights Management, Sony/ATV Music Publishing LLC, Warner Chappell Music, Inc.
145 Cunda Sutta, Samyutta Nikaya 47:14.
146 From 'Auguries of innocence', in *The Complete Poems*, pp.506–10.
147 D. Ladinsky, 'Absolutely clear', from *The Subject Tonight Is Love: 60 Wild and Sweet Poems of Hafiz*, Penguin Compass, New York 2003, p.50.
148 Rumi, *Selected Poems*, Penguin, London 2015, p.336.
149 Virgil's *Georgics*, book IV.
150 Rilke, *Sonnets to Orpheus*, book 1, sonnets 20–1.

Chapter 13

151 W. Shakespeare, sonnet 116. Viewed in H. Vendler, *The Art of Shakespeare's Sonnets*, Harvard University Press, Cambridge, MA 1997, pp.487–93.
152 The Buddhist deity Guhyasamaja in the act of ecstatic love-making (*c*.1400–1500), China. Asian Art Museum, San Francisco.
153 There is research-based support for this observation in Lewandowski, *Stronger Than You Think*, chapters 3 and 7.

154 An aphorism quoted in 'Peace is a fire' (section on work and action), which is reprinted in Sangharakshita, *Aphorisms, the Arts, and Late Writings*, p.18.
155 Visakha Suttas (Udana 2:9 and 8:8) and Majjhima Nikaya 24.
156 Anguttara Nikaya 4:55.
157 *Rajan Sutta: The King*, in *Udana* 5:1, available at http://www.accesstoinsight.org/tipitaka/kn/ud/ud.5.01.than.html, accessed on 18 March 2026.
158 Shantigarbha, *I'll Meet You There*, pp.122–3.

Chapter 14

159 P. Collins, 'In the air tonight'. Lyrics © Concord Music Publishing LLC.
160 H.C. Noyes, 'The goose story', *ARCS news* 7:1 (January 1992), p.1.
161 Based on Gary Lewandowski's Self-Expansion Questionnaire (SEQ), in Lewandowski, *Stronger Than You Think*, chapter 7.
162 A. Seid, 'Nonviolent Communication skills and divorce', available at https://www.nonviolentcommunication.com/learn-nonviolent-communication/nvc-divorce/, accessed on 19 March 2026.

Chapter 15

163 Martin Luther King's acceptance speech, on the occasion of the award of the Nobel Peace Prize in Oslo, 10 December 1964. Available at https://www.nobelprize.org/prizes/peace/1964/king/acceptance-speech/, accessed on 19 March 2026.
164 *Itivuttaka: The Group of Ones* 24–7, available at https://www.accesstoinsight.org/tipitaka/kn/iti/iti.1.024-027.irel.html#iti-027, accessed on 19 March 2026.
165 J. Kwong and P. Levitt, *No Beginning, No End: The Intimate Heart of Zen*, Harmony Books, New York City 2003, p.16. The exact sentence doesn't appear in his writings; however, the idea of intimacy with all things as a sign of Enlightenment is a core theme in his teachings. Dōgen held that true Enlightenment is found in fully experiencing and being present with all phenomena, reflecting the interconnectedness of all existence.
166 Dante, *The Divine Comedy*, 'Paradiso', canto 33, lines 143–5.

Index

Introductory Note

References such as '178–9' indicate (not necessarily continuous) discussion of a topic across a range of pages. Wherever possible in the case of topics with many references, these have either been divided into sub-topics or only the most significant discussions are listed. Because the entire work is about 'love' and 'relationships', the use of these terms (and certain others which occur constantly throughout the book) as an entry point has been minimised. Information will be found under the corresponding detailed topics.

abbot 109–10
abduction 183–4
absorption, meditative 4, 112, 169, 208
abundance 133, 238
accumulation 31, 67
acrobats 181–2
actions 27, 38–9, 67, 141, 143–9, 151, 204, 262
  skilful 61–2, 163, 192
addiction 32, 35–6, 38, 183, 185, 193–5
adolescence 31, 39–40
adultery 183–4, 210
adults 40, 139, 184, 187
affection 18, 33, 47, 121, 124, 127, 172, 246
  sticky 24, 63
age 40, 64, 121, 132, 166, 184, 217, 245
agreements 117, 181, 185–6, 195, 211, 239
ahimsa 18
air 4, 33, 100, 102, 128, 130, 163, 166, 225, 254, 263
aliveness 77, 260
ambivalence 40, 119
Amitabha 265–6
amygdala 36, 160
Ananda 87, 104–5, 107
anatta 54, 139, 142
anger 46, 51, 179, 222, 240
anthropology 25, 106, 129
anxiety 65, 131, 217, 224, 232
Aristophanes 90–1, 126
arms 79, 225, 228

arrows 23, 79–80, 89
arts 15–29, 93, 98–101, 114, 217, 261
arupaloka 208
ascent of beauty 92–3, 97, 103
asubha 87, 94–8, 169
attachment 24, 27, 32, 34–6, 39, 54, 67
  figures 39, 106
  passionate 24–5
  theory 36, 39
attendants 107
attributes 19, 177
autonomy 145, 155, 180
aversion 8, 46, 67
awakening 59, 62, 72–3, 78, 191, 222–3, 260, 263
Awakening Heart/Mind 72, 260, 266
awareness, mutual 162, 178

babies 40, 45, 77, 127, 210, 217
baggage 240, 244
Bahiya 86
balance 39, 47, 51, 163, 182, 201, 238, 251
Baldwin, James 197–8, 212
bamboo pole 181–2
beauty 83–7, 89–99, 101–5, 111–13, 117, 121–3, 125–6, 133
  ascent of 92–3, 97, 103
  ethical 85, 87
  images of 100, 121
  physical 79, 84–5, 92, 102
beings 18–20, 45–6, 50, 58–9, 61–2, 71–8, 102–3, 124–5
beliefs 8, 103, 197, 210, 241, 254
beta-endorphin 36–7
Bhante 113–14
biological glue 33, 36, 45, 125
biosphere 78, 262
birds 90, 106, 120, 246
birth 40, 54, 67, 171, 198, 261
Blake, William 20–3, 28–9, 106, 119–22, 177, 219, 230, 261
blaming 146, 156, 162, 221, 223, 253
blessings 8, 195, 210, 260, 262, 264–5
bliss 23, 28, 86, 170, 261
blood 23, 82
  colour of 82, 265
Bodhicaryavatara 62, 169
bodhicitta 72–3, 223, 260, 266
bodhisattva 62, 68, 71–88, 109–13, 219, 265
  path 73, 76, 219
bonds 169, 178, 187, 202, 225
boundless heart 19, 45, 124
boundless love 29–30
bows 79–80, 89
brahmacarya 105, 114–15, 208
brahmas 59, 105, 114, 208
brahmavihara 59–63, 67–8, 73–5, 79, 82, 115, 130
brains 32–4, 36–9, 129, 160
briars 119–20
bridges 198, 208
brothers 40, 55, 106, 237
Brown, Brené 31, 156
Buddhaghosa 47, 50, 56, 63–4
Buddhist perspective 33, 52, 169, 174–5
Buddhist texts 6, 22, 261
Buddhist tradition 5, 24, 33, 55, 92, 96, 113, 183, 203

Buddhists 6, 28, 41, 58, 105, 111–12, 196, 216, 218, 228
  ideal 71–2, 219
Burning House 65, 204
Burunat, Enrique 38

camaraderie, spiritual 104, 108
capacity 8, 15–16, 40, 42, 84, 127, 175, 262
care 17, 19, 121, 125, 128, 143, 248–9, 262
caregiver 34–6, 39
caste 202–3, 259
celebrations 3, 89, 130, 220
celebrities 32, 66
celibacy 115, 191, 209
cherishing 18, 29–30, 73, 124, 132, 142, 240, 264
children 31–5, 39–40, 45–6, 53, 109–10, 124, 177–8, 253
  raising 33–4
Christianity 120, 210
climate 65, 259
clod 21–2, 29, 119, 174
closeness 127, 156, 160, 178, 188, 190, 194, 229–30, 245
clothes 150, 155, 163
clouds 19–20, 25, 74, 90, 125, 240
CNM (consensual non-monogamy) 211
coercion 24, 48, 156–7, 160–1, 175, 184, 252
Cohen, Leonard 3–5, 47
colours 28, 69, 79, 82, 122, 197, 265
comfort 5, 34, 40, 47, 126, 177
commandments 48, 120, 204
commitment 115, 123, 228–9, 258
common humanity 17, 143, 198, 220
communication 158, 160–1, 166, 229, 242, 245, 248, 250, 252
communion 16, 126
community 32, 34, 41, 87, 199, 205, 255, 262
  spiritual 8–9, 33, 107, 204
companions 104–5, 108, 223, 260
  spiritual 105, 108
companionship 104, 107, 172
company 9, 106, 108, 163, 176, 179, 220
compassion 5–6, 58–61, 73–5, 103–4, 142–4, 218–19, 228–9, 262–3
  fatigue 58, 68
completeness 143, 216
conditioned existence 6, 93
conflicts 161, 193, 204, 218, 229, 238, 248, 253–4
consciousness 54, 95, 99
consensual non-monogamy (CNM) 211
consent 116, 191–3, 211, 232, 242, 248
contentment 49, 55, 185–6, 207–8
conventional morality 203–4, 207, 210
conversations 132, 169, 212, 235, 244, 247, 264
  difficult 212, 254–5
cooperation 33, 111, 145, 157
copying, social 25, 106
couples 155–6, 165, 200, 202, 230, 233–4, 242, 244, 246, 252
courage 15, 77, 178

craving 24–5, 45, 63, 71, 108, 170, 183–5, 231
criticism 156, 160–1, 165–6
cruelty 59, 63, 108
culture of love 257–9, 261, 263, 265
Cupid 23, 89

daughters 22–4
death 54, 111, 114, 116, 140, 150–1, 217, 219
defensiveness 157, 165–6
delusion 5, 80, 259–60
depression 37, 40, 139, 146, 219, 222, 224
despair 21, 46, 131
destruction 78, 81
  rite of 81–2
devas 86, 95, 207–9
development
  healthy 20, 127
  spiritual 48, 72, 76, 92, 106, 229, 236–7, 258
devotion 28, 39, 113, 116, 123, 181, 210, 228, 234
dhammachanda 24–5
Dharma 40, 71, 74–6, 79–80, 82–4, 98–9, 111–12, 114–15, 234–5
  life 208–9, 228
  practice 228–9, 234
dhyana 108, 208
dignity 78, 128, 173, 190, 231, 254
disappointments 146–7, 167, 178
disciples 55, 73–4, 110, 228, 234
discomfort 22, 64, 75
disconnection 159, 162
discriminating wisdom 265–6
dislikes 50, 52, 253
distress 64–5, 143
divorce 166, 210, 252–4
  Giraffe 242, 255
doctrine 111, 139
domination 80, 173
doorways 117, 122–8, 130–2, 225
dopamine 36–8
drugs 36–7, 106
drums 81, 123
duty 17, 90, 150, 258

earth 19, 26, 113, 245, 260, 262–3
ecological emergencies 65, 259
eightfold path, noble 105, 180
emancipation 72
emotional energies 99, 265
emotional experience 90, 160
emotional health 41, 218
emotional resources 35, 126
emotional warmth 2–3, 18, 46, 124, 127, 216, 229
emotions 38–9, 46, 54, 83, 99, 170, 202, 249
  negative 24, 79
  skilful 10, 67
empathic joy 59, 61, 75, 79, 82, 130
empathic listening 158–60
empathy 3, 56, 67–9, 129–30, 159–62, 212, 244, 254
empowerment 78, 148, 238
emptiness 41, 73, 76, 82, 128, 139
enemies 51, 53, 58, 61, 63, 65–6, 80, 107
  near 63–4, 66–7, 70
enemy images 51, 249–50, 255

energy 77, 79, 148, 163, 165, 196, 234, 237
  emotional 99, 265
enjoyment, vicarious 66, 70
Enlightenment 23–5, 47–8, 54–5, 78–80, 82–4, 86–7, 95–6, 101–7
  Buddha's 86, 111
  ultimate potential 103, 125
environment 8, 37, 204, 234
equanimity 59–60, 63, 67, 70, 79, 82, 130
equity 229, 237
eros 89–91, 121, 128–9
eternal law 1, 6, 258
eternity 28, 91
ethical beauty 85, 87
ethical principles 18, 207
ethics 9, 192, 235–6
Eurydice 225–6
evidence 31–2, 131, 139, 201
evolution 33, 52, 125, 129
excitement 2, 185, 206
exercise 11, 140–1, 145, 148, 249–50
existence
  conditioned 6, 93
  sentient 94
existential knowledge 17, 20
experience 46–7, 60–1, 63–7, 76–8, 98, 101–3, 138–41, 222
  human 32, 60, 143, 221
  life 129, 178–9
  of love 32, 35, 117, 200, 257
  of partnership 1, 230
  personal 116, 185

faculty 16, 84, 93
fathers 22, 40, 90, 234
failure 16, 222, 254
faith 15, 48, 104, 205, 211
feelings 36–8, 41–2, 55–8, 64–6, 153–4, 159–61, 245–7, 249
  painful 51–2, 144
  transformed 146, 223
final thoughts 257–9, 261, 263, 265
five stages 50, 58, 69
flavours 7, 20, 59, 79, 87, 107, 131, 141, 220
flowers 28, 75, 79, 89, 94, 104, 119–20, 122, 178, 257
forces 6, 8, 33, 73, 76, 80, 191, 240, 243, 259
freedom 17, 22–3, 72, 77–8, 124, 173–5, 180, 244
friends, spiritual 104–5, 107–8, 205, 231
friendship 89–117, 121, 128
  spiritual 76, 92, 104–7, 112, 117, 191, 231
Fromm, Erich 15–20, 126
fulfilment, ultimate 88, 103–4
FWBO (Friends of the Western Buddhist Order) 41

game 32, 39, 206
garden 122, 124–5, 127, 259
  love 117–35, 175, 259
gateway 97, 122–3, 126, 128
gay 200, 206
gender 197, 199, 207
generosity 7, 50, 112, 164–5, 192, 204, 207, 234–6, 238

genes 37–8, 91, 183
gifts 42, 49, 55, 62, 110, 121, 157–8, 160, 164, 245, 262
giraffe 153–4, 161, 242
giraffe divorce 242, 255
glue, biological 33, 36, 45, 125
goddesses 75, 80, 123, 216
gods 32, 47, 90–1, 207–8, 265
 angry 207, 209
going for refuge 8–9, 203, 228, 258
goodwill 6, 46, 54, 187
gratitude 61–2, 141, 151, 155, 163–4, 167–8, 234, 262
great love 68, 71–88, 239
greed 5–8, 23, 78, 80, 172, 204, 207, 259–60
Green Tara 110, 112–13
grief 87, 146, 191, 216–22, 224–6
group-dwelling mammals 25, 106
groups 33, 66, 125, 156, 200, 203–4, 207, 258
growth 17, 25, 103, 144, 147, 190, 197, 204

habits 24–5, 106, 171
Hafiz 220–1
hands 11, 40, 76, 79, 116, 127, 209, 260
happiness 8, 18, 49–50, 61–2, 65–8, 70, 77, 156, 174, 176, 236, 242
harmony 47, 100, 145–7, 208, 218
hatred 1, 5–7, 23, 51–3, 170, 172, 248–9, 258–60
health 32, 49, 109, 126, 174, 242
 emotional 41, 218
 mental 35, 39, 126
healthy development 20, 127
heart 45–55, 69, 77–8, 82–4, 129–30, 222–3, 249–50, 262–5
 boundless 19, 45, 124
Heart Sutra 41–2, 128
heaven 21–2, 29, 95, 97, 174
hell 21–2, 29, 174
helpfulness 8, 123, 258
helplessness 59, 219
Hendrix, Jimi 7–8
heroin 36–7
higher planes 95, 208
Holmes, Sherlock 32, 38–40, 42
homosexuality 90, 205–6
honesty 111, 130, 151
hormones 37–8, 169
horrified anxiety 58, 64–5, 68, 70
houses 149, 222, 232, 237–8, 257
human babies 33–4
human beings 32, 52, 145, 176, 234, 259
human experience 32, 60, 143, 221
human potential 20, 100, 243
human soul 21, 119
humanity 16–17, 150, 178, 255, 259
 common 17, 143, 198, 220
humans 33, 77, 80, 90–1, 125, 127, 129, 207
humour 170, 186–7
hurt 31, 42, 116, 137, 139, 165, 176, 178–80, 185, 235, 241, 248–9, 252
hypocrisy 131

idealism 15, 26–7
ideals 34, 83, 92, 105, 107, 123, 131
identification 27, 209
identities 9–10, 139, 172, 197, 199, 203, 212
ignorance 6–7, 82, 186, 192, 204, 207, 210, 218
images 21–2, 24, 101–2, 112–13, 121–2, 243, 249, 259
  of beauty 100, 121
  enemy 51, 249–50, 255
imagination 27–8, 67, 100–1, 113, 119, 121, 178, 249
immortality 27, 91
impermanence 93–4, 97, 170, 229–30, 264
impurity 95, 170
India 81, 86, 106, 109–10, 138, 202
indifference 61, 68
  fixed 63, 66
individuality 17, 49
Indo-Tibetan Buddhist Cultural Institute (ITBCI) 111
infants 29, 34–6
inhibitions 36, 160
innocence 21, 29, 119
insecurity 223, 260
insubstantiality 71, 76, 93–4, 97
intensity 42, 45–7, 51, 53, 244
intentions 9, 76, 129, 148, 150, 159, 192, 236, 246, 250, 260
  kind 132, 138
interconnectedness 100, 195, 219, 223, 262
intimacy 56, 148, 160–1, 194, 244, 253, 263–4
intimate relationships 26, 142, 165
isolation 22, 143

Jackal 153–4
jakri 81
jealousy 46, 172–3, 182, 210
jewels 8–9, 34, 107, 115, 123, 203, 228–9, 258
joie de vivre 126, 264
journey 3, 31, 101, 217, 223, 260
joy 28, 58–9, 65, 67–8, 100, 119–21, 178–9, 219–20
  empathic 59, 61, 75, 79, 82, 130
judgements 130, 143, 145–6, 158, 160, 247, 249–50, 255

Kalimpong 109–10
kalyana mitra 105, 108–9, 114, 231
kalyana mitrata 76, 92, 105, 107–8, 112–14, 116
kamachanda 24–5
Kamadeva 23, 79
kamaloka 95, 207–8
Kant, Immanuel 97
Karaniya Metta Sutta 11, 45, 48, 58, 236
karma 52, 57, 67, 77, 207
karuna 58–65, 67–8, 70, 73–4, 115, 130
karuna bhavana 61, 70, 142
kind intentions 132, 138
kindness 33, 50, 68, 109, 132, 143, 145, 244
kings 59, 86, 225, 235, 259
Kisa 217

kisses 4–5, 11, 28, 176, 228, 230, 266
knowledge 15, 17, 130, 178, 206, 251
  existential 17, 20
koans 2, 29, 229
Kurukulla 79–80, 82–3, 89, 265

laksanas 93, 97
languages 26, 101, 121, 150, 153–5
  of love 3–5, 121
laughter 37, 121, 123, 183, 186–9, 202, 233
law, eternal 1, 6, 258
laypeople 55, 115
lettuce 19
LGBTQ+ 200, 205–6
liberation 97, 104, 122, 198
life, spiritual 72, 92, 96, 99, 104–8, 116, 231, 262
life-energy 144–5
life experience 129, 178–9
lifestyle 49, 115, 203, 228, 258
lightness 126, 222
limitations 144, 151, 167, 232–3, 236, 251
lips 157, 176, 187, 234
listening, empathic 158–60
living beings 8, 50, 75–6, 82–3
lobha 24
loneliness 129, 220
long-term relationships 165, 169, 185, 187, 193–4, 236, 248
longings 51, 78, 170, 185, 216, 221–3, 245, 249
loss 4–5, 21–2, 116, 138, 166, 174, 191, 216–18, 220–2, 224
lotuses 102–3, 125–6
lovableness 125
love, *see also Introductory Note*
  boundless 29–30
  culture of 257–9, 261, 263, 265
  experience of 32, 35, 117, 200, 257
  languages 3–5, 121
  magic 80–1
  maternal 53, 60
  mode 7–10, 123, 155, 237, 240, 242, 258
  possessive 174, 266
  of power 7–8
  power of 7–8, 43
  romantic 32, 53, 128, 201, 203, 209, 211
  science of 31–43
  and sex 183–95
  shadow side of 169–82
  unbounded 69, 243
loveableness 56, 58, 68
lovelessness 239
lover 3–4, 131, 150, 170–1, 173, 176–7, 200, 210, 261
loving-kindness 46, 50, 56, 58, 79, 82, 257, 261
lust 22–3

magical transformation 79
magicians 74, 81
maha 72, 76, 82
mahamaitri 73, 76, 83
maharaga 82–3
Mahayana 28, 71–3, 87
maitri 6, 73, 105
Mallika, Queen 235

mammals 33–4
group-dwelling 25, 106
Manjusri 71, 74–5
mantras 37, 112, 216
Mara 22–4
daughters 22–4
marriages 161, 201–3, 210, 227, 237, 241, 253–4
maternal love 53, 60
maturing 18–20, 29–30, 73, 124–5, 142, 240, 262
maturity, spiritual 236, 244
mediation 230, 246
meditation 49, 56, 59, 63, 94–5, 123, 208, 234
practice 188–9
meditative absorption 4, 112, 169, 208
Meghiya 107–8
memories
painful 31, 53
traumatic 199, 212, 217
men 22, 90, 115, 139, 177, 183–4, 187–8, 197, 201–2, 206, 209
mental health 35, 39, 126
metta 6, 10, 45–8, 50–64, 66–8, 73–4, 105, 112–13
metta bhavana 55–6, 64, 68–9
Metta Sutta 73
mindfulness 7, 10, 143–4, 161, 180, 182
misconduct, sexual 183–4, 196, 206–8, 210
misfortune 65, 81, 140, 225
monasteries 80, 110
money 114, 149, 184, 237–8
monks 55, 75, 95, 104–5, 107, 115, 181, 234
monogamy 209–10, 212
moon 74, 81, 188, 261
morality
conventional 203–4, 207, 210
natural 203–4, 207, 210
morals 27, 210
mortality 35, 140
mothers 19, 40–1, 45, 53, 77, 121, 124, 234
motivation 16, 32, 38, 57, 129, 149, 151
mountains 19, 26, 39, 260
mourning 130, 132, 146, 212, 217–19, 221, 223–6, 255
mudita 59, 61–3, 65–8, 70, 115, 130
mudita bhavana 62, 70
murder 29, 172
music 3, 123, 224, 229
mutual awareness 162, 178
mutual responsibility 149, 182
mutuality 229, 236–9, 249
mysteries 3, 92, 230, 262

Nanda 95
natural morality 203–4, 207, 210
near enemies 63–4, 66–7, 70
needs, unmet 53, 146–7, 161–2, 177, 194
negative emotions 24, 79
neural fingerprints 38, 60
neurochemicals 36, 38, 160
neutrality 66–7, 70
Nirvana 25, 48, 99
no-self 54–5, 139
noble eightfold path 105, 180
nonviolence 8–9, 18, 123–4, 182, 258

Nonviolent Communication (NVC) 1, 65, 130, 145, 153, 155, 158, 211
norms 200–1, 203
nourishment 103, 194
NVC, *see* Nonviolent Communication
nymphs 95–6

objects 16–17, 23–6, 47, 81–3, 97, 100–1, 144–5, 176–8
obligations 148, 150, 258
openness 49, 127, 161
opposites 7, 56, 63, 65, 94, 236–7
ordeals 39, 261
ordination 113–14
orgasm 90, 183, 193
oxytocin 36–8, 160

pacification, rite of 82
pain 51, 67, 77, 132, 218–20, 223, 240–1, 244–5
painful feelings 51–2, 144
painful memories 31, 53
Pali Canon 55, 95, 191
parents 8, 35, 39, 41–2, 63, 177–8, 184, 253; *see also* fathers; mothers
partners 153–69, 173–80, 184–90, 210–12, 228–34, 236–40, 243–51, 253–5; *see also* *Introductory Note*
  potential 187, 200
  romantic 186, 262
  sexual 89, 201
partnership, *see Introductory Note*
Pasenadi, King 235
passion 4–6, 46–7, 72, 80–3, 92, 201, 261, 265
passionate attachment 24–5
patience 68, 182, 261
peace 1, 7–8, 23, 48, 55, 68, 86, 259
peace of mind 33, 49, 238
pebble 21–2, 29, 119, 174
pema 24, 63
perspective 27, 32, 76, 90, 147, 155, 163, 260
  loss of 23
philosophers 97, 129
physical beauty 79, 84–5, 92, 102
pity, sentimental 64–5, 68, 70
planet 33, 132, 164, 175, 229, 242
plants 19–20, 125, 127, 259
Plato 3, 89, 93, 97, 129
playfulness 193, 248
poems 21–2, 26–8, 57, 84, 119–20, 137–8, 217, 227
poisons 5–6, 47
polyamory 200, 209–12
possession 23, 94, 172, 231
possessive love 174, 266
possessiveness 27, 46, 172–3
posture 11, 80, 158
power 8, 10, 17, 80, 100–1, 116, 163–4, 172
  of love 7–8, 43
  love of 7–8
  mode 7–10, 24, 144, 156, 237, 242, 258
precepts 108, 115, 131, 184–5, 195–6, 204, 207–9, 228
preciousness 140–1
preferred strategies 156, 180, 238

prejudices 67, 207
protection 33–4, 39, 73, 210
protectors 62, 112
psychologists 84, 156
pujas 41, 216

qualities 2, 48–9, 84–5, 87–8, 162–3, 193, 240–1, 261–2
  enlightened 85, 102
  skilful 61, 68, 70
  unique 18, 124
quality time 121, 179–80

racism 197, 199
raga/Raga 22, 24, 82
rape 183–4
reactions 51, 53, 145, 177, 231
reality, shared 131, 253
refuge 8–9, 40, 73, 166, 199, 203, 228, 258
  going for 8–9, 203, 228, 258
regrets 75, 145–7, 184, 207, 246, 255
rejection 166–7, 179
relationships, *see also Introductory Note*
  healthy 187, 194
  intimate 26, 142, 165
  long-term 165, 169, 185, 187, 193–4, 236, 248
  sexual 116, 172, 188, 211, 231
  survival-necessary 36, 45
release 62, 96, 101, 108, 189–90
resentment 52, 63, 65, 147–8, 157, 165, 232–3, 238
resources 10, 38, 49, 157, 164, 237–8, 254, 259
  emotional 35, 126
responsibility 8, 17, 19, 46, 166, 169–70, 204, 255
  mutual 149, 182
revelation 31–2, 42, 86, 92
rewards 37, 149, 178, 192, 258
Righteousness 98, 123
Rimpoche, Dhardo 109–14
risks 19, 35, 45–6, 124, 126, 130, 156, 201
rites
  of destruction 81–2
  of fascination 80–4, 95
  of pacification 82
  of prospering 82
rituals 80–1, 200, 202, 210, 220, 224, 255
  devotional 41, 216
rock concerts 10, 55
Rogers, Carl 18, 160
role play 153–4
romantic idealism 26–7
romantic love 32, 53, 128, 201, 203, 209, 211
Rosenberg, Marshall 130, 153, 155, 166, 194
rubies 220, 222, 265
rules 32, 48, 200, 202–3, 225, 242
Rumi 84, 123, 154, 220
rupaloka 208

sadness 132, 146, 223
safety 10, 125, 150, 175–6, 182, 249
samadhi 74
samsara 6, 79, 87, 93–9, 219, 223
Sangha 8, 33–4, 40, 83, 107, 115, 173, 203, 219, 258

Sangharakshita 93, 97, 99, 110–13, 115–16, 124, 139, 180
Sanskrit 72–3, 92, 104–5
santusti 185
science of love 31–43
seasons 19, 99, 125, 220, 226
security 49, 78, 121, 125–6, 175–6, 190, 240, 253
self-compassion 138, 142–3, 146–8, 151, 159, 171, 244, 250
self-connection 147, 162, 179, 233
self-empathy 58, 166, 212
self-empowerment 149, 254
self-forgiveness 147
self-improvement 90, 129
self-judgement 143, 150
self-love 137–51
self-value 66, 139, 172, 253
sensitivity 99, 145, 160–1, 239
sentimental pity 64–5, 68, 70
separateness 16, 263
separation 76, 208, 252–5
serotonin 36–7, 83, 187
sex 90–1, 115, 129
  addiction 193–4
  drive 183, 186
  and love 183–95
sexual activity 183, 186–8, 190, 193, 248
sexual misconduct 183–4, 196, 206–8, 210
sexual orientation 90–1, 177, 183, 197, 207, 212–13, 259
sexual relationships 116, 172, 188, 211, 231
sexuality 184, 205–6, 262
shadow side of love 169–82
shared reality 131, 253
silence 99, 113, 158–9, 241, 246
simplicity 207–8, 262
skilful actions 61–2, 163, 192
skilful emotions 10, 67
skilful qualities 61, 68, 70
skilfulness 56, 61, 66, 163
skills 1, 16, 48, 56, 200, 251
social copying 25, 106
social media 24–5, 63
social networks 34, 200
society 80, 149, 197, 199–202, 204–5, 207
Socrates 89, 91
songs 3–4, 21–2, 39, 47, 81, 129, 171, 224–5
Songs of Innocence 21, 119
soul 29, 100, 142, 215–16
  human 21, 119
space 49, 101, 162, 193, 221, 232, 237–9, 244
species 33, 91, 125, 145, 183, 259, 262
speech 9, 59, 142, 159
spiritual androgyny 208
spiritual camaraderie 104, 108
spiritual community 8–9, 33, 107, 204
spiritual companions 105, 108
spiritual development 48, 72, 76, 92, 106, 229, 236–7, 258
spiritual friends 104–5, 107–8, 205, 231
spiritual friendship 76, 92, 104–7, 112, 117, 191, 231
spiritual life 72, 92, 96, 99, 104–8, 116, 231, 262
spiritual maturity 236, 244

sraddha 84–5
sramanas 59
stars 94, 227, 261, 266
steam 51, 113
sticky affection 24, 63
stillness 100, 207–8
stomach 45, 189–90
stonewalling 165–6
stories 22–5, 31, 36, 55, 95–6, 102–3, 107, 142, 181, 194, 217, 221, 223, 226, 235
strategies, preferred 156, 180, 238
strawberries 15, 20
subha 87, 93–8
Subhuti 55
sun 18–19, 28, 97, 100, 102–3, 120, 124–5, 264–6
sunyata 73–4, 76, 82–3, 139, 232
sunyatakarunagarbha 73–4
support 39, 49, 59–60, 149, 185, 238–9, 249–50, 252–3
survival 32, 34–6, 125–6, 161, 200
survival-necessary relationships 36, 45
symbolism 81, 122
symbols 120–1, 161, 226

tanha 22, 24, 45, 71
tantric approach 68, 88
tantric tradition 79, 85
tastes 22, 190, 261
teachers 89, 109–12, 114, 116, 192, 217, 226
  spiritual 34, 218
Ten Commandments 120
tenderness 8, 112, 123–4, 222–3, 258
tensions 161–2, 199, 208, 236
texture 127, 243
thangka 110, 112
Theravadin tradition 58, 71, 110
thickets 19–20
things 75–7, 98–102, 148, 156, 162–3, 193, 195, 262–4
thirst 24, 38
threats 24, 36, 52, 160, 172
Tibet 6, 73, 80, 110
tolerance 37, 154
transcendence 53, 97, 130
transformation 5, 78, 85, 98, 209
trauma 199, 217, 248
traumatic memories 199, 212, 217
trees 19–20, 99, 121–2, 125, 138, 264
Triratna Buddhist Community 41, 99, 107, 112
Triratna Buddhist Order 1, 115, 228
trust 84, 160–1, 166, 232, 242–4, 248, 252–3, 255
truth 17, 21, 54–5, 82, 84, 98, 111, 239
twelve-step programmes 193–5

ugliness 94–6
ultimate fulfilment 88, 103–4
unbounded love 69, 243
understanding 17, 31–2, 51, 129, 160–2, 178–80, 191–2, 244–5
unenlightened beings 59, 94
unhappiness 51, 55
unique qualities 18, 124
uniqueness 201, 264–5

universe 41, 47, 84–5, 96, 176, 207, 235, 263
unmet needs 53, 146–7, 161–2, 177, 194
unsatisfactoriness 94, 97, 143
unskilfulness 19, 125
upekkha 59–60, 62–3, 66–8, 70, 77, 115, 130
upekkha bhavana 63, 66–7, 70

Vajrayana tradition 71, 74, 79, 81–3, 85, 87
values 92–3, 106, 131, 149, 157–8, 172, 193, 236–7
verbal phrases 68–9
vicarious enjoyment 66, 70
victims 8, 23, 79, 89
Vimalakirti 71, 73–5
Vimalakirti Nirdesa 73–4, 79, 88
vimokkha-mukkha 97, 122
Vinaya 191
violence 8, 144, 183–4, 200, 248–9, 252, 258
Visakha 234
vocabulary 46, 179
voices 29, 42, 74, 154, 158, 198, 221, 226, 232, 265
volition 9, 192, 203, 236
vows 72–3, 76
vulnerability 130, 151, 156

Walcott, Derek 137–8
walls 40, 42, 123, 126
warmth 82, 103, 124, 126, 186, 216, 257, 265
water 19–20, 24–6, 33, 74, 102, 126, 257, 259
welfare 58, 62, 74, 143, 164, 234, 261
wellbeing 9, 32, 56, 58, 63, 126, 131, 237–9
White Lotus Sutra 19, 125
white lotuses 102, 126
wholeness 91, 122, 126, 186, 216, 244, 261, 264
Wilde, Oscar 64, 205
wings 246, 257
wisdom, discriminating 265–6
withdrawal 159, 166
women 139, 177, 184, 187–9, 197, 201–2, 209, 211
Wordsworth, William 99–100
worldviews 156, 167, 171

WINDHORSE PUBLICATIONS

Windhorse Publications is a Buddhist charitable company based in the UK. Our books, which are distributed internationally, champion Buddhism, meditation, and mindfulness. They offer fresh interpretations of Buddhist teachings and their application to contemporary life, with subject matter and authors from across the Buddhist tradition, catering for a broad range of interest and experience. In addition to publishing titles exploring classic texts for modern audiences, we aspire to publish books that offer a Buddhist perspective on today's challenges, including social inequality, the environment and climate, gender, mental health, and more. Established in the 1970s to publish the writing of Urgyen Sangharakshita (1925–2018), the founder of the Triratna Buddhist Order, Windhorse Publications continues to be dedicated to preserving and keeping in print his impressive and influential body of work, making it accessible for future generations. As well as high-quality print and e-books, Windhorse Publications produces accompanying audio, podcast, video, and teaching resources.

Windhorse Publications
38 Newmarket Road
Cambridge CB5 8DT
info@windhorsepublications.com

For information on distribution and trade orders visit:
www.windhorsepublications.com/trade-resources/

THE TRIRATNA BUDDHIST COMMUNITY

Windhorse Publications is a part of the Triratna Buddhist Community, an international movement with centres in Europe, India, North and South America, and Australasia. At these centres, members of the Triratna Buddhist Order offer classes in meditation and Buddhism. Activities of the Triratna Community also include retreat centres, residential spiritual communities, ethical Right Livelihood businesses, and the Karuna Trust, a UK fundraising charity that supports social welfare projects in the slums and villages of India.

Through these and other activities, Triratna is developing a unique approach to Buddhism, not simply as a philosophy and a set of techniques, but as a creatively directed way of life for all people living in the conditions of the modern world.

If you would like more information about Triratna please visit thebuddhistcentre.com or write to:

London Buddhist Centre
51 Roman Road
London E2 0HU
UK
contact@lbc.org.uk

Aryaloka
14 Heartwood Circle
Newmarket NH 03857
USA
info@aryaloka.org

Sydney Buddhist Centre
24 Enmore Road
Sydney NSW 2042
Australia
info@sydneybuddhistcentre.org.au

The Radical Embrace
A Meditator's Guide to Embodying Love
Singhashri

The Radical Embrace is a powerful exploration of what it means to live and love with your whole self. With raw honesty and fierce compassion, Singhashri – a queer mindfulness teacher and activist – invites us onto a transformative path of belonging that weaves together personal narrative, social justice, and Buddhist practice. This is a book for anyone longing to feel more at home in their body, their community, and the world.

> 'Singhashri's years of spiritual exploration shine through the pages of this book, offering us a deeply embodied, trauma-informed approach to spiritual practice that is at the same time rooted in an awareness of our obligations to address social, environmental, and economic injustice. We need more dharma teachings like these.' – Bodhipaksa, author of *This Difficult Thing of Being Human* and *The Heart's Awakening*

> 'The Radical Embrace *is a powerful reminder that we are all beginners, and awakening is available to everyone. This unique and accessible dharma book invites us to dream, while offering grounded exercises to ensure we don't spiritually bypass.'* – Vimalasara (Valerie) Mason-John, author of *First Aid Kit for the Mind: Breaking the Cycle of Habitual Behaviors*

> *'This book is an intimate conversation about healing ourselves and our communities, calling us toward "a radical shift in perspective from a world based on domination to one rooted in love." As a socially engaged, gender queer, BIPOC practitioner, I found real medicine here. This is dharma for our times.'* – Viveka Chen, Dharma and Somatics Teacher/Social Justice Coach and Facilitator

> *'The radical embrace of what is possible – in the healing of becoming all of who we are, in the integration of our intergenerational and ancestral heritages, in the most expansive intentions to imbue love into our relationship with all things, and in the awakening to freedom – is beautifully and skilfully described in this book.'* – Larry Yang, author of *Awakening Together*, founding teacher of East Bay Meditation Center

Singhashri is a queer, Chilean-American-British dharma teacher, writer, and somatic practitioner. They teach an embodied and relational approach to mindfulness and compassion as a means to awakening to love, beauty, and truth, and have committed their life to supporting collective liberation for all. They are an ordained member of the Triratna Buddhist Community.

The Heart's Awakening
108 Steps to a Life of Love
Bodhipaksa

What if love wasn't just something you feel – but something you practice, step by step?

In *The Heart's Awakening*, renowned Buddhist teacher Bodhipaksa offers a transformative journey through the four *brahma viharas* – the "immeasurable" qualities of kindness, compassion, joy, and equanimity. Through 108 accessible and practical reflections, this book invites you to cultivate these qualities in your daily life, guiding you toward deeper self-acceptance, more meaningful relationships, and an openhearted connection to the world. Whether you're new to meditation or a seasoned practitioner, this book will support you to live with greater peace, joy, and kindness – one revolutionary step at a time. Are you ready to awaken your heart?

> *'With his clear insights and heartfelt approach, Bodhipaksa offers an antidote to the fears, struggles, and stresses inherent in this human experience. His latest book is a sincere and accessible step-by-step guide to opening the heart to all aspects of our lives.'* – Sharon Salzberg, author of *Lovingkindness* and *Real Life*

> *'What I love most about Bodhipaksa's writing is that he includes himself as an ordinary human being. Just like us, he also sometimes gets irritable, makes mistakes, and struggles to be happy. From this place he offers us the fruit of his decades of meditation and self-compassion.'* – Satya Robyn, author of *Coming Home: Refuge in Pureland Buddhism*

> *'This book offers the meditator an imaginative and practical approach to cultivating kindness. Bodhipaksa offers personal insights from his life and teaching, creating both an engaging and valuable resource for both teachers and practitioners alike.'* – Suryagupta, Chair of the London Buddhist Centre

Bodhipaksa is a Buddhist teacher and author. He has been practicing meditation since 1982, and has been a member of the Triratna Buddhist Order since 1993. He is the founder of Wildmind: an online meditation resource, publisher of guided meditations, and meditation center offering online instruction. He is the author of *Vegetarianism: A Buddhist View* (2009), *Wildmind: A Step-by-Step Guide to Meditation* (2010), *I Can't Believe It's Not Buddha!* (2018), and *This Difficult Thing of Being Human* (2019).

www.ingramcontent.com/pod-product-compliance
Lightning Source LLC
LaVergne TN
LVHW010615190926
848399LV00034B/328
9781915342676